S/NVQ Level **2**

Revised
Now includes
Unit 210

Children's Care, Learning & Development

Kate Beith • Penny Tassoni • Kath Bulman • Maria Robinson

www.heinemann.co.uk

✓ Free online support
✓ Useful weblinks
✓ 24 hour online ordering

01865 888080

Heinemann

Heinemann is an imprint of Pearson Education Limited, a company incorporated in England and Wales, having its registered office at Edinburgh Gate, Harlow, Essex, CM20 2JE. Registered company number: 872828

www.heinemann.co.uk

Heinemann is a registered trademark of Pearson Education Limited

Text © Kate Beith, Penny Tassoni, Kath Bulman, Maria Robinson 2008

First published 2005
Revised edition published 2008

12 11 10 09 08
10 9 8 7 6 5 4 3 2

British Library Cataloguing in Publication Data is available from the British Library on request.

ISBN 978 0 435448 50 9

Designed by Wooden Ark Studio, Leeds
Typeset by Saxon Graphics Ltd, Derby
Original illustrations © Pearson Education Ltd, 2008
Illustrated by HL Studios, Long Hanborough
Cover design by Wooden Ark Studio, Leeds
Picture research by Christine Martin
Cover photo/illustration © Corbis
Printed in China by CTPS

Acknowledgements
Every effort has been made to contact copyright holders of material reproduced in this book. Any omissions will be rectified in subsequent printings if notice is given to the publishers.

Websites
The websites used in this book were correct and up-to-date at the time of publication. It is essential for tutors to preview each website before using it in class so as to ensure that the URL is still accurate, relevant and appropriate. We suggest that tutors bookmark useful websites and consider enabling students to access them through the school/college intranet.

Contents

Acknowledgements

Kate Beith would like to thank Emma, Tom and Sam for their help and support.

Penny Tassoni would like to thank those many professionals who have given freely of their time and expertise. In particular, she would like to thank Kate Beith, Meg Marshall, Wendy Lidgate, Shirley Eden, Wendy Bristow and Louise Burnham. Thanks also go to the many students, tutors and practitioners who have given her helpful and vital feedback. She would like to thank Mary James, Julia Bruce, Beth Howard and others in the Heinemann team who have driven this writing project forward. Finally, she would like to thank the Tassoni Team, who continue to support her in her work!

Kath Bulman would like to give thanks and love, as ever, to Joanne and Andrew and her nieces and nephews for inspiration and case studies. She would like to give grateful thanks and love to Ian for keeping her sane during the creative process!

Maria Robinson would like to thank her husband for his continuing patience with her apparent permanent residence at her computer! She would also like to thank her co-writers for their patience and kindness with comments and feedback.

The authors and publisher would like to give special thanks to Maureen Smith of FutureWise Solutions Ltd, lead consultant in the recent review of the National Occupational Standards, for providing her expert advice and guidance during the preparation of this book

The authors and publisher would like thank the following individuals and organisations for permission to reproduce photographs:
Alamy; Bubbles; Corbis; Getty; Pearson Education Ltd/Gerald Sunderland; Pearson Education Ltd/ Jules Selme; Pearson Education Ltd/Tudor Photography; Sally and Richard Greenhill.

Introduction

Welcome to this handbook for **National Vocational Qualifications (NVQ) Level 2 in Children's Care, Learning and Development**. You are probably already committed to working with children so it is hoped that this book will support you in gaining a qualification in this challenging and demanding career.

About the National Occupational Standards in Children's Care, Learning and Development

The revised NVQ 2 in Children's Care, Learning and Development is made up of nationally set standards that are accredited by the **QCA** (Qualifications and Curriculum Authority). The standards cover the care and development of children from birth to 16 years. At Level 2 the qualification has **seven** units: **six** mandatory units and **one** option chosen from a list of four.

They are as follows:

Mandatory Units

201	Contribute to positive relationships
202	Help to keep children safe
203	Support children's development
204	Use support systems to develop own practice
205	Prepare and maintain environments to meet children's needs
206	Support children's play and learning

Optional Units

207	Contribute to the effectiveness of teams
208	Support the development of children and babies under three
209	Support a child with disabilities or special needs
210	Support children and young people's play

Each NVQ unit is organised in the same way:
- The **Introduction** says what the unit is about and who it is for.
- The unit is divided into **elements** which make your studying more manageable!
- Within each element there are **performance criteria**. These tell you what you have to do at work to achieve the standard. You will mostly be observed carrying out the performance criteria by your assessor.

- The **What you must know and understand** section at the end of each unit is a summary of the knowledge you must have for the unit. Your assessor will use this section to check that you understand your practice relating to the unit.

About this book

This handbook is a comprehensive summary of the knowledge you need to become competent in your NVQ. It covers all the mandatory and optional units in the qualification, so giving you plenty of choice.

The text in this book is closely linked with the section at the end of each unit entitled **What you must know and understand**. The introduction to each unit in the book is referenced to the numbered points in the standards so you can be sure that every point is covered. This will also help you and your assessor when checking off the knowledge points in your portfolio. You will also find a variety of activities in the text that will test your understanding of this knowledge. It is important that you carry out these activities as a way of supporting your portfolio of evidence.

Although this book covers the development of children from birth to 16 years, many of the practical examples focus on children in early years settings (that is, under the age of eight years).

Throughout the book, reference is made to the most well-known curriculum frameworks (usually those used in England and Scotland). However, you will need to check out the curriculum framework used in your own place of work.

Features of this book

Throughout this book there are a number of features that are designed to encourage you to reflect upon your own experience and to help you see how theory is put into practice in early years settings. They will also encourage you to research and seek out the views of other practitioners working with different age groups or in different settings.

Check it out – activities that will help you relate the knowledge you gain in the book to the workplace

Test yourself – activities and questions that will help you check that you understand the text

Did you know ? – interesting facts about children's care, learning and development

Case studies – real scenarios that will enable you to explore key issues and broaden your understanding of working in early years settings

Keys to good practice – practical ways of developing and promoting best practice in caring for children. These relate to the performance criteria and will specifically help you to improve your performance at work

Evidence collectors – support the elements and provide you with evidence for your portfolio. These are referenced to the key skills, Communication, Application of Number and Information Technology

Unit tests – questions at the end of each unit which help you to test your knowledge as you read through the book

Key skills

Throughout the text there are activities that can be used as evidence for key skills. These are highlighted with a ✓ symbol. The key skills you will need at level 2 are:

Level 1 Application of number
Level 1 Communication
Level 1 Information technology

We hope you enjoy using this book – and good luck with your course!

Kate Beith
Penny Tassoni
Kath Bulman
Maria Robinson

Contribute to positive relationships

The way that you communicate, listen and respond to the adults and children who you work with is important in every aspect of your work. By using verbal and non-verbal communication skills you will be able to show that you value both adults and children. By learning to listen, respond and communicate positively you will be able to work effectively in partnership with parents to ensure the best possible care for their children.

Children need to be able to express themselves to become confident learners. This unit looks at ways of encouraging this confidence by listening and responding to them.

What you must know and understand:

- Why it is important to give children your full attention when listening to them (K2C1)
- How you can give children the opportunity to be heard (K2C2)
- How children's communication skills develop (K2D3)
- Why it is important to give children sufficient time to express themselves in their own words (K2C4)
- How you can help children make choices (K2C5)
- Why it is important to understand the key features of effective communication (K2C6)
- How to understand the main differences between communicating with adults and communicating positively with children (K2C7 and K2C13)
- How you can show that you value adults' views and opinions (K2C8)
- How you can overcome communication difficulties (K2C9 and K2C14)
- How to manage disagreements with adults (K2C10)
- Why it is important to reassure adults of the confidentiality of shared information (K2M11)
- Why it is important to understand your organisation's policy with regard to information exchange (K2M12)

Throughout this unit you will come across the words **verbal** and **non-verbal**.

- Verbal is the way you communicate using language.
- Non-verbal is the way you communicate through gestures and body language.

Why it is important to give children your full attention when listening to them

When you communicate with the children in your care you will use four different skills:

- body language
- facial expression
- gestures
- speech.

Body language

Children will know you are listening to them before you speak.

Case study 1: Using appropriate body language

Pip, aged 8, came into the school play club after she had finished in the classroom. Annette, her keyworker, was looking out of the window with her arms crossed. Pip said, 'Hi, Annette'. Annette continued to look out of the window and replied, 'Hi, Pip – did you have a good day?' Pip was going to tell her about their dragon project and show Annette the mask she had made. She smiled when Annette turned round. Without looking up Annette busied herself by placing the paper and crayons out on the drawing table ready for the children to use. Pip hung her coat up ready to play with her friends.

1   *What did you think about Annette's body language when Pip came into the room?*
2   *Why did Pip decide not to show Annette her mask?*
3   *Can you think of ways that Annette could have shown more positive body language to Pip?*

Keys to good practice: How to use appropriate body language when working with children

- ✓ Use eye contact.
- ✓ Make sure you are on the children's level.
- ✓ Do not move too closely to a child's face or 'invade their space'.
- ✓ Try not to make communication barriers by crossing your arms.
- ✓ Ensure that children with communication difficulties such as a hearing impairment can clearly see your face if this is appropriate.

It is important to remember that cultures vary with regard to acceptable body language. In some cultures it is considered disrespectful for a child to have eye contact with an adult.

Facial expression and gestures

It is often easy to find out what someone is saying by looking at their facial expression or the way they use their hands (gesticulate). Children should be given the time and opportunity to understand people's facial expressions and gestures as part of developing their communication skills. Remember that one of the first facial expressions that a baby responds to is a smile. A variety of activities and resources can help children to explore the use of facial expressions.

This list of activities and resources can be added to:
- Peek-a-boo
- Simon says
- Games, puzzles and books about feelings – sad, happy, etc.
- Looking in mirrors and describing feelings
- Songs and rhymes
- Drama activities such as 'mirroring' a partner's facial expressions.

Check it out

Turn off the sound on your television and see if you can guess what the person is talking about without hearing the words. Your favourite soap opera will probably be a good choice of programme for this exercise!

Speech

When you are listening to children you can show you are giving them your full attention by the way you:
- give them time to say what they want to
- take advantage of unplanned opportunities to talk to them
- reflect phrases that a child has said to show you are listening, for example 'So you ate a large red apple?'
- avoid interrupting them however long they take to tell you something
- encourage them to talk without being patronising
- ask open questions that encourage children to talk and to show that you respect their opinions.
- do not finish their sentence for them
- be sensitive to any child who has a barrier to communication such as a speech disorder.

Did you know?

A speech disorder can be caused by a defect in the mouth or vocal cords. Damage to the brain can also cause speech disorders.

How you can give children the opportunity to be heard

The United Nations Convention on the Rights of the Child (signed by the UK in 1991) states in Article 12 that:

It is your role as someone who is working with children to make sure they have the opportunity to talk and be listened to, however difficult they might find this.

ALL CHILDREN HAVE A RIGHT TO BE HEARD.

Quieter children can often be overlooked, particularly in a group activity. Older children may have to raise their hand if they wish to speak but this is not so for younger children. You may need to encourage children to speak by prompting them or asking appropriate questions. Some children may really need you to give them time to build their confidence in you.

Test yourself

Make a list of the opportunities you might have in your setting for children to have an individual conversation with you. These might include:

- in the playground
- lunchtime
- quiet periods
- story sharing.

If you discuss these opportunities with your study group or tutor you might come up with ideas you have not considered.

Look at the spider diagram below to find out which group activities will give children the opportunity to be heard. These activities can easily be adapted to suit the children you are working with.

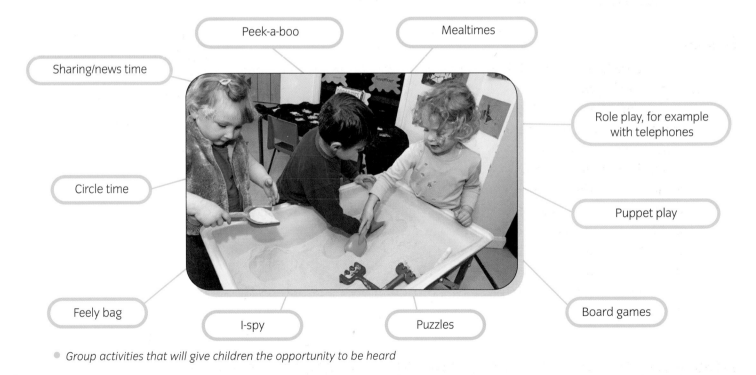

Peek-a-boo

Mealtimes

Sharing/news time

Role play, for example with telephones

Circle time

Puppet play

Feely bag

I-spy

Puzzles

Board games

● *Group activities that will give children the opportunity to be heard*

Test yourself

Consider four ways in which a feely bag activity for a small group of 6-year-olds could give children the opportunity to be listened to. Imagine that the activity is about items hidden in the bag that are connected with the seaside, for example pebbles, shells, etc.

How early speech patterns are expressed as children develop through their use of language

Children's communication skills develop in a sequence. However, not all children's speech will develop at the same rate. When you study the table below keep in mind the fact that because a child in your care is not at the pattern of speech described, it does not indicate a delay or concern.

Speech patterns are generally known as being in the pre-linguistic stage or the linguistic stage.

Pre-linguistic stage

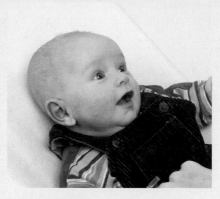

0–3 months
- Cries when hungry, upset or tired.
- Coos and gurgles when happy.
- Differentiates tones of voice.
- By 3 months reacts positively to main carer's voice.
- Begins to smile at people.

3–6 months
- Cries but can be comforted.
- Adds babbles to sounds.
- Makes sounds such as da da.
- Chuckles, laughs and sometimes squeals with pleasure.

6–12 months
- Babbles much more.
- Begins to use vowels and consonants, e.g. dadadadadada!.
- By 9 months uses sounds needed for language.
- By 10 months understands about18 words.
- Begins to gesticulate, e.g. to point.
- Begins to love games such as 'round and round the garden'.

continued on next page

12–18 months
- Main carers recognise first words.
- Words can be used to mean a number of things.
- At 15 months main carers will recognise about 10 words.

18 months–2 years
- Strings together two words, e.g. bye-bye car.
- Uses phrases, e.g. Mummy gone.
- Learns at least 10 words per month.
- At 2 years may have 200 words.

2–3 years
- Still acquires new words quickly.
- Begins to recognise more than one, e.g. cat(s).
- Makes some mistakes, e.g. sitted down.
- Starts to question, e.g. Where Mummy?
- Begins to use negatives, e.g. no doggy.

3–4 years
- Begins to copy adult speech.
- Uses more than four words in sentences.
- Vocabulary includes body parts, animals, etc.
- Makes errors in past tense.
- Understands nursery rhymes.
- Asks questions.
- Speech understood by strangers.

4–8 years
- Begins to define language.
- Uses language to recount and socialise.
- At 5 years vocabulary is about 5,000 words.
- Uses more complex sentences.
- Tells and hears jokes.
- At 8 years is more fluent as a speaker, reader and writer.

8–16 years
- Language is fully developing.
- Uses complex sentence structure.
- Able to use language to negotiate, etc.
- Able to converse in large groups.

How children's communication skills develop

Children who speak English as an additional language may take longer to develop their speech patterns as they have to learn more than one language. However, this does not mean that their language development will be affected. Children respond to the person who is caring for them and will cope with two languages if they are sensitively supported. Often young children are only able to speak their home language with their family as they associate the home language with that particular environment.

It is important that you value children who speak more than one language as it is part of the child's identity and therefore self-esteem.

Did you know?

A child who speaks two languages is called bilingual. A child who speaks more than two languages is called multilingual.

Keys to good practice: How to support differences in speech patterns with multilingual children

✓ Involve parents in your setting.

✓ Promote an understanding of the appropriate culture.

✓ Ensure that the setting is labelled with familiar words from the child's home language.

● *Supporting language*

Why it is important to give children sufficient time to express themselves in their own words

Your role in developing a child's speech is to ensure that they are given sufficient time to express themselves and that they are not hurried or interrupted. If children are not given these opportunities they might find it difficult to concentrate or reason.

Carefully look at the spider diagram below to see how children can be given time for verbal expression.

Encourage them to recall events and incidents

Give them time to socialise with their peers

Help them to use language to predict and anticipate

How to give children time for verbal expression

Provide activities where they have to learn to give instructions

Encourage them to ask for reassurance and help

Give them plenty of time to talk about things that have happened to them

Ensure they have time to ask questions

Encourage assertiveness so that they will be happy to cope with interruptions

Test yourself

In your study group look at the list below. Match the uses of language in the spider diagram against the activities.

- Interest table
- Group activity asking a local policeman/women questions
- Sensory activity smelling spices
- Snack time with snacks made by the children
- Topical debate
- Sound lotto

How you can help children make choices

As adults our life is about making choices and feeling confident about the choices we have made. You will need to help the children in your setting to express their needs and make choices so that they can develop this skill.

It is always important to make it clear to children that they can safely make their own choices.

Keys to good practice: How to help children to make choices

- ✓ Allow children to choose who they work with. If you are unable to do this make your reason clear.
- ✓ Give children time to make their own choices, for example during free play activities.
- ✓ Do not be too dominated by timetables and routines.
- ✓ If leading an activity respond positively to children's ideas and contributions.
- ✓ Ensure that children know they can choose healthy and safe activities.
- ✓ Encourage children to plan their own programme and ask them how it went.
- ✓ Make sure resources are accessible and at the children's height.
- ✓ Praise their choices.

Understand the key features of effective communication

In order to communicate with both adults and children there are a number of key features to remember.

Keys to good practice: How to communicate effectively

- ✓ Always make eye contact.
- ✓ Ensure you smile as appropriate.
- ✓ Be patient.
- ✓ Do not interrupt or finish sentences.
- ✓ Give the other person time.

- ✓ Concentrate on what the other person is saying to you.
- ✓ Ensure that your questions are open to encourage further communication.
- ✓ If you are leading a group situation, ensure that everyone is listened to and that their opinions are valued.

Respecting and listening to a child's point of view

Check it out

Observe a group time in your setting. Note the following:
- How were children encouraged to listen to each other?
- If open questions were used how did the children respond?
- How were the children given time to speak?
- Describe the body language of the practitioner leading the group.

Understanding the main differences between communicating positively with adults and with children

Whether you are working with adults or children it is important that you show sensitivity and respect.

While you may use more complicated language with adults you still need to be caring, respectful and clear.

Caring for children and adults is shown by the way you treat them. This includes smiling, saying please and thank you, and generally making them feel supported and welcome.

Test yourself

- How would you treat a new child and parent you were welcoming into the setting?
- List ways to make them feel welcome.

Being **respectful** is about valuing what adults or children think. If you communicate this respect by listening, acknowledging and thanking children and adults then relationships will be positive. Even if you don't share another adult's or child's point of view, the way you express your disagreement should not make the other person feel their view is worthless.

Case study 2: Respecting children's and young people's opinions

Jude, a youth worker at a group for teenagers, is holding a council meeting about the next club party. Both Tracy and Julia are keen for the party to be advertised locally to attract more people. Jude tells them that he understands why they want to attract more people but he is worried that if they admit strangers the party could be difficult to control. Tracy and Julia offer to sit at the door to screen any suspicious behaviour. Jude thanks them for offering but feels that they would be too vulnerable. He says that while he does not agree with them he respects the fact that they have obviously thought of ways to enable more people to attend.

1   *What do you think about the way Jude responds to Tracy and Julia's idea?*
2   *Do you think they would have felt that their viewpoint was respected?*
3   *Do you think Tracy and Julia will feel they can still express their opinions at the next meeting?*

Be **clear** simple and direct with your communication. Always give reasons and take the time to explain your thoughts or actions.

● *Clear communication is essential*

How you can show that you value adults' views and opinions

Positive relationships are the key to a successful setting. It is important that you value the opinions of the adults with whom you work.

You have to ensure that your own personal preferences and prejudices do not get in the way of your work. Try not to show any favouritism to either adult or child.

A good relationship with the parents of the child in your setting will benefit the child. Remember that the parent is the main carer of the child and that the parent's wishes must be respected.

Key terms

Positive relationships: benefit children and their ability to participate in and benefit from the setting.

 Keys to good practice: How to show parents that you value their views

- ✓ Always ensure that information they give you becomes part of the child's care programme, for example dietary needs.
- ✓ Ask for their advice, for example about items for the home corner relating to their culture.
- ✓ Share their wishes with the rest of your team.
- ✓ Listen to any concerns and manage the concerns sensitively.

Check it out

Talk to members of your team and find out ways in which they ensure that the parents of children they work with feel that they are listened to.

Make a list of these ways and share them with your study group.

Can you add to the list in any way?

Valuing the opinions of those you work with is important if you are going to work together in a positive way, but it is not always easy.

It is an important part of your role to develop the way that you value your colleague's opinions and views even if they differ from yours. If this does not happen this can have an effect on the work of your team.

 Keys to good practice: How to value the opinions of those you work with

- ✓ If you disagree, be constructive, for example 'I respect your point of view. However …'
- ✓ Avoid being personal, for example 'Why do you always look like that when …'
- ✓ Exchange ideas openly and seek colleagues' views, e.g. 'What do you think …'
- ✓ Ask for advice when you need it, for example 'How do you think I could have …'

Test yourself

Which of the following sentences do you think would show that you value the views and opinions of those you work with.

- Why on earth have you chosen to do that activity? I would never have chosen that!
- You know far more than I do about this, so can I ask your advice?
- I think that you are wrong about this, Mary.
- How do you think I should tell Ben's parents about this?

If you have not chosen any of the sentences, explain why.

How you can overcome communication difficulties

Communication difficulties can arise when children or adults have special communication needs or when people have different attitudes, beliefs and values.

Some common communication needs are:

- a physical condition such as a cleft palate
- a speech impediment such as a stammer
- a hearing impairment, either permanent or temporary
- lack of confidence
- English is an additional language
- a learning need, for example Down's syndrome.

By being aware that you need to support a child or adult with communication needs you will be showing that you recognise their right to effective communication.

If you work with a child or adult who has communication needs you should find out how that person needs to be supported. You may need to find information from:

- the parents of a child
- SENCO
- research as appropriate.
- the adult concerned
- health professionals

Other barriers to communication could be caused by:

- personality clashes
- gender differences
- close friendships.
- differing views on practice
- cultural differences

It is your responsibility to ensure that you put aside any differences in order to create a positive working relationship. Seek advice from your line manager if you cannot cope with the effect of any communication barriers that might exist with adults in your setting. It is sometimes better to ask for objective advice.

Did you know?

Persona dolls are a positive way of encouraging children with emotional barriers to communicate and express their feelings. The dolls are individually made with their own personality and story and can help children to cope with difficult situations. They may be used in circle time or on a one-to-one basis, and can help to develop positive self-esteem and confidence.

How to manage disagreements with adults

There will always be times when you disagree with adults in your setting. The way that you cope with these disagreements is very important.

 Keys to good practice: How to cope with disagreements with adults

- ✓ Always remain calm and polite.
- ✓ Listen carefully and respect the other adult's point of view.
- ✓ If you need to have a discussion do so in a private space.
- ✓ Always ensure that your supervisor is aware of any difficulties.
- ✓ Avoid making personal comments.
- ✓ Seek another adult to mediate if you cannot agree.
- ✓ Ensure children are never aware of any disagreements.
- ✓ Refer to your setting's grievance procedure if a disagreement cannot be resolved.

Why it is important to reassure adults of the confidentiality of shared information

You may have already encountered a situation in your setting where you have been asked to maintain confidence over an issue. This may have been from a parent or colleague. When people give you confidential information they are showing that they trust you. Therefore what you do with this information is an essential part of your role and that of your setting.

Carefully read the diagram below to find out how to reassure parents and colleagues that any information shared will be treated confidentially.

 Check it out

Ask if you can see your setting's policy with regard to confidentiality.

How are you encouraged to follow this policy in your work setting?

Before you are told anything, always tell the adult that you will have to share the information with your supervisor. The adult can then decide if he or she still wants to talk to you.

Talk to them in a private place.

How to reassure adults that shared information will be treated confidentially

Assure them that information will not be discussed with anyone outside the setting.

Always check with your supervisor before you pass information on to parents as you may unknowingly breach confidentiality.

Case study 3: Sharing confidential information appropriately

Siobhan is asked by one of her fellow trainees, Charlotte, if she can talk to her in private. As they go to college together every week Siobhan thinks that Charlotte just wants to chat about her boyfriend and agrees to meet Charlotte in the staffroom during their lunch break. They will be the only staff on their break. However, Charlotte tells Siobhan that it is something to do with work. Siobhan feels uncomfortable and tells Charlotte that she may have to share information with her supervisor as she may not be able to keep it to herself. Charlotte immediately bursts into tears and tells Siobhan that she is very unhappy with the way one of the members of staff is treating her. Siobhan promises not to tell anyone but encourages Charlotte to go and tell her supervisor. Charlotte agrees to talk to her the next day.

1   *How do you think Siobhan reacted to the situation?*
2   *What do you think Charlotte felt when Siobhan told her she may have to share her confidence?*
3   *Do you think Charlotte could have dealt with the situation on her own?*

Understand your organisation's information exchange policy

When you exchange any information your setting should have clear guidelines as to how this is done. Exchange of information can be very positive if carried out appropriately. Your setting will have guidelines on how to exchange information in writing but you should also understand the importance of verbal communication, including emergency communication exchange.

Keys to good practice: How to exchange information with adults positively

- ✓ Always find out what the adult's preferred name is that you should use.
- ✓ Ensure that information is exchanged in an appropriate environment.
- ✓ Be very clear about what you are communicating.
- ✓ Make eye contact.
- ✓ Nod or smile and lean forward slightly to show you are listening.
- ✓ Sometimes repeat what the other person says.
- ✓ Speak clearly.
- ✓ Reassure adults.
- ✓ Give adults time to ask questions or make comments.
- ✓ Consider how to verbally exchange information with an adult who speaks English as an additional language.

If you have to exchange information that is negative you should try to start with something positive, for example 'James has tried very hard to play with the other children today. However, we did have to talk to him about …'

In this way you will help the parents to understand that James' behaviour has not been completely negative. Remember that it is natural for people to focus upon negative information.

There will probably be plenty of opportunities in your setting for information to be exchanged with carers in a positive way. Study the chart below and tick the items that your setting carries out. You might add some more to the list!

Open days or evenings	☐
Fund-raising events	☐
Focus groups	☐
Information sessions	☐
Topical workshops	☐
Celebrations	☐
Social functions	☐

● *Social parents' evenings are a good way to exchange information*

 Keys to good practice: How to exchange emergency information

- ✓ Stay calm.
- ✓ Ensure you are talking to the correct person.
- ✓ Clarify who you are.
- ✓ Give a reason for your call.
- ✓ Explain what is happening.
- ✓ If you leave a message, leave a contact telephone number.

 Check it out

Find out from your supervisor what your setting's policy is with regard to verbal information exchange and emergency information exchange.

This activity will require you to understand how important it is that you contribute to positive relationships with the children in your setting.

Design a booklet that will encourage new practitioners to communicate clearly with children. Your booklet must refer to:

- using language the child will understand
- how children must be valued
- how children can be encouraged to make choices
- preferred ways of communication
- using different methods of communication
- acting as a role model.

Use the computer to design the booklet. Make sure it is simple and attractive. If you use photographs ensure you have gained permission.

End-of-unit knowledge check

1 What are verbal skills?
2 What are non-verbal skills?
3 What is appropriate body language?
4 Name three ways in which you can show a child that you are listening to him or her.
5 What does gesticulate mean?
6 List three opportunities for individual conversation with a child in your setting.
7 How could a feely bag activity encourage listening skills?
8 How do children's communication skills develop?
9 What is a child called who speaks two or more languages?
10 What does it mean to speak English as an additional language?
11 Why is it important to allow children to make choices?
12 Where was Highscope developed?
13 What are the three things you need to be when communicating with children?
14 Name two communication barriers.
15 When should you seek another adult to mediate in a disagreement?
16 How would you deal with confidential information from a parent?
17 Where should you talk confidentially to a parent?
18 Why should you sometimes nod or smile when exchanging information?
19 How should you communicate in an emergency?
20 Name two events that could encourage the exchange of information with parents?

Help to keep children safe

An essential part of your role is to help ensure the safety of children. When working with children you will have daily responsibility for maintaining a safe environment, contributing to the protection of children and ensuring that risks and hazards are dealt with and reported promptly according to procedures. However, the final responsibility lies with your manager or supervisor.

You need to know how to keep children safe during day-to-day work activities including outings. When accidents, emergencies or illnesses occur you need to know how to respond appropriately. Supporting the protection of children from abuse is a vital part of any childcare worker's role, and you must be familiar with, and have the ability to set in motion your settings safety and welfare procedures.

What you must know and understand:

- Why it is important to follow the safety, protection and emergency procedures of your setting (K2S15, K2H16, K2S17, K2S18 and K2P25)
- How to safely lay out (...) rooms, equipment, materials and outdoor spaces (K2D22)
- How to use safety equipment to protect children and to promote safety with animals and in the outdoors (K2H23 and K2S33)
- How to make sure that the setting and equipment are appropriate (K2H19, K2H20 and K2H28)
- Why it is important always to practice good hygiene (K2H24)
- How to supervise children safely according to their age, needs and abilities (K2H26)
- Why it is important to follow the correct emergency policies and procedures for accidents and emergencies (K2H27 and K2S1118)
- How to recognise when children are ill and what to do about it (K2H29)
- Why it is important to be familiar with all emergency procedures (K2H30)
- Why it is important to know about the types and possible signs and indicators of child abuse (K2S31 and K2S32)
- How to encourage children to be aware of their own bodies and understand their right not to be abused (K2S34)
- Why it is important to apply boundaries and rules for children's behaviour (K2S35)
- How to encourage positive behaviour and deal with unwanted behaviour (K2S36)
- Why it is important to consider safety issues and concerns when planning, preparing and implementing outings for children (K2S38)

Why it is important to follow the safety, protection and emergency procedures of your setting

Children are at risk from many threats to their safety as they grow up. As children grow up they face many threats to their safety. They depend on the people caring for them to protect them from those threats. All settings that offer care or education to children from birth to 19 years have to have **procedures** for safety, protection and emergencies.

These may include procedures for:

- **accidents** and illnesses
- food preparation
- dealing with strangers
- fire safety
- **personal hygiene practices**
- child protection
- health and safety
- arrival and departure of children
- electrical appliance checks.

Accidents to children are so common that it is too easy to assume that nothing can be done to stop them happening. It would be impossible to prevent every single minor bump and graze – but it is possible to eliminate the majority of **risks** and protect the children in your care. The skill of protecting children from injury involves a thorough knowledge of child development. Children can move onto a new stage of development before carers realise it, and can be at **risk** of injury. For example, a baby of 6 months can roll over; if left on a high surface, the baby could easily fall off onto the floor below.

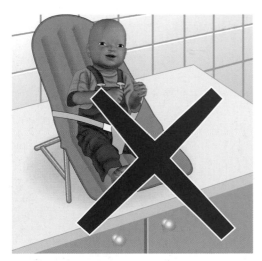
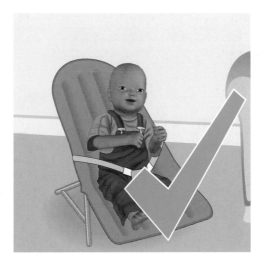

● *It is important to think about the everyday dangers that children face*

Did you think of some of these?

- exposure to drugs
- poisoning
- sudden infant death syndrome
- exposure to passive smoking
- illnesses
- bullying
- abuse.

Unit 202, Help to keep children safe

25

Anyone caring for children has a huge responsibility to protect them from danger. You need to be aware of the possible dangers and set a good example to children.

All settings need to follow a systematic approach to protecting children from harm. When making plans, it is helpful to think about the following questions:

- How many children are involved and what are their ages?
- Is the building or area suitable for all the children?
- Is the area safe? Does it meet all necessary safety regulations?
- Has everyone been trained to be safe in their work with children including how to deal with emergencies?
- Are there clear procedures to keep the children safe from all relevant risks?
- Are activities and **outings** planned with safety in mind? Are all staff clear about what they have to do?
- Are the activities and outings carried out safely?
- Do the children understand what they have to do to help keep themselves safe?
- Are activities and outings reviewed, especially if any incidents have happened?

When you are working with children – even as an assistant – you need to be constantly aware of safety issues. You are responsible for reporting anything that you feel is a risk to the children in your care to your supervisor or manager.

Check it out

What other dangers to children, apart from accidents, can you think of?

Did you know?

Accidents are the greatest single threat to life among children: about 350 children aged under 15 years die every year in the UK. Accidents are also a major cause of disability and ill-health, with over 100,000 children being admitted to hospital and over two million visiting accident and emergency departments every year. (Source: Child Accident Prevention Trust 2003)

Key terms

Outings: visits outside the setting.

Check it out

Look at the picture below.

1 List all the hazards you can see.
2 How would you make the room safer for young children?

Standards relevant to maintaining a safe environment

There are a number of legal and regulatory requirements that you need to know about to help protect children and adults in any setting. These include the following:

- Health and Safety at Work Act 1974.
- Product safety marking.
- Motor Vehicles (Wearing of Seatbelts) (Amendment) Regulations 2006.
- Control of Substances Hazardous to Health (COSHH) Regulations 2002.
- Reporting of Injuries, Diseases and Dangerous Occurrences Regulations (RIDDOR) 1995.
- Childcare Act 2006 – This sets out the statutory framework for assessment of settings, including health and safety, in the Early Years Foundation Stage (EYFS), in force from September 2008. This information was previously covered in the National Standards for Childcare and Education Settings (Ofsted).
- Smoking ban – UK-wide in indoor public places from July 1st 2007. Already in force in Scotland from March 2006, and Wales and Northern Ireland from April 2007. EYFS includes a legal requirement that children always be in a smoke-free environment.
- Food hygiene legislation 2006 (European directives).

As an early years worker, you have an important part to play in the safety of the children in your care. Parents and carers are trusting you to help look after their children. There are often differences in the legal requirements between different countries in the United Kingdom. You must make sure to find out if there are any differences where you work – especially in the National Care Standards. The new statutory Framework for Early Years Foundation Stage (EYFS), which takes effect from September 2008, now includes legislation and standards for keeping children safe in England and Wales.

Key terms

Environment: the place, setting or service where you work with children.

Check it out

Look again at the five requirements shown in the diagram. Find out what is included under each of the requirements in the National Standards that apply in your area.

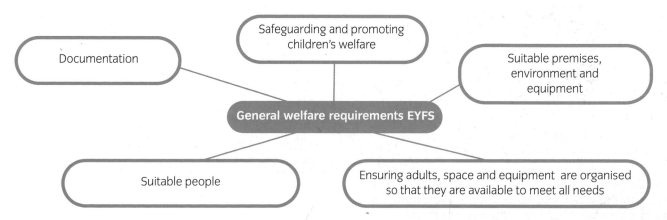

- *The general welfare requirements that cover the safety of children in England and Wales*

Keys to good practice: How to ensure safety in your setting

✓ Always ensure you know your setting's safety policy and procedures.

✓ Check – every day and before each use – that equipment is clean, unbroken and working.

✓ Double-check doors and safety gates every time you go through them.

✓ Always challenge and check up on visitors if you do not know who they are or why they are there.

✓ Report breaches of safety rules – even by colleagues. They could be putting a child's life at risk! 'If in doubt, shout' is a good rule to follow if you feel that children's safety is at risk in any way.

✓ Refuse to work outside the legal ratio of adults to children. Never be left alone with a large group of children.

Check it out

1 What is the legally recommended ratio of adults to children for the setting you work in?
2 Do you have the right numbers or more adults than needed?

How to safely lay out and organise rooms, equipment, materials and outdoor spaces

The way a room is organised depends on many factors including what it is being used for, the ages of the children and the type of room. This section looks at the safety aspects of planning a room.

There are several basic principles that you should consider when planning a room. These include:

- making sure that all the children can access everything; think about children with restricted mobility or limited vision
- making sure that doors and fire exits are unobstructed
- allowing sufficient space around tables for children to move around safely
- making sure that staff have good visibility so that they can supervise children easily
- making sure that 'messy' activities are situated near washbasins and on suitable flooring
- ensuring that free-standing furniture, such as cupboards, cannot topple over on to children.

If you are working with children who have special needs, some adaptations may be necessary to the environment so that they can safely join in with all the activities. The type of adaptations will depend on the individual needs of the children. Talking to the parents or professionals who may be working with the child to find out the particular needs is the best approach.

As part of the preparation for an outdoor session, you should carry out the following checks to ensure that the outdoor setting is safe.

- **Equipment**: large apparatus such as swings and slides should be wiped down and checked for any signs of wear and tear.
- **Access and fencing**: outdoor areas should be fenced off to prevent children from wandering away and also to make sure that strangers or animals do not have access. Fences and gates should be checked before allowing children outside.
- **Plants and animals**: some plants are poisonous and others such as nettles and thistles can sting or scratch children. Regular checks on the plants in the area are important. You should also look out for any signs of animal droppings including cats' and dogs' faeces. Disinfect any area that has been soiled. If sandpits are contaminated, do not allow children into them until the sand has been changed.
- **Dustbins**: some outdoor settings can be close to bins and dustbins. It is important that lids are kept on bins and wherever possible they should be moved out of reach of children. In summer there is also the added danger of wasps and other insects hovering around bins.
- **Sun protection**: children will need adequate protection from the sun. Hats and sunscreen should be used in very sunny weather.

How to use safety equipment to protect children and to promote safety with animals and in the outdoors

Safety equipment

Many items of equipment are used to keep children safe in early years settings. Regular checks on all safety equipment should be carried out, and **manufacturers' instructions** should be closely followed, especially if items need maintaining or cleaning. In general, it is considered good practice to buy new equipment to be sure that it conforms to the latest safety regulations. Second-hand or older equipment needs to be carefully checked as some items can become less effective through wear and tear.

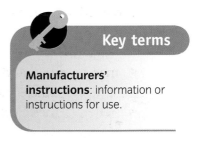

Key terms

Manufacturers' instructions: information or instructions for use.

Type of equipment	Purpose
Bath mats	Prevent children and babies from slipping in the bath.
Car seats/booster cushions	Help to protect children and babies if a car suddenly brakes or is involved in an accident. Car seats have to be correctly fitted. Seats must be correct for the age of the baby or child.
Cooker guards	Prevent children from tipping over pans.

continued on next page

Type of equipment	Purpose
Electric plug covers	Prevent children from putting their fingers or objects into plug sockets.
Fire guards	Used around heaters and radiators to prevent children from being burnt.
Highchairs	Help young children to sit safely at mealtimes. Include harnesses to strap children in.
Reins and harnesses	Prevent children from straying into a road or dangerous area when they are outside. Also used in pushchairs and highchairs to prevent children from falling out.
Safety gates	Prevent babies and children from falling downstairs or from having access to certain areas.
Window and cupboard door locks	Prevent children from opening cupboards and windows.

● *Safety equipment for babies and children*

Safety with animals

While children can learn a lot from and enjoy contact with animals, any setting that cares for animals will have to pay particular attention to health and safety. Some diseases are associated with animals, and it is important before introducing a new pet to make sure that you are aware of any risks. For example, a risk of caring for cats and dogs is the danger that children can become infected with one of the worms that can be present in these animals' faeces.

 Keys to good practice: How to minimise the risk of infection when caring for animals

✓ Feed animals away from kitchen areas.

✓ Use separate utensils for feeding animals.

✓ Make sure that animals are not allowed near children's food or sleeping areas.

✓ Follow recommended care routines for animals, for example vaccinations, worming, flea control measures.

✓ Ensure that children wash their hands thoroughly after handling any animal.

✓ Regularly clean animals' cages or areas.

In addition, children have to be taught that animals are not playthings. This means that an adult should closely supervise all contacts between animals and children so that the animals are treated with respect. Good supervision should prevent children from being bitten or scratched by distressed or irritated pets.

How to make sure that the setting and equipment are appropriate

The Kitemark

Many items that we use every day have been tested for safety by the British Standards Institute (BSI). If an item has a Kitemark it means that BSI has independently tested and confirmed that the product complies with the relevant standard and is safe and reliable. The manufacturer pays for this service and their product is tested and assessed at regular intervals.

Products are not legally required to carry a Kitemark, but many everyday appliances such as fridges, electrical plugs and crash helmets have them.

Many products such as toys must meet **legal requirements** before they can be sold within the European Union, and must carry a CE marking. A CE marking shows that the product meets European rules but it is not a European safety or quality mark. Some products carry both a Kitemark and a CE marking. This tells you that BSI has also tested them against the appropriate standard.

The Health and Safety at Work Act

The Health and Safety at Work Act (see page 000) have clear principles to ensure health and safety at work. Employers and employees have a responsibility for the safety of a workplace. This means that when you are working in a childcare setting (or anywhere else) you have the right to expect that you will not be exposed to any dangers to your health and safety. You must also make sure that you deal with or report any hazards that you see.

The legislation covers all of the following:
- buildings and services – design and maintenance
- cleanliness of the environment and of food preparation areas
- safe storage and use of equipment
- working practices that promote health and safety
- provision of a safety policy.

 Key terms

Legal requirements: the laws governing safety in your home country.

 Check it out

1 Pick a room in your place of work. How many items can you find that display the Kitemark? Make a note of them.
2 Pick five of the items you have listed. In a group discuss why you think they need to conform to British Standards.
3 Did you find anything that you thought should have the Kitemark that didn't?

If you notice anything that could be a source of danger you must report it immediately and/or take steps to protect other people. You must also co-operate with your employer on health and safety issues, for example by not using unsafe equipment or taking note of warning notices. Blocking fire exits with toys or uncovering electric sockets, for example, is a very serious offence because it goes against safety regulations and can cause death or serious injury.

Accidents are less likely to happen when:

- potential dangers have been minimised, for example kettle flexes are kept well away from worktop edges, ponds are properly covered or filled in
- children are not over-protected and are allowed to develop skills to keep themselves safe
- adults are good role models and set a safe example
- children are never left alone
- toys and equipment have the Kitemark or safety mark on them to show they are of a good standard.

COSHH

Legislation called COSHH (Control of Substances Hazardous to Health) covers substances that can cause ill-health. COSHH lays down a step-by-step approach to the precautions to prevent injury or illness from dangerous substances. Such substances must have labels on them. The examples below show that substances are dangerous and need to be kept in special containers and carefully stored.

very toxic or toxic

harmful or irritant

corrosive

- *Warning signs shown on hazardous substances*

Thousands of people are exposed to hazardous substances at work. If the exposure is not prevented or properly controlled, it can cause serious illness and sometimes even death. This clearly is unacceptable in a childcare setting. Although you may not think there are many dangerous substances in your setting, there will be some, such as cleaning products, that pose the risk of poisoning for children.

The effects of hazardous substances on children and staff include:
- poisoning by drinking toxic liquids from bottles mistakenly thought to contain water or soft drinks – sometimes with fatal results
- cancer, which can appear many years after first exposure to carcinogenic (cancer-causing) substances at work
- infection from bacteria and other micro-organisms ('biological agents').

Maintaining safety in the setting

Being aware of potential dangers to a child's health and safety is not enough – you must plan activities and routines with safety in mind. Some of the things to think about are listed below.

- Regularly check equipment for broken parts and sharp edges.
- Make sure that large equipment and toys are arranged to allow safe use by all children.
- Check outside play areas daily for broken glass, syringes and other dangerous litter.
- Check toilet and washing facilities regularly for cleanliness and supplies of toilet paper and soap.
- Make sure that all locks, catches, etc. that stop children leaving the building alone are working.
- Do not store dangerous items, for example knives or bleach, in cupboards and shelves that are accessible to children.
- Always follow procedures for dealing with spillages of urine, faeces, blood and vomit.
- Follow the procedures for dealing with visitors to the setting – reporting, signing in, etc.
- Follow good practice in the preparation of food and drink.

Did you have these in your list?

Check it out

Imagine you have been given the responsibility for the daily safety checks in the toddler room at the nursery where you are working. Your supervisor has asked you to write down your checklist of points for safety in the room. Make your list showing the checks you would carry out to ensure the safety of all the children in your care.

Buildings and maintenance
- Doors opening into entrances and exits from the building must not be capable of being opened by young children.
- Emergency exits must be clear and easy to open from the inside.
- Floors should not have any loose rugs or pieces of carpet.

Cleanliness of the general environment
- There should be a high standard of cleanliness throughout the building.
- Spillages should be immediately cleaned.
- Toilet areas should be regularly cleaned and checked.

Food preparation areas
- All staff dealing with food should have a food hygiene certificate.
- All regulations relating to food storage should be followed.

Safe storage and use of equipment

- Cupboards at 'child level' should not contain cleaning items, knives, tools or any other potentially dangerous items.
- Toys with very small parts should be kept well away from children under 3 years of age.
- Children should not be able to touch heaters and radiators.

Outdoor areas

- Outdoor slides, swings, etc. should have safe, impact-absorbing matting provided and should be checked for safety.
- Gates should not be able to be opened by young children.
- Sandpits should be kept covered when not in use.

Working practices that promote health and safety

- Adults must not leave bags or coats containing medicines within reach of children.
- Adults must not bring hot drinks into the same room as children.
- All stairs should have fixed guards at the top and bottom.
- Children using babywalkers, bicycles, etc. should be supervised at all times land should wear helmets where appropriate.

Case study 1: Health and safety outside

Lee is working in a childcare setting that also has an after-school club for older children. The older children enjoy ball games in the outdoor play area. Last night he was concerned that some of the bigger boys had been using the swings meant for younger children. When he goes outside he notices that the outside gate has been left open and there is a dog wandering around the play area, especially in the sandpit.

1. *Should Lee allow the children outside to play?*
2. *What action should Lee take now?*
3. *What might the manager of the setting do to stop the things happening that concern Lee?*
4. *Design a notice reminding the supervisors of the after-school club about the health and safety requirements.*

It is important that all items used by children are suitable for them – this means suitable for their age and stage of development.

A safety Kitemark is only an indication of the level of safety of an item when the item is being properly used. So the most important factor in ensuring safety is the person using the item or the person responsible for them – that means you!

A child is not interested in and often not able to read the instructions on a game or piece of equipment. So the responsibility rests with you. You can very easily make following the instructions part of the activity, especially with an older child. This also helps the child to learn about safety requirements and the importance of reading instructions.

● *Helping a child with instructions*

Why it is important always to practice good hygiene

All children pick up infections and become ill from time to time as their immune systems develop. However, many illnesses are caused by poor hygiene practices. The hospital superbug is mostly a result of doctors and nurses not washing their hands properly.

You don't need to know the science behind all different types of infections, but you do need to know how infection is passed on from one person to another.

The picture below shows some of the ways that bacteria and viruses can be passed on to others. Just think of all the times you may pass infection from one source to another. How can you help to protect yourself as well as the children you are working with?

Did you know?

In a survey one in three men and one in five women admit they don't wash their hands after going to the loo or before preparing food.

Bacteria left on a doorknob by one person can be picked up by the next 14 who touch it – then passed on to everything they touch. (Source: *Good Housekeeping*, August 2004)

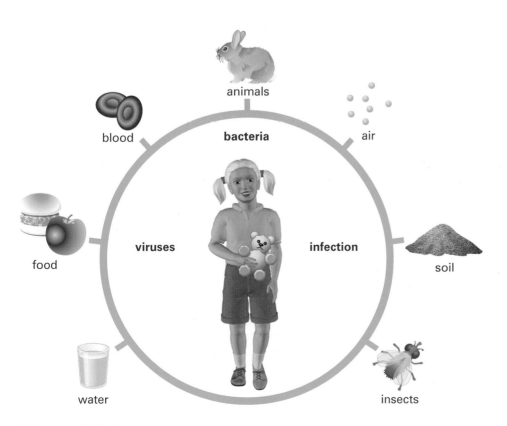

● *Sources of infection*

✔ Keys to good practice: How to avoid infection

✓ Always wash hands after using the toilet, changing nappies, handling animals and before handling food.

✓ Dispose of dirty nappies and other soiled items correctly.

✓ Cover coughs and sneezes and dispose of tissues correctly – then wash your hands.

✓ Always cover any cuts or grazes that you may have and use plastic gloves when dealing with children with cuts or grazes.

✓ Follow food hygiene precautions to the letter – never use food or drink that has any risk of being contaminated.

✓ Take care when handling animals – make sure that children don't let them lick their faces and that they always wash their hands after handling animals.

✓ Take care that gardens and sandpits are not contaminated by animal faeces.

The number of people, including children, who are infected with the HIV virus or hepatitis is rising. There are many reasons why a child may be infected, but the important thing is to minimise the risk to you and to other children. If you follow basic good hygiene practices as outlined above, you will not be at risk from HIV or hepatitis. These infections are carried in the blood or other bodily fluids. Another person can only be infected by direct contact with that fluid through an open wound. If you always wear gloves when changing nappies and carrying out first aid, and always keep cuts and grazes covered you will not be at risk of infection.

Did you know?

HIV is not transmitted by casual physical contact, coughing, sneezing, kissing, sharing toilet and washing facilities, using eating utensils or consuming food handled by someone who has HIV, nor is it spread by mosquitoes or other insect bites.

How to supervise children safely according to their age, needs and abilities

The key factor in protecting children in your care from accidents and injury is that you understand the risks they are exposed to, especially in relation to their age and stage of development. You should then be able to help to identify risks for situations and certain groups of children.

There are common accident risks for all children. These include potential injury from:

- falls
- choking
- suffocation
- burns and scalds
- cuts and bruises
- drowning
- poisoning
- being out and about
- car accidents.

Check it out

Think about the different ways children at different stages of development can injure themselves in these ways. How could the children you care for be injured in the ways shown above?

 Common accident risks for children

If you think about a child's stage of development and have a good understanding of that stage, you should be able to predict how the child could be injured and so take steps to prevent it. This sounds easy – and with a little thought and a lot of understanding it can be. All too often you hear parents or carers saying after an accident, 'but I didn't know he could do that yet …'

Case study 2: Preventing accidents

Lily, aged 2, is tall for her age. She is also extremely curious and has just discovered that she can now just reach the door handles at home and feel the pattern on them. She lives in an old house with a cellar and a front door that opens onto a busy main road. When she is out and about she doesn't always like to have her hand held, preferring to 'do it herself'.

1   *Can you think of any dangers that Lily might be at risk from?*
2   *Why do you think these are dangers to Lily?*
3   *What steps should her parents be taking to protect her from possible injury?*

The following table shows the common accidents that occur at different ages, why they occur and, most importantly, what you need to think about when supervising children.

Age/stage of development	Common accidents	Reasons	Prevention
Birth to crawling Very dependent and vulnerable – but can move more than you think.	Falls from raised surfaces.	Even small babies can move by wriggling, the risk increases as the baby grows.	Never leave a baby unattended on a raised surface or put a bouncing chair on a raised surface.
	Suffocation.	Babies cannot push covers or other items away from their face.	Do not use duvets or pillows for babies under 1 year.
	Choking.	Young babies cannot deal with large volumes of fluid or hard objects.	Never 'prop feed'. Never leave a baby alone when giving solids. Keep small objects from a baby's grasp. Endure older children don't put anything in a baby's mouth.
	Strangulation.	Ribbons, jewellery or wool could get caught in a cot or car seat, for example.	Never put ribbons or jewellery around a baby's neck Check clothing is not too tight.
	Burns and scalds.	A baby's skin is 15 times thinner than an adults – so they burn much easier.	Never have hot drinks near young children. Test bath water. Never use microwaves for heating feeds. Keep the baby well covered and protected from the sun.
	Drowning.	Babies can drown in as little as 5cm (2 inches) of water.	Never leave a baby in water without an adult present, even if using a bath seat.
Crawling to walking – about 6–15 months Mobile at last!	Falls downstairs, from raised surfaces, highchairs, cots.	As a baby starts to become mobile he or she wants to explore but lacks understanding of danger, e.g. from stairs, furniture, etc.	Always guard stairs. Use a five-point harness. Never leave a baby on high surfaces.

Did you know?

In 2002 over 27,700 babies under 6 months were injured in accidents. (Source: Child Accident Prevention Trust, 2003)

continued on next page

Age/stage of development	Common accidents	Reasons	Prevention
Crawling to walking about – 6–15 months (continued)	Suffocation from bedding, plastic bags and choking by food and small objects.	A baby can still get trapped in bedding. A baby will explore plastic bags, which are seen as a toy. A baby uses the mouth to explore, putting anything new into the mouth – anything larger than a 2p piece will cause choking.	Do not use a duvet on a baby under 1 year. Keep plastic bags out of reach. Always stay with a baby who is eating or drinking. Keep small items out of reach. Teach older children not to put anything in a baby's mouth. Never allow a child under 6 to have peanuts.
	Strangulation.	Clothing is still a risk. Unexpected items can cause problems to a mobile baby, e.g. washing lines, window blind cords, belts, etc.	Never put anything around a baby's neck and check clothing. Keep blind cords, etc. short and out of reach, and never next to a cot or bed.
	Burns and scalds.	With increased mobility a baby can now reach things on surfaces, e.g. drinks, radiators, ovens, and can pull on kettle flexes and pan handles. When sunny, it is difficult to keep a mobile baby in the shade. A baby has no understanding of what 'hot' is and cannot learn from experience at this stage.	Take the same precautions as for a young baby. Use a coiled flex on kettles and a safety gate to bar access to the kitchen when cooking. Take extra care with clothes, sun creams and hats in the sun. Keep out of the sun between 11am and 3pm. Fit guards and keep all sources of burns and scalds out of reach.

Did you know?

In 2002 38,300 babies under a year old were taken to hospital after a fall, and 17,000 with burns and scalds. (Source: Child Accident Prevention Trust, 2003)

continued on next page

Age/stage of development	Common accidents	Reasons	Prevention
Crawling to walking – about 6–15 months (continued)	Drowning.	Out of curiosity a baby may peer into water containers. A baby enjoys water play and being left alone in the bath.	Supervise water play very closely and empty water containers immediately when finished with. Never leave a baby alone in the bath or with older children.
	Cuts and bruises.	First mobile movements are often unsteady and poorly co-ordinated. Out of curiosity a baby may grab anything that takes his or her attention, even if it is big and heavy.	Move dangerous and/or heavy items that are a risk. Carefully position furniture with hard or sharp edges so that there is less chance of injury.
	Falls and injuries during transport.	A car seat may not be correctly secured. A baby may fall out of a pram or pushchair if no harness is used. Baby walkers are associated with a range of injuries, especially falls and burns.	Always secure a baby in the correct car seat, and use harnesses in prams. Do not use baby walkers.
Toddlers – about 1–3 years Very inquisitive and full of energy. Short attention span and totally absorbed in themselves. Not old enough to understand the concept of danger, and do not always learn from experience.	Falls downstairs and from windows.	New-found climbing skills and increased manual dexterity mean toddlers can get upstairs, onto window sills, and can open catches.	Use good safety gates and window locks that cannot be opened by the toddler. Teach the toddler to climb stairs but don't allow him or her to use them alone. Don't put furniture underneath windows.
	Suffocation and choking.	A toddler may want to play with plastic bags. A toddler may be still learning to chew and still putting things in the mouth.	Keep plastic bags out of reach or destroy them. Take precautions as for younger children. It is important to still avoid peanuts as the oil in them can cause swelling of the bronchial tubes.

Did you know?

By law, babies and toddlers must be in a proper car seat when travelling in the car – even for very short journeys. (Source: Child Accident Prevention Trust, 2007)

continued on next page

Age/stage of development	Common accidents	Reasons	Prevention
Toddlers – about 1–3 years (continued)	Poisoning.	Curiosity and increasing skills mean a toddler has access to poisonous substances, medicines (despite child-resistant tops), chemicals and berries.	Keep all medicines and chemicals locked away and out of reach. Keep chemicals in original containers. Don't keep medicines in handbags or by the bed. Check gardens for poisonous plants.
Did you know? In 2002 over 212,000 children aged 1–3 attended hospital after a fall and 22,500 after a suspected poisoning. (Source: Child Accident Prevention Trust, 2003) 20 children a day are admitted to hospital with suspected accidental poisoning. It can take only 5 seconds for a toddler to suffer third degree burns from hot water from the bath tap. (Source: Child Accident Prevention Trust, 2007)	Strangulation.	A toddler may get the head into but not out of gaps. Clothing may have poor necklines, cords, etc.	Supervise climbing games. Check necklines and loose cords, etc.
	Burns and scalds.	Curiosity is still an issue – pans and irons are a hazard. A toddler starts to imitate adults. A toddler is able to use matches if found. A toddler's skin is still easy to burn, e.g. in a hot bath, etc.	Take precautions as for babies of 6–15 months, but with extra vigilance.
	Drowning.	A toddler has increasing mobility, independence and curiosity – especially of garden ponds. Drowning is possible in very small amounts of water.	Closely supervise a toddler around any water. Ensure there is secure fencing around ponds. Empty water containers when they are finished with. Stay with a toddler in the bath.
	Cuts and bruises.	Fingers can easily be trapped in door jambs. Toddlers may cut themselves while trying to imitate adults using scissors, knives or razors.	Be aware of the risk of doors when little fingers are around. Toddlers could run into low glass in doors. Keep scissors, etc. out of reach. Board up low-glass doors.

continued on next page

Age/stage of development	Common accidents	Reasons	Prevention
Toddlers – about 1–3 years (continued)	Out and about.	Toddlers may want to experiment with their car seat or buggy harness. Toddlers may be left alone in a car. Toddlers may run off when out on the street.	Use the correct seat and harness, and discourage messing with fastenings. Never leave toddlers alone in a car. Use a harness and reins when out on the road. Start simple road-safety training.
About 3–5 years Improving co-ordination and increasing understanding of action and consequence. May well forget safety instructions when tired or distracted. Still enjoy testing their abilities and finding unusual ways to use toys and other objects!	Falls downstairs, from windows and from play equipment.	Children are attracted to stairs and windows – they use their powerful imaginations to be Superman, etc. Children test their own skills by climbing higher and so are at risk of falling further.	Do not allow stairs to be used for playing. Fit window locks and tell children about the dangers. Choose playgrounds with impact-absorbing surfaces. Tell children how to use equipment properly.
	Choking and suffocation.	Children may want to eat on the move Ice cubes and small sweets pose a danger. Peanuts are still a risk.	Encourage children to sit still while eating and not to run with sweets in their mouth. Avoid peanuts with children under 6.
	Poisoning.	Children could confuse sweets with medicines and berries. Children have increased skills at overcoming locks and resistant caps.	Keep medicines, etc. locked away. Teach children not to eat anything they pick outside without checking with you.
	Burns and scalds.	Copying adults, there is danger from hot foods, liquids, taps and candles. Children understand the concept of 'hot, do not touch' but can forget when practising their manual skills of turning and switching.	Keep dangerous items out of reach, especially matches and candles. Teach children what to do if a fire or smoke alarm goes off. Use thermostatic valves on taps.

Did you know?

In 2002 over 4,400 children aged 3–5 were injured in road accidents and 527 were injured in fires; two died. (Source: Child Accident Prevention Trust, 2003)

continued on next page

Age/stage of development	Common accidents	Reasons	Prevention
About 3–5 years (continued)	Drowning.	Any open water remains a threat, especially as children become more independent. A child can be left in the bath from 4 years, but an adult should be nearby.	Supervise children closely near water. Fence off ponds. Teach children to swim.
	Cuts	Children can now be taught to use scissors and knives safely. There is still a risk with sharp objects if they are not used safely in play.	Keep sharp objects out of reach. Teach children how to use them safely.
	Out and about.	Children do not have the understanding or experience to deal with traffic. They may have started to ride a bicycle.	Never allow children under 5 on the road alone – on foot or on a bike. Teach road safety, but aware of children's limits of remembering and understanding. Ensure children always use a helmet when on a bike.
About 5–7 years and onwards Risk-assessment skills improving, but still impulsive and may overestimate ability. More external influences on behaviour.	Falls, choking, poisoning, burns and scalds, drowning, cuts and bruises, accidents when out and about, road accidents, cycle accidents.	Injuries at this age are often due to children being keen to help and copy adults, but misjudging their abilities. Boisterous play can result in accidents. The increasing influence of friends – persuading them to 'have a go' – can increase the risk.	As for ages 3–5, ensure dangerous items are hard to reach Encourage children to start taking some responsibility for their own safety, but the extent of this will vary. Realise that repeating a rule doesn't mean a child understands or will follow it; this improves as the child gets older, but outside influence can 'overrule' this.

● *Common accidents, why they occur and how they can be prevented*

It would be very easy to respond to all the risks children are exposed to by not allowing them to explore or experiment. But just think about how that would affect a child's development.

Any activity a child does has some risk attached, even something as simple as painting! If the activity is well planned and organised with thought given to possible dangers, the risk of accidents or injuries should be minimal.

The secret is to balance the risk of an activity against the benefit to and safety of the child. This is known as risk assessment.

Test yourself

Consider two common, popular activities – painting and outdoor play on large equipment. What are the potential dangers from each point?

Painting:
- Water spilt on floor
- Children moving around with paint brushes
- Cleaning up after the activity.

Outdoor play:
- Children running around
- Height of equipment
- Recent rain.

Make a list of why children might be injured as a result of any of these points and identify what you could do to prevent injury?

Did you know?

The figures in the table above are only a part of the picture. Every year some 2 million children – about one in five – are seen in accident and emergency departments after an accident. Around 320 children die each year as a result of accidents and many more suffer long-term disability.

Case study 3: Risk assessment for outdoor activities

Jasmine is planning an outing with a colleague to the local woods with two groups of children from her childcare setting. She hopes that she can include some nature work, physical-skill development and art work with the children. She is planning to take a group of six 4-year-olds from the pre-school group and a group of eight 7- and 8-year-olds from the after-school group.

1 List the different safety risks for each of the groups.
2 What will Jasmine need to think about for each group?
3 How much freedom will each group be able to have in the area of wood Jasmine plans to work in?

Keys to good practice: How to use equipment safely

✓ Ensure you can see all children.

✓ Keep moving around so that you can see all activity.

✓ Check that the children do not become over-excited.

✓ Ensure that the equipment is used correctly.

✓ Encourage children to rest when tired.

When you are supervising indoor and outdoor activities it is important that equipment is of the highest safety standard to avoid any risk of a child being injured. Space must be allowed for children to run, hop, skip, throw and so on. Space will obviously vary according to availability but no room should be overcrowded. This means that you need to think about the size of the groups of children that are using an area.

Check it out

Ask your supervisor if you can read the health and safety policy of your setting. Think about how you would need to refer to it when checking the safety of planned activities.

 Keys to good practice: How to ensure children's safety

Equipment safety

✓ Always ensure that objects and equipment are regularly checked for wear and tear, such as fraying ropes and rusting joints.

✓ Check that equipment is clean and dry, especially slides, steps, etc.

Personal safety

✓ Ensure that each child has the space to move freely without bumping into other children or objects.

✓ Ensure that the appropriate adult/child ratios required by your social services department are maintained for adequate supervision.

✓ Ensure that swings and rope ladders are used by one child at a time. All other children should be discouraged from playing nearby in case they are hurt by a swing or rope.

✓ Ensure all children are visible.

Safety of the environment

✓ Check that outdoor areas are free from harmful **waste** such as dog faeces (which can cause eye damage to young children), broken equipment and litter.

✓ Ensure that surfaces are soft and safe, to encourage freedom of movement.

Key terms

Waste: unwanted materials such as used nappies, body fluids, dressings, cleaning cloths.

While you are maintaining their safety, it is important that children are given the freedom to develop their skills. They should have adult support but not too much intervention.

Why it is important to follow the correct policies and procedures for accidents and emergencies

Young children tend to have accidents and injure themselves. Even a simple banging of heads when two children run into each other could be serious if the carer failed to notice symptoms that something was wrong. Sadly some children have died because the people caring for them have not known what to do.

All childcare settings must have at least one person qualified in first aid. As a childcare worker you have a responsibility to take a first aid course that specialises in first aid for children. You should also keep your first aid knowledge up to date. If you haven't done a first aid course there are some basic procedures you must know about.

- If a child is injured, tell someone in charge immediately.
- If you are at all worried about a child after an accident, you should ring for an ambulance.

● *Inform your manager*

What is an emergency?

An emergency is whenever someone is injured or seriously ill, or is in danger of being so.

Examples include:

- choking
- swallowed poisons
- severe bleeding
- allergic reactions
- convulsions
- head injuries
- broken bones
- unconsciousness.

Basic first aid

Keep calm

1   Assessing the casualty
    - **Danger** – are you or the casualty in danger?
    - **Response** – is the casualty conscious?
    - **Airway** – is the airway open?
    - **Breathing** – is the casualty breathing? If not, get someone to dial 999.

2   Act on your findings and call for help!

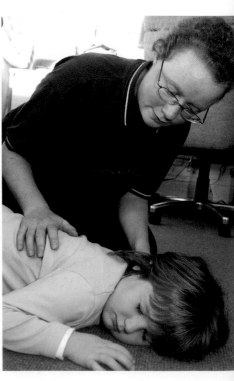

● *Calmly assess the casualty*

Casualty conscious, breathing present

1 Treat any injuries.
2 Call for help if needed.

Casualty unconscious, breathing present

1 Treat any life-threatening injuries.
2 Place in the recovery position.
3 Call for help.

Recovery position

● *Recovery position*

An unconscious casualty who is breathing and has no other life-threatening conditions should be placed in the recovery position.

● Turn the casualty onto his or her side.
● Lift the chin forward in open airway position and adjust the hand under the cheek as necessary.
● Check the casualty cannot roll forwards or backwards.
● Check the casualty's breathing and pulse continuously.

Note: if you suspect an injury to the back or neck, place your hands on either side of their face. With your fingertips gently lift the jaw to open the airway. Take care not to tilt the casualty's neck.

If the casualty is a baby less than a year old, hold the baby in your arms. Make sure the head is tilted downwards to prevent the baby from choking on the tongue or inhaling vomit. Keep checking for breathing and call for help. Take the baby with you if you need to go into another room or the telephone.

Casualty unconscious and not breathing

Open the airway and call for help.

Opening the airway

1 Open the airway by tilting the head, removing any obvious obstructions in the mouth and lifting the chin.
2 Look, listen and feel for breathing.
3 Keep the chin held up and put the casualty in the recovery position.
4 Call for help.

Opening the airway is the single most important first aid action for anyone who is unconscious, whether it is an adult or child. It is a simple action that can and does save lives.

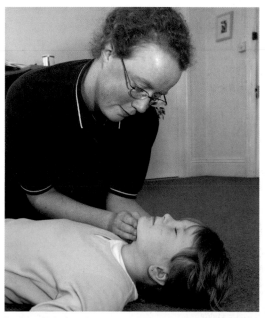
● *Opening the airway*

Bleeding

Bleeding from wounds should be controlled as follows.

- **Elevate** the wound.
- **Press** on the wound (over clean material if at hand).
- Apply a **dressing**.
- If there is a foreign body in the wound, leave it and press around the wound to stop the bleeding. Do not try to remove it as this may make the wound worse.
- Treat the casualty for **shock**, reassure the casualty and keep him or her warm. Lay the casualty down, lower the head, raise the feet and loosen tight clothing.

When a child is bleeding, make sure you:

- **reassure** the child and encourage the child to relax.
- **do not** move the child unnecessarily.
- **do not** give food or drink.
- retain normal body heat by covering the child with a blanket or coat.
- if serious, or there is doubt, call an ambulance.

Other common emergencies

The table below shows some other common emergencies that may affect children in your care and how to deal with them. However, this is not a substitute for attending a first aid course.

In the case of an accident, in addition to taking action to help the casualty, you or someone else needs to:

- send for a qualified first-aider if you are not qualified yourself
- call for your supervisor
- calm the other children
- inform the child's parents
- record the incident in the accident book.

Ambulances

When dialling 999, always have ready:

- the details of the accident and injury
- the age of the child
- where the injured child is.

In serious incidents involving breathing difficulties or severe bleeding, an ambulance should be summoned as soon as possible – preferably while first aid is being given.

Emergency	Treatment
Cuts and grazes.	• For minor cuts and grazes wash with clean water to remove dirt. • Cover with an appropriate dressing.
Head injury.	• Control any bleeding by applying pressure with a pad. • Lay the casualty down. • Take or send the casualty to hospital. • Monitor the level of consciousness, vomiting, etc.
Convulsions. Often the result of a high temperature in a child.	• If the child is hot, help to cool the child by removing clothing. • Protect the child from injury – clear surrounding objects. • Sponge the child with tepid water. • Place the child in the recovery position. • Dial 999 for an ambulance.
Back injury. Always suspect after a fall from a swing, slide, tree, etc.	• Do not move or attempt to move the child. • Steady and support the neck and head. • Dial 999 for an ambulance.
Allergic reaction to stings, medicines or irritants – red blotchy skin, swelling of face and neck, problems with breathing leading to anaphylactic shock.	• Dial 999 for an ambulance. • Put the child into a comfortable position. • Monitor the airway, breathing and pulse.
Choking in young children – may go very quiet and blue around lips. May be very noisy breathing and coughing.	• Lean an older child forward or put a baby over your knee face downwards and give five back slaps between the shoulders. • Remove any obvious obstruction from the mouth. • Next, give five chest thrusts: stand behind the child, make a fist against the lower breast bone, grasp the fist with the other hand and press it sharply into the chest. • For a baby, press two fingertips on the lower half of the breast bone. Check ABC. Dial 999 for an ambulance.
Asthma attack or breathing difficulties.	• Make the child comfortable. The child should be seated in the position most comfortable away from other children in a quiet area. Let the child use an inhaler if he or she has one – usually a blue reliever. • Encourage the child to breathe slowly. If the attack doesn't subside, call for medical help.
Suspected broken bones or sprains.	• Support the affected limb with a sling (if an arm) or padding. • Take the child to hospital or call an ambulance.
Burns and scalds.	• Cool the burn with cold water for at least ten minutes. • Cover the burn with a sterile or clean dressing or even a clean plastic bag. • For any burn or scald on a young child call an ambulance or take the child to hospital.
Poisoning – drugs, plants, etc.	• Dial 999 for an ambulance. • Try to find out what has been taken and keep the evidence. • If unconscious, check the airway and put the child in the recovery position.

• *Common emergencies and how to treat them*

First aid boxes

Always make sure you know where the first aid box is kept and what is in it.

A good first aid box should contain the following items:

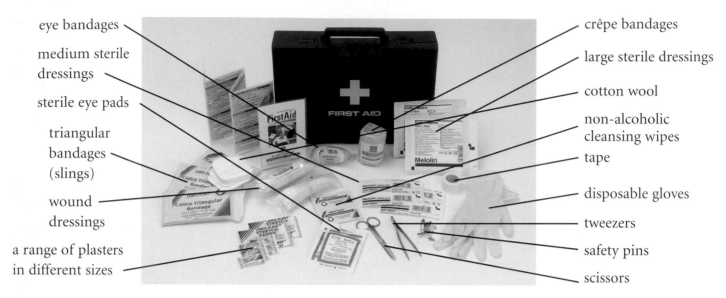

eye bandages
medium sterile dressings
sterile eye pads
triangular bandages (slings)
wound dressings
a range of plasters in different sizes

crêpe bandages
large sterile dressings
cotton wool
non-alcoholic cleansing wipes
tape
disposable gloves
tweezers
safety pins
scissors

Procedures after an accident or emergency

The child should have a record card with emergency contact numbers of parents, grandparents or other relatives. They should be people who are usually easy to contact, and who in turn can contact the parents if necessary.

The person in charge must get in touch with the emergency contact as soon as possible and tell that person about the incident, and where the child is being taken. If the child has to go to hospital before the parents arrive someone the child knows well should go to the hospital with them.

Even a minor accident should be entered in the accident book. The accident may need to be reported to the Health and Safety Executive. A full report is needed. In any incident the person in charge should look at what happened to see what could be done to prevent a similar incident happening again.

Check it out

1 Find out where the first aid kit is at work. Is it easy to find?
2 Do the contents match the list above? Is anything missing? Are there any extra items, and if so what are they for?
3 What is the procedure following an accident to a child in your setting?

Case study 4: A child is injured

You are looking after two children, Samir aged 2 and Ahmed aged 5, at their home. Their parents have gone shopping for the afternoon. At 2 pm, during a game with a ball, Ahmed trips and falls heavily on his left leg. You see that his leg is swollen and it looks a strange shape.

1 *What do you do immediately?*
2 *What, if anything, do you do with Ahmed's leg?*
3 *What do you do with Samir?*
4 *Who do you contact first and how?*
5 *Now imagine this incident had happened at school. What else might have to be done?*

How to recognise when children are ill and what to do about it

You should always make sure that you follow the routines that help to protect children from illness, for example careful hand washing and cleanliness of toilet areas.

Parents may ask for advice about their children when they are ill or appear unwell. Always suggest they take their child to the doctor. Doctors prefer to see a child, even if for a minor illness, rather than miss a serious illness such as meningitis.

When a child is taken ill in your care, the parents or guardians must be informed. As a student or junior worker you should always check with your supervisor. You can provide support to a child who is ill while his or her parents are coming by sitting quietly with the child, perhaps reading a story.

Often after an illness a child may need to take medicine while at nursery or school. Most settings have a policy that parents must give written consent for their child to have medicines administered by the nursery nurse or teacher. Childcare workers are not allowed to give medicines to children without this written permission under any circumstances.

● *Comforting a sick child*

Why it is important to be familiar with all emergency procedures

As part of the 1974 Health and Safety at Work Act and its Regulations, your setting will have a safety policy if it employs five or more staff. The policy will cover emergency procedures in the event of a fire, accident or other emergency. There are many different types of emergency and it is important to know what the different procedures are, especially for fires, a security incident or if a child goes missing.

Evacuation procedures

A building may need to be evacuated in the event of a fire, gas leak or bomb scare. All adults need to know what to do. In most settings, one member of staff is responsible for these procedures and will need to make sure that all staff are aware of the evacuation procedures. Evacuation practices need to be held regularly and relevant signs and notices must be kept in place. Drills and practices should always be taken seriously so that any difficulties can be reviewed.

Check it out

Find out what the emergency procedure is at your setting.

1 How is the alarm raised?
2 Who contacts the emergency services?
3 Who takes out the registers and checks them?
4 What are the safest exit points?
5 Where is the assembly point?
6 How often is there an emergency practice?
7 How are visitors to the setting made aware of evacuation procedures?
8 How are children reassured during evacuation practices?
9 Is there a notice like the one on page 52 in view?

IN CASE OF FIRE

Close doors and windows and try to get the children out of the premises by the normal routes.

Do not leave the children unattended.

Do not stop to put out the fire (unless very small).

Call the fire brigade by telephone as soon as possible as follows:
1 Lift the receiver and dial 999.
2 Give the operator your telephone number and ask for FIRE.
3 When the brigade replies give the information clearly, for example 'fire at the Elms Nursery, 23 Berry Road, Stockton, XY5 3ZA, situated between the Black Dog Pub and DIY centre'.

Do not replace the receiver until the address has been repeated by the fire operator.

 Keys to good practice: How to carry out a practice evacuation

✓ Have an evacuation practice every three months.

✓ If there are problems with the procedures repeat the practice or seek advice from a fire officer.

✓ Reassure children during a practice by staying calm and explaining what is happening.

✓ Praise children and thank them for their help in carrying out the evacuation.

✓ Provide an absorbing activity, such as reading a story or playing a game, to help the children to settle down quickly after the practice.

Why it is important to know about the types and possible signs and indicators of child abuse

Most of this unit focuses on your role in protecting children and keeping them safe in the setting you work in. One very important part of keeping children safe is recognising when they are not safe outside of the childcare setting.

You need to use several very important skills:
- observation – recognising when a child's behaviour has changed, for example
- having a thorough knowledge of normal patterns of development and behaviour
- knowing when to be concerned for a child's welfare and safety
- knowing your role and responsibility when abuse is suspected.

The Early Years Foundation Stage framework contains clear guidance about child protection. Prior to this, the National Standards for Under Eights Day Care and Childminding contained requirements relating to the area's child protection committee.

It is one of the most important responsibilities of a childcare worker to report suspicion of abuse to an appropriate person. You are most likely to be the worker in close contact with a child on a daily basis so will be the most likely person to spot the warning signs of possible abuse. Dealing with any suspicions promptly and appropriately is vital.

Abuse can happen as a one-off incident or can be a regular feature of a child's life. Abuse can take place anywhere and by anyone, but the majority of abuse is carried out by someone the child knows.

In 2000 the NSPCC published the results of a national survey of 3,000 young people aged 18 to 24 about their experience of a wide range of issues and found that:

- 7 per cent had been physically abused by a carer
- 6 per cent had suffered emotional and psychological maltreatment as children
- 6 per cent had been seriously physically neglected
- 4 per cent had been sexually abused
- 80 per cent of physically abused children have also witnessed domestic violence in their homes
- a significant number of children face repeated pathological and multiple forms of abuse at the hands of parents or carers.

(Source: Cawson P., 2002, *Child Maltreatment in the Family*, NSPCC)

Evidence of signs and symptoms (on pages 54–57) does not necessarily mean that a child has been abused; but they can help responsible adults to recognise that something is wrong. The possibility of abuse should be investigated if a child shows a number of these symptoms, or any of them to a marked degree. It is important to realise that a child may be the victim of a combination of different kinds of abuse.

Think about a child who is neglected. The child will not be properly clothed and fed. Do you think the child will feel loved and protected? The child may well be suffering from emotional abuse as well as neglect.

It is also possible that a child may show no outward signs of abuse and may be trying to hide what is happening from everyone.

If you have any suspicions about the welfare of a child in your setting, share it with your supervisor or designated person. Your fears may be unfounded, but it is better to be overcautious in passing information on than to ignore warning signs. It is very important to handle the issues in a sensitive manner and not upset the child concerned.

Did you know?

At the end of March 2004 there were 32,100 children on child protection registers in England. The most commonly recorded risk was for neglect (39%) followed by physical abuse (19%) and emotional abuse (17%) (Source: Statistics of Education; referrals, assessments and children and young people on child protection registers; DFES, 2005)

Did you know?

In 2003 the Laming Report found that far too often children are identified as causing concern, but that different agencies do not share information with each other. As a result children die from abuse unnecessarily. Victoria Climbie, the little girl who promoted the Laming report, had been seen by many different childcare workers from the health, social and education services. She still died at the hands of her aunt and her aunt's boyfriend. The new Children Act (2004) aims to make sure that services work together to share information to try to stop such deaths happening.

Check it out

Find out what is happening in your area as a result of the Children Act (2004) and the Laming Report. Does your area have a Children's Director responsible for the protection of all children?

However, not every sign means a child is being abused. Have you cared for children who always appear a bit grubby and maybe smell a little, but are happy and loved by parents? Some physical signs such as darkened areas can be birth marks and not bruising, for example some infants of Asian or African heritage can have a dark bluish area on their lower back and/or buttocks. This is sometimes known as a Mongolian Blue Spot.

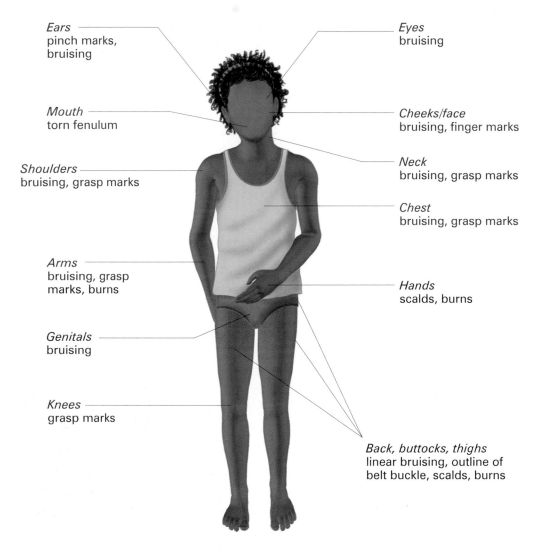

Ears
pinch marks,
bruising

Mouth
torn fenulum

Shoulders
bruising, grasp marks

Arms
bruising, grasp
marks, burns

Genitals
bruising

Knees
grasp marks

Eyes
bruising

Cheeks/face
bruising, finger marks

Neck
bruising, grasp marks

Chest
bruising, grasp marks

Hands
scalds, burns

Back, buttocks, thighs
linear bruising, outline of
belt buckle, scalds, burns

● *The usual position of injuries in cases of child abuse*

Physical abuse

Physical abuse is when a child is physically hurt or injured. Hitting, kicking, beating with objects, throwing and shaking are all physical abuse. They can cause pain, cuts, bruising, broken bones and sometimes even death.

Signs and symptoms

- Unexplained recurrent injuries or burns
- Wearing clothes to cover injuries, even in hot weather

- Refusal to undress for games
- Bald patches of hair
- Repeated running away
- Fear of medical examination
- Aggression towards self and others
- Fear of physical contact – shrinking back if approached or touched.

Case study 5: Suspicious bruising

Ollie, aged 5, has been away from school for two days due to 'being unwell' according to the note from his mother. You are helping him to get changed for PE in the hall and he jumps when you are pulling his jumper off. The back of his upper arms and his back are covered in deep purple bruising. When you gently ask how they happened, he shrugs and says he fell off his bunk bed.

1 What should you do now?
2 Who should you talk to about this?
3 Who should you not talk to about the incident?

Many signs of physical abuse can be confused with genuine accidental injuries. However, they are often not in the places or distribution you would expect, or the explanation does not fit, or you may see the outline of a belt buckle or cigarette burn. Suspicion should be aroused if the parents have not sought medical advice soon after the injury occurred.

Case study 6: Jumping to conclusions

Usha was very upset when she took Ashok, her 9-month-old son, to the local hospital's accident and emergency department. She had slipped on the stairs carrying Ashok downstairs and he had obviously broken his upper leg as she fell with him. An X-ray confirmed that Ashok had a fracture to his femur and would need several weeks in hospital. To Usha's horror the doctor and nurses started to suggest she had deliberately hurt her son and called in the social services department. In her distress Usha did not immediately remember that her neighbour had been in the house when the accident happened, and luckily could confirm that what she said was true.

1 Why do you think the doctor involved social services?
2 What do you think they should have done?

Emotional abuse

Emotional abuse is when a child is not given love, approval or acceptance. A child may be constantly criticised, blamed, sworn and shouted at, told that other people are better than he or she is and rejected by those the child looks to for affection.

Signs and symptoms

- Delayed development
- Sudden speech problems – stammering, etc.
- Low self-esteem ('I'm stupid, ugly, worthless', etc.)
- Fear of any new situation
- Neurotic behaviour (rocking, hair twisting, self-mutilation)
- Extremes of withdrawal or aggression.

Neglect

Neglect, which can result in failure to thrive, is when parents or others looking after a child do not provide the child with proper food, warmth, shelter, clothing, care and protection.

Signs and symptoms

- Constant hunger
- Poor personal hygiene
- Constant tiredness
- Poor state of clothing
- Unusual thinness
- Untreated medical problems
- No social relationships
- Stealing food
- Destructive tendencies.

 Case study 7: Possible neglect

Lewis is 6 years old and has an older brother, Jason, who is 11. Their parents both have drinking problems. Sometimes there is nothing to eat in the house. Jason is often left alone to look after his younger brother. The school they both go to has noticed that they are always tired and appear very thin. Their clothes are often dirty and Lewis is often in the same clothes for a few days. One day when Jason comes to collect Lewis from the classroom to go home, Lewis bursts into tears and says he doesn't want to go home.

1 *What do you think Lewis's teacher should do?*
2 *What do you think should have already happened?*

Sexual abuse

Sexual abuse is when a child is forced or persuaded into sexual acts or situations by others. Children might be encouraged to look at pornography, be harassed by sexual suggestions or comments, be touched sexually or forced to have sex.

Signs and symptoms

- Sexual knowledge or behaviour that is inappropriate to the child's age
- Medical problems such as chronic itching, pain in the genitals, venereal diseases

- Depression, self-mutilation, suicide attempts, running away, overdoses, anorexia
- Personality changes such as becoming insecure or clinging
- Regressing to younger behaviour patterns such as thumb sucking or bringing out discarded cuddly toys
- Sudden loss of appetite or compulsive eating
- Being isolated or withdrawn
- Inability to concentrate
- Lack of trust or fear of someone they know well, such as not wanting to be alone with a babysitter or child minder
- Starting to wet or soil again, day or night
- Become worried about clothing being removed
- Suddenly drawing sexually explicit pictures
- Trying to be 'ultra-good' or perfect; overreacting to criticism.

Bullying and harassment

This is also a form of abuse that affects older children particularly. It can continue for a long time and can include one or more of the following:

- emotional bullying – the most common type – including not speaking and excluding (sending to Coventry), tormenting, ridicule, humiliation
- physical bullying including pushing, kicking, hitting, pinching and other forms of violence or threats
- verbal bullying including name-calling, sarcasm, spreading rumours, persistent teasing
- racist bullying involving racial taunts, writing graffiti, gestures
- sexual bullying involving unwanted physical contact or abusive comments
- homophobic bullying including hostile or offensive action against lesbians, gay males or bisexuals, or those thought to be lesbian, gay or bisexual.

Bullying can be carried out by one person against another, or by groups of people 'ganging up' on a person. Bullying is not always delivered as a personal, face-to-face attack, but can also be delivered through technology, such as mobile phones and the Internet. This is known as cyber-bullying.

Persistent bullying can result in:

- depression
- low self-esteem
- shyness
- poor academic achievement
- isolation
- threatened or attempted suicide
- running away.

Did you know?

An estimated 77,000 under-16s run away from home each year putting themselves in considerable danger of physical or sexual assault. Some 80 per cent of runaways say it is due to family problems. More than 20,000 of the runaways are under 11 years. Runaways under 11 are more likely to have experienced physical abuse at home.

Case Study 8: Dealing with children who have been bullied

Leanne, aged 13, contacted a telephone support service after years of constantly being bullied at school. She often had things stolen from her, especially new school bags or trainers. The two girls who were bullying her had started at primary school by calling her names and following her home. More recently they had started to push her over if she walked past them and were spreading unpleasant rumours about her father. Leanne has started to miss going to school to avoid meeting the bullies. The telephone counsellor explained to Leanne that it was her right to be educated without fear and encouraged Leanne to ask a friend to go with her to talk to the head of her year.

1   *Why do you think it has taken so long for her to tell someone?*
2   *How do you think this has made Leanne feel about herself?*
3   *What do you think you could have done if you were working at Leanne's school?*

How to encourage children to be aware of their own bodies and understand their right not to be abused

The United Nations Convention on the Rights of the Child, signed by the United Kingdom, aims to make sure that all children are treated equally and fairly.

These rights include:
1   the right to life and the best chance to develop fully
2   the right to enjoy a decent standard of living
3   the right to a free education
4   the right to be as healthy as possible
5   the right to live in a safe, healthy, unpolluted environment and the right to safe, nutritious food and water.

● *It is an undeniable right that all children are fairly treated, loved, protected and helped to develop to the best of their ability*

The Government *must* protect children from:

- doing work which could be dangerous or which could harm their health
- doing work which interferes with their education
- dangerous drugs
- being abducted or sold
- sexual abuse.

Children may be separated from parents/carers *only* if it is in the child's best interests. If separated, for example in care (looked after), the child has the right to keep in regular touch with his or her parents and siblings unless it would be harmful to do so.

If you are aware of the rights of children, you will be able to think about how you can help to protect children and also help them to protect themselves.

 Keys to good practice: How to help keep children safe

✓ Teach children how to keep themselves safe.

✓ Encourage them to share worries about abuse with their friends and to tell a trusted adult.

✓ Make sure they know that being abused is never their fault and that abuse is never right.

✓ Promote services such as Childline or the NSPCC Child Protection Helpline to older children.

Helping to protect children

Very young children and babies need protecting by adults, and when abuse happens the carers responsible need a lot of support and help. Abuse happens for all sorts of reasons. One of the best ways of preventing abuse is to ensure that all parents feel good about themselves and have the support they need when things go wrong for them. This is the role of more senior workers but it is important to be aware of this issue.

You can help by knowing that to feel safe and protected, children need to feel good about themselves. They need to have a good level of self-esteem and helping a child to develop this is an important skill of a childcare worker. A child who has high self-esteem will do better in many aspects of development. Self-esteem can be helped by:

- giving lots of praise and encouragement
- encouraging independence with lots of opportunities to try things out
- teaching children how to be assertive – that means having their own needs met but still respecting those of others
- encouraging co-operation, respect and tolerance between children, and giving a positive example yourself.

 Did you know?

In July 2004 the Children's Rights Director for England produced a report about keeping children safe. Many children felt that the risk of abuse was greatest when they were being looked after by people they didn't know (although this is not the case).

The children in the report all felt good about being asked for their views. These are some of their statements.

- Pay attention and talk seriously to children.
- Don't patronise us – explain so we can understand – don't talk complex.
- Don't always believe an adult over a child.
- We want to be looked after by adults we can trust.
- Treat us individually – children are not all the same.

(Source: Morgan, R. (2004) 'Safe From Harm: Children's Views' report, CSCI)

It is important to be available to talk with children about any concerns they may have. If they are upset by a reported case of abuse, be as reassuring as possible. These cases are very rare, even though it is hard to believe when they are constantly in the media. Stress that almost all children lead safe and happy lives and only a very tiny percentage of adults want to hurt children in any way.

To be able to tell someone that they are unhappy with someone else's behaviour, children need help to use the right language, to draw pictures or show an adult on a doll, for example.

Using correct anatomical language, at a level appropriate to the child, is important when you are talking about bodies. However, you also need to be aware of the many different terms used by people for a part of the body such as the genitalia or for functions such as passing urine.

Simple, age-appropriate sessions, linked to other activities, on how the human body works help children to understand what their bodies can do and raise awareness of what is normal and what is not.

You need to help children to understand that they have a right to be safe, and to have people they can tell if they are not feeling safe.

What is safe though? What is OK and what is not OK? Childcare settings – along with agencies such as the NSPCC, Childline and Kidscape – are very important in educating children about looking after themselves. The important fact for all children is that they should never feel uncomfortable about someone they are with or about something being done to them.

Have a look at this code for safety from Kidscape. Do you think it can be useful for all children?

The Keepsafe Code

1 Hugs
Hugs and kisses are nice, especially from people we like. Even hugs and kisses that feel good and that you like should never be kept secret.

2 Body
Your body belongs to you and not to anyone else. This means all of your body. If anyone harms you or tries to touch your body in a way which confuses or frightens you, say *no*, if possible, and tell.

3 No
If anyone older than you, even someone you know, tries to touch you in a way you don't like or that confuses you, or which they say is supposed to be a secret, say *no* in a very loud voice.

4 Run or Get Away
Don't talk to anyone you don't know when you are alone, or just with other children. You don't have to be rude, just pretend you didn't hear and keep going. If a stranger, or a bully, or even someone you know tries to harm you, get away and get help. Make sure you always go towards other people or to a shop, if you can.

5 Yell
Wherever you are, it is all right to yell if someone is trying to hurt you. Practise yelling as loud as you can in a big, deep voice by taking a deep breath and letting the yell come from your stomach, not from your throat.

6 Tell
Tell a grown-up you trust if you are worried or frightened. If the first grown-up you tell doesn't believe or help you, keep telling until someone does. It might not be easy, but even if something has already happened that you have never told before, try to tell now. Who could *you* tell?

7 Secrets
Secrets such as surprise birthday parties are fun. But some secrets are not good and should never be kept. No bully should ever make you keep the bullying a secret and no one should ask you to keep a kiss, hug or touch secret. If anyone does, even if you know that person, tell a grown-up you trust.

8 Bribes
Don't accept money or sweets or a gift from anyone without first checking with your parents. Most of the time it will be all right, like when you get a present for your birthday from your grandma. But some people try to trick children into doing something by giving them sweets or money. This is called a bribe – don't ever take one! Remember, it is possible that you might have to do what a bully or older person tells you, so that you can keep yourself safe. Don't feel bad if that happens because the most important thing is for you to be safe.

9 Code
Have a code word or sign with your parents or guardians, which only you and they know. If they need to send someone to collect you, they can give that person the code. Don't tell the code to anyone else.

(Source: www.Kidscape.org.uk)

Keys to good practice: How to respond to a child's disclosure of possible abuse

✓ Find out to whom you should report any concern you may have about the safety of a child in your setting.

✓ Make sure you understand your setting's child protection policy and procedure.

✓ Always pass on any information that may be related to possible abuse to the correct person.

✓ Never promise to keep a child's disclosure a secret.

Test yourself

1 Bruising is always a sign of physical abuse. True or false?
2 You should never promise to keep a child's secret. True or false?
3 All childcare settings must have a designated _____ who is responsible for reporting cases of suspected abuse to _____.
4 Name an organisation involved with helping children to be safe.

Why it is important to consistently and fairly apply boundaries and rules for children's behaviour

You can probably think of a time when one person has expected one type of behaviour from you and another a different type in the same situation. You may have memories of one of your parents allowing you to stay up late but the other expecting you to be in bed by a certain time. No two people have the same expectations and exactly the same rules for children, but

Check it out

1 How could you use the Keepsafe Code in your setting?
2 Could you put it into a picture format with titles?
3 Can you think how you could get the children to practise actions for the Keepsafe Code?
4 What else might you need to do with the children so that they understand about hugs and touching that they are not comfortable with?

What procedures are followed in your setting when there is suspicion of abuse of a child? Make sure you have a copy in your file and that you have read it and asked your supervisor if you are not sure about anything in it.

Boundaries can become unclear

it is important that children know the simple rules and **boundaries** for their behaviour.

Studies show that children can be very confused by adult rules and often do not understand what they have done wrong. If they are punished they will be angry and upset and will not know how to behave next time in that situation.

The United Nations Convention on the Rights of the Child states that children have a right to be protected from all forms of mental and physical violence and deliberate humiliation. A child who is punished for an act one day that was ignored the previous day, or who has no sense of boundaries or rules because they are at the whim of an adult, is not having that right protected.

All children need to know what the boundaries and expectations of them are. Limits have to be set, very often for safety as well as social reasons. Children will test these limits, but it is important to keep to them even though a child may complain at the time. All children need a routine that applies to meals, bedtimes and play times, but the routine needs to be responsive to special events. Rules, routines and boundaries will be different in very family and in every childcare setting, although they should be built around the basic needs to keep a child safe, well and active. It is obviously important that a child knows when rules are different in different places, and that they know why if they are old enough.

These 'rules' need to be simple and easy to understand, and more importantly all adults need to know them and keep to them. Simple rules that could apply to any setting might include the following:
- no walking around with scissors
- no hitting other children
- no snatching of toys from other children.

These are important rules for young children – but can you think how you could turn these negative commands into positive guidelines for **positive behaviour**?

Think about the children in your setting. Who do you think of when asked who the naughty ones are? Who is known as the clumsy child, or the class joker, or the clever one, or the helpful one? It is very easy to stereotype people – to put them into 'boxes' according to how we expect them to behave. If you are known for being naughty and the only way you get attention is when you are naughty, what will you do? It doesn't take much imagination to come up with the answer. What were you stereotyped as at school?

Key terms

Boundaries: limits for behaviour.

Key terms

Positive behaviour: behaviour that is welcomed and supports children.

Check it out

1 What is the behaviour policy in your setting?
2 Is there a simple list of rules or code of conduct for the children? If so, who developed them? Were the children involved?
3 Compare your setting with other settings. What are the differences?
4 How do you think the rules could be improved?

Any stereotype is unfair on a child – or an adult for that matter!

 Little angel or little devil?

Always being known as the perfect child can be just as limiting as being known as a naughty child. Other children may resent the constant attention to the good children and react with more negative behaviour to attract attention.

Case study 9: Reinforcing negative behaviour

Lucy, aged 6, always seems to be in trouble. If something gets broken at home or her little brother starts to cry, she gets the blame. At school, the girl next to her blames Lucy for stopping her working, and Lucy never finishes her work on time. At playtime Lucy is always the last one to go out as the teacher chooses children in order of how good they have been. The teacher has now told Lucy that she won't be in the Christmas play because she is too naughty.

1   *What is happening to Lucy?*
2   *How do you think Lucy feels?*
3   *What do you think the teacher, and Lucy's parents, could do differently?*

Imagine never being the object of positive attention, but only of negative attention – in other words constantly being shouted at, told off and punished. This is not ideal attention, but it is attention and for some children it is better than none. For many children with behaviour problems, this is the cycle they have got into. From their first entry into nursery some children become known as the 'naughty one', and their reputation sticks. I am sure this sounds familiar to you.

How to encourage children's positive behaviour and deal with unwanted behaviour

It is important to remember that children are naturally curious and enthusiastic. Children learn by trying things out, but some adults may view this as naughty. As a childcare worker you need to know what a child understands at different ages. You need to be able to explain what is normal and inquisitive to parents rather than naughty behaviour from their child.

For example, a newly mobile baby learns by experimenting. For months they have only been able to observe the world around them. That fascinating black box on the table has a slot in it that the baby's mother puts a box into. How natural to see if the sandwich left on a plate while the baby's mother answers the door also fits into the video recorder! Obviously there are serious accident risks here as well – the same curiosity can be extended to pulling that curly wire leading to the kettle or iron.

● *Experimenting can be a problem!*

Children will generally behave positively if treated positively. This means praising and encouraging the behaviour that you want, and giving children attention when they are behaving 'well'. The more a child understands the reasons for wanting them to do things, and they are shown attention and respect, the more they will want to please. It is far preferable to be told you are doing well and someone is proud of you, than to be told off and told you are useless.

So, how can you help to create an atmosphere where children want to behave well?

- Show children how to behave by example. They learn by copying.
- Keep rules simple and minimal. Let older children help to make the rules.
- Be positive – tell children what you want them to do, not what you don't want.
- Set routines so that children know what is expected of them and when.
- Praise, encourage and listen to the children.
- Change the environment, not the children. Remove precious or fragile objects from the reach of very young children.
- Only make demands that are reasonable for the children's ages and situation. Remember that when children are ill or tired their needs change.
- Don't shout or use physical force. Physical force is illegal for a childcare worker and harmful from parents. Shouting achieves nothing other than having to shout louder next time.
- Use diversion tactics with very young children. Distract them with a new activity or interest. Negotiate and explain the reasons to older children.
- Remember to laugh whenever possible – it often helps to defuse a situation.

What is seen as good behaviour is relative – relative to time, place, the age of the child and the relevant culture. What is perfectly acceptable behaviour in one family would be condemned as unacceptable in another. You may have experienced this in your parents' attitudes to staying out late, friendships, helping at home, etc. as compared to the attitudes of other parents. Events in a child's life can have an impact on the child's behaviour regardless of whether the events are serious or trivial.

 Case study 10: Scribbling on the wall

Harry wandered into the room and saw the big fat crayons on the table. He went over to pick up the red one. He looked around for a second, and then started to scribble on the wall. At that moment Harry's mother came into the room.

1 *Was Harry being 'naughty'?*
2 *If you knew Harry was 18 months old, would your opinion be the same as if he was 5 years old?*
3 *How would you deal with the situation?*

Potentially upsetting incidents that might affect children's behaviour include a new baby in the family, moving house, parents separating or rowing, access visits by absent parents, a poor night's sleep, minor illness, a parent losing a job, a new teacher or class, moving schools and so on. Any change in routine can upset a child. It is your responsibility to be alert for changes in a child's behaviour and report these to a senior person.

All childcare establishments have an accepted code of behaviour, which is explained to children and parents, but within each establishment there will be individual differences of interpretation among staff.

It is important to be clear about the behaviour policies and procedures of your setting, and to work within them. If you are working in a child's home, make sure you know the parents' 'rules' and try to be consistent with them.

Behaviour policies and procedures

Children need security to thrive and develop. Going for the first time to playgroup, nursery or school is a momentous event in any child's life. Children should not have to cope with inappropriate behaviour in the form of abuse, racism or sexism. Being on the receiving end of abuse or racism has a damaging effect on a child. It can affect self-esteem and confidence, especially if it is not challenged by carers. It is the responsibility of every childcare worker to make sure this does not happen. Childcare settings therefore need to have clear policies and procedures relating to many things, but in particular to behaviour. This does not mean to say that a long list of rules should be drawn up in nursery that children have to learn. Children as young as 4 or 5 will understand simple rules related to caring for others, not being unkind, and not taking items belonging to others.

All childcare settings have stated policies and procedures dealing with issues such as bullying, stealing, deliberate damage, etc. and these are known and understood by staff. Children and parents should be aware of the associated rules where appropriate – when the children are very young just the parents will need to be aware of the rules. Clearly, policies will depend on the age of children who attend.

Methods to deal with unwanted behaviour

Unwanted behaviour usually has a cause. Have you ever been in a classroom with a teacher who shouts all the time? Have you ever seen a parent who seems to shout and tell a child off all the time? In comparison, think of a quietly spoken parent or teacher who seems to have well-behaved children. A carer's behaviour can greatly influence the behaviour of the children.

The way you deal with behaviour in a setting can have an impact on the response of the children. Ignoring bullying, racism or disruption provides a poor role model for children and encourages equally bad behaviour. In contrast a fair adult, who deals with issues promptly and fairly and shows respect for all the children, will encourage a calmer, happier setting.

The best way to encourage good behaviour in a child who continues with unwanted behaviour is to make a fuss about the good behaviour and pay a

Key terms

A **policy** is the statement of what is expected or is provided in a setting, for example: 'All children will be treated with respect.'

The related **procedure** might state, for example: 'Cases of children taking items not belonging to themselves must be reported to the member of staff in charge of that group. Parents must be informed.'

The related '**rule**' might be: 'All children are expected to look after their own and other people's property. Children should not bring their own toys into nursery.'

lot of attention to it. The best way to stop the bad behaviour is to ignore it. Pay attention and give plenty of praise to a child when he or she is behaving in an appropriate way.

Ignoring bad behaviour can at times be hard, if not impossible. You might manage to ignore the behaviour, but your colleague might not be able to and might stand the child in the 'naughty' corner.

Rewards

Working on a child's inappropriate behaviour requires a lot of co-operation and teamwork, with both parents and staff involved. Observations are needed to decide on the exact nature of the problem behaviour, and targets must be set to improve it through positive behaviours. Through a series of rewards for good behaviour, targets are gradually raised. This method is called 'behaviour modification'. Even as a student, you can use some of the skills developed from this method.

The next time you are working with children, try to listen to other staff and yourself to see if you and they spend more time praising children or telling them off. It is important to try to look for something to praise, even if it is only that a child has sat still for a few moments, done a good painting or shared something.

Most schools have a merit or reward system, with children being given small rewards such as stickers. An example of a merit chart is shown below.

Check it out

Think about the different ways of dealing with unwanted behaviour you have seen.

How effective were they? Why?

Name	My Merit Stars
Ashook	★ ★ ★
Ayesha	★ ★
Barnaby	★ ★
Ben	★ ★ ★ ★ ★
Carlo	★
Catherine	★ ★ ★
Desi	★ ★
Ellie	★
Frank	★ ★ ★
Georgy	★ ★ ★ ★

● Merit chart for good behaviour

Consider safety issues and concerns relating to outings for children

When you are planning outings, safety is as important as the value the children will get out of the activity. Safety depends on:

- appropriate staffing levels for the number and ages of the children
- where you are going
- how you will get there
- what you intend to do once there.

You will need to carry out a risk assessment identifying any potential hazards on the journey or at the location.

Just imagine taking a group of children out together without any planning, preparation or thought for safety. Would it be possible for you and your colleagues or the children to enjoy the outing?

Outings can vary from a walk in the park to feed the ducks with nursery age children, to a visit to a living museum with primary school children, through to an outing to a theme park or even an overnight stay with young people. The arrangements and issues will be different for each of these, but whatever the scale of the outing, you need to think about the following:

- choosing a suitable venue, which will depend on the planned outcomes
- risk assessment of the outing
- consulting with staff and children if old enough
- informing parents and having consent forms signed if needed
- arranging transport if needed
- lists of children and adults on the outing and the ratios
- information about the venue
- travel and insurance details
- first aid cover
- appropriate clothing
- food and equipment
- contingency plans – the 'what if' plans.

Think about the different issues for each of the following cases:

- a group of six 3-year-olds on a walk to the park
- a group of 25 7–8-year-olds on a visit to an outdoor farm
- a group of 20 13–14-year-olds going to a theme park
- a group of 15–16-year-olds on a day trip to France.

Check it out

What is included in the planning of outings in your setting? Does it differ for different age groups?

Case study 12: Organising an outing to the park

A new countryside park area has been opened near to the Blue Jays childcare centre. It boasts of lots of items of interest for children to enjoy including a wildlife observation area, pond dipping, an interactive information centre and picnic area.

Your manager decides it would be a good idea to take a group of children aged 4–12 years during the holiday club scheme period. You are asked to go along and have a look at the area to see what the safety issues of the planned outing might be.

The park is very large, with all the areas of interest spread around an 8-square-kilometre space. Apart from the main entrance, there are two other exits out of the wire perimeter fence. The pond dipping looks very interesting – the pond is large and has a steep bank on one side and a shallow approach on the other. There are two wooden jetty areas to walk on to look into the pond more easily.

The information centre has a lot of computers set up with interactive quizzes on wildlife and a film show on the facilities. All the activities are placed around a maze arrangement with the exhibits in separate areas.

The picnic area looks over a lake with lots of bird life. It is on a raised platform with a railing around and 15 wooden steps down to the lake.

You agree that the children will enjoy the outing and that there is plenty to keep all of them occupied. But you are worried about some of the safety aspects.

1 *Make a list of the possible safety hazards at the park.*
2 *Group the risks according to the ages of the children in the group.*
3 *Are there some risks that are more of a problem to the younger children or the older children? Which ones?*
4 *What plans will have to be made to protect the children?*
5 *How do you think you will be able to work with colleagues to make sure the children all have a safe and enjoyable day?*

Written records/snapshot observations

Written records are brief descriptions of what a child is doing. They are popular with parents as they provide a written picture of their child. This is perhaps why they are also known as **snapshot observations**.

Brightlands Day Nursery
107 St. Georges Road
Cheltenham
Gloucestershire
GL50 3ED

Brightlands

Ravi is standing up in front of Michaela, who is sitting on a chair. Ravi seems to be looking down at Michaela. She is saying 'Shall we dress up?' Michaela nods and smiles, Ravi smiles too and they both walk over to the dressing-up corner.

Ravi takes a pink dress, grasping it in her right hand, and places it on the floor. She pulls the back of the dress open with both hands. She steps into the dress using her right foot first and pulls up the dress gradually to a standing position, placing her right arm into the dress and then her left.

Ravi walks over to the nursery nurse and looks up. She asks 'Can you do my buttons up?' and turns around.

● *Example of a written record*

How they work

The observer either notices something that is interesting and starts to write it down, or has already decided what skill or area of development to look for. The observer simply writes down what he or she can see as it is happening. Most observers can only do this for a couple of minutes at a time.

It can be useful after a few recordings to read through what you have written to check that it makes sense while it is still fresh in your mind, especially if your handwriting is hard to read. Always include the start and finish time of each burst of recording.

Advantages	Disadvantages
• No preparation is needed. • You can record anything that is of interest. • It can provide a rounded picture of a child. • You can use this method to record any area of development.	• Different observers pick up on different things. • It is hard to write down exactly what a child is doing while also watching the child. • You need to be able to write quickly. • It can be hard to find the right language to describe what you are seeing. • Observations are not continuous as the observer usually has to have breaks in order to keep writing.

● *Advantages and disadvantages of written records*

Time samples

You look at what a child does over a period of time, such as a morning or part of an afternoon. This means that you gain a more complete picture of the child.

Time	Activity	Social group	Comments
11.00	Snack time	Whole group	Anna is sitting with her legs swinging on a chair. She is eating an apple. She is holding it in her left hand and she is smiling. She puts up her hand when a staff member asks who wants a biscuit.
11.15	Outdoor play Climbing frame	Anna and Ben	Anna is on the top bar of the climbing frame. She is smiling at Ben. She is calling 'Come on up here!'
11.30	Taking coats off	Anna, Ben and Manjit	Anna unzips the coat and pulls out one arm. She swings around and the coat moves around. She laughs and looks at Manjit

● *A time sample*

How they work

This type of observation needs some planning, as the observer needs to be free to keep an eye on the children. A sheet is prepared with the times marked out. At each of the times on the sheet, the observer watches what the child is doing and records it on the sheet. This provides a snapshot view of what the child is doing. It is possible to record the activity of more than one child.

Advantages	Disadvantages
• They can provide a lot of informationabout a child. • They are interesting observations to carry out. • You can use time samples to look out for particular skills or to focus on areas of development. • More than one child can be observed.	• A piece of significant behaviour may not be recorded if it falls outside of the time slot. • The observer may find it hard to do anything else but record.

● Advantages and disadvantages of time samples

Event samples

This observation method is used to look at how often and in what circumstances a child shows a particular behaviour. Some settings use this method to look at unwanted behaviour such as biting. It can also be used to find out about how often a child talks or plays with other children.

Event	Time	Situation	Social group	Dialogue
1	9.16 am	Curren is hovering near the painting	Susan + 2 children table	A–C 'Do you want to come and paint a picture too?' C–A nods head
2	9.27 am	Curren is finishing painting	Susan + 2 children	A–C 'Have you finished?' C smiles 'It's a lovely picture. Tell me a little bit about it.' C–A 'It's my mum. Can't take my apron off.' A–C 'Wait still, I'll do it.' Curren hands apron to Susan and runs over to sand area
3	10.12 am	Curren is waiting for his drink snack time	Curren is sitting next to Ahmed. Jo is handing out drinks	A–C 'Milk or squash, Curren?' C–A 'Milk.' A–C 'Can you remember the magic word?' C–A 'Thank you.' A–C 'Good boy.'
4	10.19 am	Curren is putting on his coat in the cloakroom area	Jo + 5 children	C–A 'Can't put coat on.' A–C 'Keep still. There you are. You can go out now.'
5	10.36 am	Curren is waiting for his turn by the slide	Jo + 2 children	A–C 'Good boy. It's your go now.' C smiles C–A 'I go fast down now.'

● This event sample was drawn up to look at how often and when a child played co-operatively with others

How they work

A prepared sheet is drawn up in advance after considering carefully the type of information that needs to be collected. A column is put down for each piece of information. When the behaviour is seen, the person who has seen it should fill in the sheet.

Advantages	Disadvantages
• They can help you to understand the reasons behind a child's behaviour. • They can be repeated to see if a certain behaviour is increasing or disappearing. • They can be used to record other aspects of children's development.	• An adult may not always be present at the time of the behaviour. • An adult may forget to fill in the event sample or may not know that he or she should be looking out for a particular behaviour.

● *Advantages and disadvantages of event samples*

Keys to good practice: How to carry out observations

✓ Ask your supervisor before carrying out any observation or assessment on a child.

✓ Carry out observations and assessments in line with your setting's policy.

✓ Observe children sensitively and unobtrusively.

✓ Write up your observations in a sensitive and non-judgemental way.

✓ Avoid making any negative judgements about children.

✓ Make sure that any conclusions are based directly on the observations.

✓ Remember that observations and assessments are confidential.

Aspects of children's development

Why the role of play is important in development

When considering what children of different ages need, it is interesting to see how many times 'opportunities to play' keeps coming up. This is because play is a key way in which children learn about themselves and others. It is also an important way in which children learn many skills that will help their development. A good example of this is a baby playing with a rattle. The sound of the rattle helps the baby to learn about sounds, but because it is interesting, it also makes the baby want to reach out and touch it. Every time the baby shakes the rattle, the baby is learning control of the hands.

Children at 4 years

By the age of 4, most children have made huge steps forward in their development. They will be fairly fluent in their speech and should be easily understandable to adults who do not know them. There will still be the odd grammatical mistake and interesting pronunciation of words, for example 'I wented swimming', 'I tooked it', 'bestest', but by and large they will have mastered the spoken language.

Most children's behaviour will be co-operative, but this is dependent on getting plenty of praise and recognition from adults. Most 4-year-olds enjoy being with other children and will be starting to plan their play with definite ideas of what they want to do. Most are also learning to be independent. They can dress and feed themselves and organise their play if given the opportunity. They also enjoy being with responsive adults, especially when given responsibility and encouragement.

● *Co-operative play with others*

Most children will be attending some pre-school provision such as a playgroup, nursery or crèche. This is important for them as they are beginning to find out about friendships. They will also be learning, often without realising it, as activities will be planned for them. Many children during this year will be starting school. For some children, this is a difficult transition as they have to adapt to being part of a much larger group.

● *Skilful use of the hands*

● *Good at steering and pedalling*

What you might observe in children of 4 years

- Children who are settled into the routine of the setting and are able to separate from their parents easily (if they have been in the setting or a few months)
- Co-operative play between children along with the odd squabble and argument
- Responding well to adult praise and recognition
- Seeking out particular playmates
- Asking questions and enjoying talking
- Speech and pretend play that models adult life
- Riding on tricycles, climbing and enjoying simple ball games
- Drawings that have meaning for the child and are recognisable
- Skilful use of the hands to do activities such as threading, pouring and using scissors
- Concentration when an activity has caught their interest
- Enjoying singing and knowing some nursery rhymes

Children of 4 years need:

- opportunities to play with other children
- sensitive adult help and direction when appropriate
- opportunities to explore new play materials, objects and equipment
- times to relax and enjoy favourite activities
- a wide range of different play activities and equipment
- time to play outside as well as inside
- opportunities to look at books, draw and paint
- practical activities that help children learn about number and their environment
- adults who act as good role models as children copy their behaviour
- times when adults listen and chat to children
- praise and acknowledgement from adults
- a safe environment that encourages them to be independent.

Children at 5–6 years

In these years, the rapid physical development comes to an end. Instead children gain in confidence and co-ordination. Other skills, such as spoken language and social skills, also develop. A good example of this is the way that children begin to enjoy hearing and making jokes.

At around 5 years, most children have begun formal education. This can be a difficult transition period for some children, especially if they are not interested in learning to read and write. For children who are ready, learning to read and write can prove exciting and they may enjoy the intellectual challenge of a classroom. As well as school, some children will be doing activities such as swimming, dance or music. They may attend after-school clubs where they can play with other children. Ways in which children play is also starting to change, with them keen to work out rules of situations and enjoy playing games with rules.

Friends are important to children of this age. Many will start to have established friendships and preferences. Staying for tea or overnight helps children to learn about other families. However, children still rely on their parents to meet many of their emotional needs.

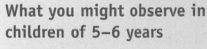
● *Increased fine manipulative skills*

What you might observe in children of 5–6 years

- Enjoyment of jokes
- Beginning to work out some words that they see often – this might be their name or the word 'milk' on a bottle
- Keen to understand and use rules, for example that the child has to wait for his or her turn
- Some friendship preferences
- Ability to kick and control a ball
- Better formed handwriting and increased fine manipulative movements

● *Beginning to read and write*

● *Starting to enjoy playing games with rules*

Children of 5–6 years need:

- opportunities to play with other children
- boundaries that they can understand
- opportunities to listen to stories and to share books
- a balanced diet and sufficient sleep
- adults who encourage independence and are sensitive to their needs
- adults who are able to supervise and support play
- activities outside of school including playing with friends.

Children at 7–9 years

Children's development in this period continues but is more gradual. While children continue to grow in height, the main changes are in the way they think and reason. This can be seen in the way that their games and play become more organised and they make up rules as well as follow rules. Children start to be able to solve simple problems and enjoy practical situations in which they have to work things out for themselves. Most children are co-operative and enjoy being given responsibility. They respond well when adults give clear explanations for rules and when their behaviour is praised.

Reading and writing become easier, although there will be variations in the speed at which children become competent and confident.

Children are also becoming more physically skilled. This results in children being able to do things more quickly, confidently and accurately. Putting on a coat, for example, is now an easy task, as is cutting out with scissors or drawing a simple picture.

Friendships are becoming increasingly important. Many will have groups of close friends and some girls will have 'best friends'. The lack or temporary absence of a friend starts to become an issue. Children may only want to attend a club if they know a friend is also likely to be there.

● *Co-operative play is seen*

● *Skillful and precise hand movements*

As most children are at school, life in the classroom and playground is a major influence on them. This is also a period in which children really start to compare themselves with others. They may notice which children are the fastest runners, best readers or quickest at finishing tasks. This can start to affect their confidence and even enthusiasm.

What you might observe in children of 7–9 years

- Clear differences in play activities that interest boys and girls, for example boys might enjoy kicking a ball around while girls might prefer acting out characters
- Co-operative play with children having stable friendships
- Verbal arguments, persuasion and negotiation
- Telling jokes and enjoying chatting
- Play that involves turn taking
- Enjoyment of playing and making up games with rules
- Understanding of rules and consequences
- Children who tell others the rules and are keen to point out when rules have been broken
- Skilful, precise and confident hand movements, for example detailed drawing, colouring and making models
- Co-ordinated physical movements including aiming and throwing a ball, moving their legs to make a swing move, riding a bicycle
- Beginning to read books silently
- Writing short stories and text with less adult help required
- Painting, drawing and making models independently
- Enjoyment of stories, imaginative play and small world play

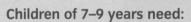

● *Friendships are important*

Children of 7–9 years need:

- sensitive adults who can spend time listening to children
- opportunities to play with other children
- toys and equipment that stimulate children's development
- opportunities for creative play
- times to organise own play and games
- adults who can support, but not interfere in children's play
- praise and acknowledgement that makes children feel special and nurtured
- support and encouragement during tasks that the child finds difficult.

Children at 9–11 years

This period in most children's lives can be summed up as the 'calm before the storm'. Most children are fairly confident and have mastered many skills, and they will often have decided what they are good at. They can now read, write, draw and use some logic. They are often skilled communicators and enjoy having friends. This is a time when many children feel quite settled, although early puberty in girls is not uncommon.

What you might observe in children of 9–11 years

- Detailed and representational pictures where children enjoy drawing
- Stories and writing that show imagination as well as being easy to read and reasonably grammatical
- Problem-solving, for example how to play co-operatively, use materials fairly
- Strong and consistent play preferences, for example collecting cards or stickers, playing football, acting
- Enthusiasm when given areas of responsibility

● *Draws detailed and representational pictures*

● *Good hand–eye co-ordination*

● *Enjoys playing with friends*

Children of 9–11 years need:
- information about puberty
- opportunities to try new activities and experiences, and develop new ideas
- time to be with friends
- opportunities to develop problem-solving and organisational skills
- praise and encouragement from adults
- adults who look for ways of encouraging independence
- a range of toys and equipment that will stimulate children including books, drawing materials and construction toys
- opportunities to make dens, hideouts and engage in physical play.

This period in children's lives marks the start of their growing independence. While parents remain important, children begin to show signs of wanting to grow up. They may, for example, now ask to walk home or get buses home by themselves. Some children also begin to question rules at home and may try to push the boundaries.

Children's relationships with others of the same age become increasingly important. This can put a lot of pressure on children as their friends may have very different ideas to their parents.

Children will be starting secondary school. The new school will often be larger and the curriculum more formal. They may have a series of teachers during the day, rather than just one or two.

This period also marks physical changes for children as their bodies prepare for adulthood. Puberty in girls usually begins at around 11 years, while in boys it may not start until they are 13 or 14 years old. The physical changes can cause embarrassment and anxiety, creating further pressure.

● *Argues with parents*

● *Enjoys 'childish' activities*

● *Enjoys time with friends*

What you might observe in children of 11–13 years

- Enjoyment when with their friends
- Growth and changes to their bodies
- More confidence around the home and in familiar situations
- Arguments with parents as children start to become independent
- Times when children are grown-up and times when they enjoy 'childish' activities, for example sitting on a swing, watching cartoons, playing games

Children of 11–13 years need:

- opportunities to take control and be given responsibility
- clear boundaries that they can see the sense of and have helped to negotiate
- adults who can listen carefully to them and are sensitive to their needs
- praise and encouragement to support their self-esteem
- opportunities to relax and also to take exercise
- a balanced diet with sufficient protein and iron for growth
- times when they can enjoy being a child again, rather than a young person.

Young people of 13–16 years

In this period, young people inch closer to adulthood. By around the age of 15 or 16, the physical development of girls will be complete. For most boys, puberty will start from around 14 years and is likely to take around three years to complete (see diagram on page 000).

Pressure in school is likely to increase as most young people are preparing for exams and may be starting to think about their future. At around 16 years, young people will need to decide whether to leave school and education and take a job. Some children in this period will have developed skills that are on an equal with adults, for example the ability to use computers or to draw.

Being with friends is likely to be more important than being with family members. Young people who do not have a group of friends are likely to feel that they are missing out and may become anxious. This is a time when young people are also exploring their own identity. They may have tastes in music and clothes, and prefer activities that are different to their parents'. This may cause clashes as try to develop their own personality and space.

Young people also want to be independent and may test the boundaries at home and at school. As the transition to adulthood is not complete, young people will also at time revert to 'child-like' comments, activities and games.

While for some young people, this period can be one of anxiety and conflict, for others it can be an enjoyable period as they spend time with friends and are able to dream a little about the future.

● *Confidence and enjoyment when with friends*

What you might observe in young people of 13–16 years

- Confidence and enjoyment when with friends
- Thoughts and ideas that are different to their parents'

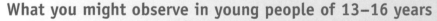

● *High level of skills in sport, drawing, computing and so on*

- Uncertainty about themselves
- High level of skills in some subjects, for example drawing and painting, using computers proficiently
- Mood swings

● *Thoughts and ideas that are different to their parents'*

Young people of 13–16 years need:
- adults who listen and are sensitive to their needs
- opportunities to discuss boundaries
- opportunities to take control and become independent
- time to relax and enjoy being with friends
- information about drugs, alcohol and sex
- a balanced diet and opportunities to find out about healthy eating
- opportunities to take exercise
- information about careers and educational opportunities.

Areas of children's development

The skills that children learn are often grouped into four key areas:

- physical development
- cognitive development
- **communication** and language development
- personal, social and emotional development.

This section looks at each of these areas of development and will help you to understand the range of skills that children acquire. It also looks at some of the theories that have helped practitioners to understand these areas of development.

Key terms

Communication: verbal and non-verbal communication including gestures and facial expression.

Understanding what each of the areas of development might include

Before looking at the areas of development, it is worth understanding the types of skills that are usually associated with them.

Physical development

This area of development is about learning how to master physical movements. Running, drawing and tying a knot are all examples of movements that most children will gradually learn.

Cognitive development

This area of development is also known as intellectual development. It is a complicated area, but is essentially about the way in which children learn to think, handle information and express themselves. Being able to remember someone's name, understand and use symbols, for example drawings and letters, and add up are all examples of cognitive skills.

Communication and Language development

This area of development is about learning to communicate with other people and to understand their communications. Talking, reading and writing, and using gestures are all examples of skills that most children learn.

Personal, social and emotional development

This area of development is about relationships and also understanding yourself. Being able to feel sorry for someone, knowing what behaviour is acceptable and also being able to control your emotions are examples of skills that children learn.

How areas of development are connected

No single area of development is more important than the others. For many skills that children need to develop, more than one area of development is involved. A good example of this is the ability to play hopscotch. This is a game that several children might play together. It involves being able to jump on one foot. The spider diagram below shows some of the skills that are involved and how these might link to the areas of development.

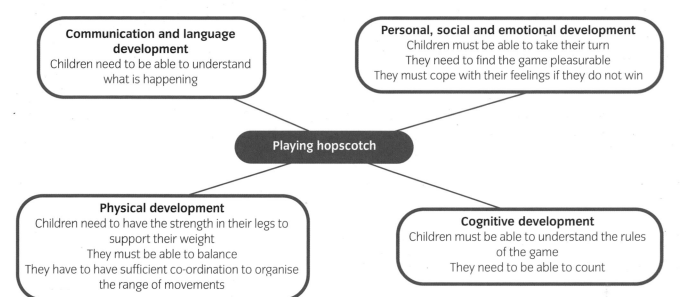

Communication and language development
Children need to be able to understand what is happening

Personal, social and emotional development
Children must be able to take their turn
They need to find the game pleasurable
They must cope with their feelings if they do not win

Playing hopscotch

Physical development
Children need to have the strength in their legs to support their weight
They must be able to balance
They have to have sufficient co-ordination to organise the range of movements

Cognitive development
Children must be able to understand the rules of the game
They need to be able to count

Physical development

The control that most people have over their bodies is quite remarkable and yet most people take it completely for granted. Watch a young baby, though, struggling to pass a rattle from one hand to the other and you will soon see how skilled you have become. Physical development like many other areas of development is a journey, but it is a relatively fast one. By 5 years old, most children have a good level of control over their bodies.

Physical development and the link to growth and maturation

While this section on physical development looks principally at the skills that children acquire, there is also a link to growth and maturation. Young babies can, for example, suck their toes, but later on this become very difficult as the body's proportions change. In the same way, some physical development cannot take place until some maturation processes have occurred. In young children, a good example of this is toilet training. This is a skill, but the brain has to be mature enough to be able to send signals to and from the bladder.

The importance of physical development in children's lives

Physical development is something that is easy to take for granted. It is an essential part of children's development. The spider diagram below shows the importance of physical development in children's overall development.

Key terms

Development: the way children gain skills and abilities.

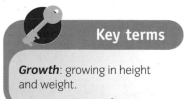

Key terms

Growth: growing in height and weight.

Builds children's confidence
When children can do things for themselves, they are more likely to gain in confidence. They can do things how and when they want.

Helps children to socialise
As play is quite active, especially in the early years, children will benefit if they are physically able to join in. Children may construct a train track together or follow each other on tricycles.

Helps children to become more independent
Children are able to dress themselves, get out toys and equipment, and go out and see friends.

The importance of physical development in children's overall development

Allows children to express themselves
Physical movements can be one way in which babies and young children can express themselves. Babies may signal with their arms that they wish to be lifted up, while toddlers may throw themselves to the ground to express their frustration. In older children, physical skills will enable them to dance, play musical instruments, paint and ride a bike.

Links to cognitive development
In children's early years, a significant amount of learning is practical and requires physical movements. There is also research that suggests that early physical movements also help to develop the brain.

Different types of physical skills

To gain control over their movements, children need to master different types of movements and skills.

How the body changes shape as it grows

The diagram below shows how the human body changes shape as it grows. This does not mean that babies' heads get smaller, but that other parts of the body grow more and so the overall shape changes.

Key terms

Gross motor skills: large movements of whole limbs as well as the ability to bear weight on them, for example walking, crawling and climbing.

Fine motor skills: small movements involving the hands and fingers, such as holding a pencil or unscrewing a lid off a bottle.

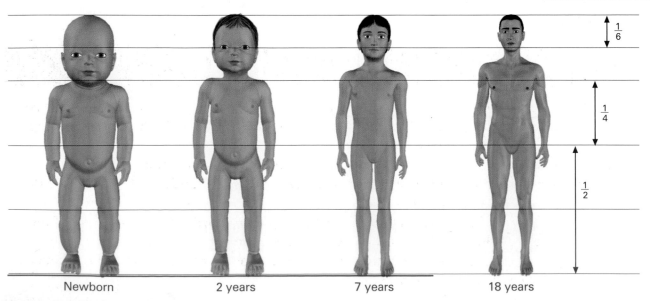

| Newborn | 2 years | 7 years | 18 years |

● *How the body changes shape as it grows*

Principles of physical development

Three principles of physical development have been observed in young children.

1 **Physical development follows a sequence:** This means that children do not suddenly jump stages. A good example of this is the way in which babies need to be able to support their heads before they can learn to sit up or to crawl.

2 **Physical development begins with the control of head movements and continues downwards:** This is particularly true of babies' development and it is thought to be a survival mechanism. Babies need to be able to turn their heads to feed. The downward pattern of development also applies to the process of ossification. This is the way in which children's bones, which at first are soft, become harder. This is a long process that does not finish until the teenage years. During this process the bones in the hand harden before the bones in the feet.

3 **Development begins with uncontrolled gross movements before becoming precise and refined:** Young babies, for example, are able to reach out for an object with the whole arm before they can use their fingers to grasp it.

How children aged 0–1 develop physically

The first year of life sees rapid physical development. Babies begin with a range of reflexes. The reflexes are actions that happen without the baby thinking about them (see below). Over the first few months, some of these reflexes begin to disappear and babies learn to control their movements instead. Muscle tone also increases, which allows babies to become stronger. By the end of their first year, most babies are mobile, able to sit up and can reach out and handle objects easily.

Growth in the first year is also rapid. Most babies grow about 30cm and will also triple their birth weight. This rapid rate of growth continues into their second year.

Key terms

Co-ordination: co-ordination is linked to the way in which the brain is able to pass messages and take in information. Hand–eye co-ordination, for example, is about the way in which information from the eyes is used to help the hands do something such as thread a bead on a string.

Balance: this skill is also linked to the way in which the brain is able to handle information. Balance is an important skill to master in order to gain mobility.

Key terms

Pattern of development: rate and sequence of development.

Rate of development: speed at which development takes place.

Sequence of development: order in which development occurs.

Age	Developmental pattern
Newborn	<ul><li>A newborn baby has many developmental reflexes that are designed to help him or her survive, for example, being able to cry and suck. These gradually disappear as the baby gains voluntary control of his or her body.</li><li>Rooting reflex – moves mouth if face is touched to look for food.</li><li>Startle reflex – throws out hands and legs as if trying to catch something if he or she hears a sudden sound.</li><li>Grasp reflex – fingers automatically tighten around anything put in the palm of the hand. The grasp is so tight that baby can be lifted up.</li><li>Crawling reflex – when placed on front, knees are tucked underneath. This is because of being curled up in the womb.</li></ul>

continued on next page

Age	Developmental pattern
6 weeks	• Starting to have more periods of alertness. • Looks at carer, stares at bright lights. • Is soothed by carer's voice. • Follows objects and faces at close range. • Arm and leg movements are jerky.
3 months	• Smiles and coos. • Kicks legs strongly and moves arms. • Movements are less jerky, although still not co-ordinated. • Can find hands and bring them to the mouth. • Looks at and plays with fingers. • Is alert and looks around. • Can lift and turn head from side to side when lying on front. • Can hold a rattle for a short time, although cannot co-ordinate arms to bring it to mouth.
6 months	• Smiles, laughs and makes sounds. • Follows adults' movements. • Grasps objects. • Beginning to roll over. • Pulls up legs with hands when on back. May put foot in mouth. • Sits up with support, although some babies are starting to sit up for short periods without support. • Pushes head, neck and chest of floor when on front.
9 months	• Sits up well without support. • Can reach out for toys from sitting. • May be crawling or shuffling on bottom. • Uses fingers and thumb to pick up objects. • Can bang objects together. • Babbles and starts to understand words such as 'bye-bye' and 'no'.
12 months	• Most babies are mobile – either crawling, rolling or bottom shuffling. • Starts to walk by holding on to furniture; this is often called cruising. • May stand alone for a few seconds. • Points to objects using index fingers to show adults. • Understands name and simple instructions. • Drinks from cup; tries to feed using spoon and fingers.

• *Summary of physical development from 0–12 months*

How children aged 1–3 develop physically

In this period, children's physical skills continue to develop relatively quickly. Somewhere between 12 and 15 months, most children will start to walk. The pattern of gaining control over larger movements before smaller ones continues. Some movements are also made possible because the bones in the body have started to harden or have now formed. These processes do not finish until the end of adolescence and this is one reason why older children become stronger. The wrist, for example, of a 1-year-old contains only three bones, while there are nine bones in an adult's wrist.

The brain is also developing and growing. It is responsible for sending and co-ordinating messages between different parts of the body. Somewhere between 18 months and 3 years, children will become ready for toilet training. The timing depends on when the brain is developed enough to send the necessary signals. Hand–eye co-ordination is another skill that is reliant on the signals sent to and from the brain, as is the ability to walk without bumping into objects.

Age	Fine manipulative skills	Gross manipulative skills
12 months	<ul><li>Picks up objects with thumb and forefinger</li><li>Picks up and holds toys such as rattles</li><li>Points to objects</li><li>Holds cup with help</li><li>Puts small objects in a container</li></ul>	<ul><li>Mobile – either crawling, rolling or shuffling</li><li>(Some children may be walking)</li><li>Sits up unsupported for long periods</li><li>Walks with assistance</li><li>Tries to crawl up stairs</li></ul>
15 months	<ul><li>Holds and drinks from cup with help</li><li>Builds tower of two blocks</li><li>Makes marks with crayons</li><li>Tries to turn pages in books</li></ul>	<ul><li>Crawls down stairs feet first</li><li>Walks independently</li><li>Seats self in small chair</li></ul>
18 months	<ul><li>Strings four large beads</li><li>Turns door knobs and handles</li><li>Pulls of shoes</li></ul>	<ul><li>Bends down from waist to pick up toys</li><li>Rolls and throws a ball</li><li>Walks down stairs with adult help</li><li>Pushes and pulls toys whilst walking</li></ul>
2 years	<ul><li>Uses a spoon to feed him or herself</li><li>Zips and unzips large zippers</li><li>Places five rings on a stick</li><li>Puts on shoes</li><li>Draws circles and dots</li><li>Builds a tower of five to six bricks</li><li>Begins to use a preffered hand</li></ul>	<ul><li>Kicks a ball that is not moving</li><li>Climbs on furniture</li><li>Puts together and pulls apart snap-together toys</li><li>Walks up and down stairs confidently</li></ul>

continued on next page

Age	Fine manipulative skills	Gross manipulative skills
3 years	• Turns pages in a book one by one • Holds crayon and can draw a face • Uses a spoon without spilling • Washes and dries hands with help • Puts on and takes off coat	• Walks and runs forwards • Walks on tiptoes • Throws large ball • Kicks ball forward • Jumps from low steps • Pedals and steers a tricycle
4 years	• Buttons and unbuttons own clothing • Cuts out simple shapes • Draws a person with head, trunk and legs • Puts together 12-piece puzzle	• Walks on a line • Aims and throws ball • Bounces and catches large ball • Runs, changing direction • Hops on one foot • Pedals and steers a tricycle confidently

● *Summary of physical development from 12 months to 4 years*

Toilet training

Helping children to move out of nappies is mainly a question of getting the timing right. Beginning too early can leave children worried and confused as they cannot do what adults around them are expecting. Beginning too early also leaves adults frustrated as children may have frequent accidents and refuse to go near the potty. Understanding when children are ready is not simply a matter of age, but is more about physical readiness. A few children are ready at 18 months, but the majority of children will be ready somewhere between 2 and 3 years. Fortunately, there are some signs that you can observe to help you know when children are ready:

- dry nappies after a child has had a nap or sleep
- long intervals when the nappy is dry
- awareness from the child that the nappy has been wet or soiled
- interest in using a potty
- ability to communicate the need to use a potty.

Some practitioners in other countries also note whether children are able to walk up steps using alternate feet. This is a sign that the brain has sufficiently matured to handle complex information from different parts of the body.

How children aged 4–7 develop physically

In this period, children's movements become more co-ordinated and smoother. This is because the brain has developed further and is able to process information more quickly. This can be seen in the way that children are faster at dressing and have fewer accidents, for example stumbling or bumping into things. As a result of improved co-ordination, children often gain in confidence.

Age	Fine manipulative skills	Gross manipulative skills
5 years	• Forms letters, writes own name • Draws recognisable pictures of trees, houses, people and animals • Colours in pictures neatly • Dresses and undresses easily • Completes 20-piece jigsaw puzzles • Cuts out shapes using scissors quite accurately • Draws around a template	• Skips with a rope • Runs quickly and is able to avoid obstacles • Is able to use a variety of large equipment – e.g. swings, slides • Throws large ball to partner and catches it • Hits ball with bat or stick
6–7 years	• Is able to sew simple stitches • Cuts out and shapes accurately and neatly • Handwriting is evenly spaced and may be joined • Drawings are detailed and representative • Makes a simple sandwich • Ties and unties laces	• Rides a bicycle without stabilisers • Runs • Chases and dodges others • Hops, skips and jumps confidently • Kicks a ball with direction • Balances on a beam or wall

● *Summary of physical development from 5–7 years*

How children aged 8–12 develop physically

Children's physical skills continue to develop and will often depend on their interests. This means that a child who enjoys football or tennis will begin to show increasing skill.

Children's fine motor skills are also good and children who enjoy drawing or making things are able to make very precise movements. In terms of boys' and girls' strength, there is little difference. This is because hormone production is very low. This begins to change once the body begins to produce more hormones.

From about 10 years, many girls' bodies will be starting the process of puberty, which for most girls finishes at around 15 years. For boys this usually starts later at around 13 or 14 years and finishes at around 16 years. Puberty usually begins with another growth spurt, but the body does not all grow at the same rate. Hands and feet are usually the first to reach adult size, followed by the arms and legs and then the trunk. As well as the increase in growth, the body also becomes stronger. This is partly due to the hardening of the bones in the body, but also to the increase in muscle strength and hand grip.

Age	How modelling influences children
4–7 years	Children in this age group are still modelling adults, but they also copy older children and each other. A child may see another wave a ruler around and then copy that child. This is why when one child goes to the toilet, it is likely that other children suddenly have a need to go as well! Children are also copying what they have seen on television or other media. They may run around pretending to be Spider-man!
	It is important that children can also learn positive skills and attitudes. They may notice the way in which an adult writes, mixes paint or tidies up and then try to copy it.
8–12 years	Modelling continues, but television and other media may also have an effect. Children may want products that they have seen advertised. This is known as 'pester power' by the manufacturers. It means that children may want particular brands of crisps or clothes.
13–16 years	Young people continue to be affected by modelling. Peer group modelling can mean that young people experiment in negative ways. They may try smoking if they see that a popular person in their group smokes. Older brothers or sisters who may be trying drugs or involved in sexual relationships may influence them. The media also influence young people as they try to fit in with an 'image'.

Communication and language development

Being able to communicate and also to understand others is an essential skill. Most children quickly acquire this skill and by the age of 4 years are becoming fairly competent speakers. The spider diagram below shows the skills that children need to master in order to become skilled communicators.

Facial expressions
Children need to understand what facial expressions mean. They also have to use them when they communicate.

Vocabulary
Children need to learn the meanings of words. They need also to know when and how to use them.

Pronunciation
In a spoken language, children need to be able to create the sounds that they are hearing. Babies begin this process by babbling and practising sounds. Older children often make the odd mistake as they learn how to say a new word.

Gestures and body language
As well as words, children need to know what someone is feeling. Body language and gestures are ways of communicating feelings and moods.

Key skills involved in communication and language

Taking turns
Good communication is a process. It involves listening, thinking and also responding. Babies learn how to be responsive if adults play with them and encourage them to babble.

Grammar
Speaking and writing requires knowledge of grammar. Words have to be put in the right order to make sense. Children have to know about plurals and past tenses. Fortunately, children seem to learn the grammar of their language fairly naturally if the people they are with are speaking in sentences.

Tuning in and listening
Babies need to work out the sounds that are needed in the language they will be learning. Older children need to be able to listen and make sense of what is being communicated to them.

Pitch and intonation
The sound of your voice is important. Through pitch and intonation, you let everyone know how you are feeling. It also helps other people to stay interested. Through early babbling, babies learn how to modulate their voices.

How babies learn to communicate

From the moment babies are born, they are tuning into sounds. They quickly start to turn their head in the direction of sounds and soon recognise their main carers' voices. In their first year they learn the key skills of communicating, which include eye contact, facial expression and smiling. Bit by bit, babies start to work out what words mean. By the age of 9 months, many babies are able to understand key words such as 'bye-bye' or 'drink'.

While they are tuning into the language, babies are also practising their speech. They start by cooing, but quickly move onto babbling. From 6 months, even the babbling becomes more complex and increasingly sounds like the language they are hearing. From 12 months, babies start mixing babbling with recognisable words. By 18 months, children often have ten or more words.

How young children build their language

Once children begin to use words, they quickly start using them more and more. The amount of babbling goes down and the number of words increases. From 2 years onwards children may learn tens of new words each week.

From single words, children start to put two words together. 'Cat gone' or 'Drink no' are examples of the way children are able to make mini-sentences. This is known as 'telegraphese'. From this point, children soon make whole sentences. By 3 years, their speech is likely to be understood by someone who does not know them. From 4 years, children are likely to sound fairly fluent, although the odd mispronunciation or mistake will carry on until children are around 7 years.

How older children use language

Once children have become fluent users of language, they soon start to be able to use it to their advantage. They may start to pester adults, argue back as well as enjoy jokes and even make them up.

Once children have mastered spoken language, their next step is to learn how to read and write. Most children will be ready to do this at around 6 years, although they may sometimes be encouraged to start earlier. Learning to read is quite a skill and relies on children being able to remember visual signs as well as being able to link sounds with signs. Writing is linked to reading so many children need to learn how to read before they can write easily.

Age	Pre-linguistic stage
0–3 months	• Cries to show hunger, tiredness and distress. • Recognises different tones of voices. • Coos and gurgles when content. • By three months can recognise carer's voice and is soothed by it. • Smiles in response to others' faces.
3–6 months	• Still cries to show distress, but is more easily soothed. • Babbles and coos. • Babbles consist of short sounds – e.g. 'ma ma da da'. • Laughs, chuckles and even squeals.
6–12 months	• Babbling makes up half of a baby's non-crying sounds • Strings vowels and consonants together to makes repetitive sounds, e.g. 'memememe, dadadadadada'. • Babbling becomes more tuneful and inventive, and by 9 months most of the sounds used are the ones needed for the language being learnt. • At 10 months understand about seventeen words – e.g. 'bye-bye'. • Uses gestures to ask for things – e.g. points hand and whines to show adult what he wants. • Enjoys games – e.g. pat-a-cake.

Age	Linguistic stage
First words **12–18 months**	• First words appear at around 12 months, although will only be recognisable as a word to carer – e.g. 'dede' to mean 'drink'. • Words are used to mean more than one thing depending on the intonation the baby uses – e.g. 'dede' is used to mean 'I want a drink', 'My drink is finished'. (Linguists call these one-word expressions holophrases.) • By 15 months children will have about 10 words that their carers can understand.
18–24 months	• Two words are put together – e.g. 'Bye-bye dog'. • Telegraphic speech appears, with children using key words in a grammatical way – e.g. 'Dada come.' • Children's vocabulary increases with children learning 10–30 words in a month. • By 2 years, most children have 200 words.
2–3 years	• Quickly learns new words. • Uses plurals – e.g. 'dogs'. • Makes errors – e.g. 'sheeps', 'drawed'. • Starts to use negatives – e.g. 'There no cats'. • Starts to use questions – e.g. 'Where cats?'
3–4 years	• Imitates adult speech patterns accurately – e.g. 'We liked that, didn't we?' • Speech is understood by strangers. • Sentences contain four or more words and are grammatical. • Vocabulary is large, with children knowing parts of their bodies, names of household objects, animals. • Errors are still made especially when using past tenses – e.g. 'I taked it'. • Knows and understands nursery rhymes. • Enjoys asking questions.
4–8 years	• From 4 years on, children develop and refine language. Mistakes become fewer and children start to enjoy using language as a means of socialising with others, expressing their needs and recounting what they have done. • By 5 years vocabulary is about 5,000 words. • Uses complex sentences correctly. • Enjoys telling and hearing jokes. • Understands that language can be written with symbols. • By 8 years most children are fluent speakers, readers and developing writers of their language.

● *Language development*

How adults help babies to learn to communicate

Communication and language development does not just happen on its own. Cases where children have been badly neglected have shown this. From the moment they are born, children need adults who talk to them, point out things of interest and spend time with them. It might seem strange, but babies really need to hear adults talking even when they cannot yet reply. Most adults do this instinctively with young babies. They raise the pitch of their voices and use facial expressions. Adults are also good at simplifying sentences and repeating key words. This helps babies and toddlers to understand them.

How adults develop young children's communication

Once children have a few words, adults can help them by showing interest in what they are saying. Adults can listen to what children say and repeat it. Sometimes they might repeat it so that children can hear the phrase correctly. This helps children to learn without knowing it. This is better than telling children that they have said something wrong.

Adults can also help young children's communication by exposing them to new words. You might plan activities that broaden children's vocabulary by, for example, showing them a collection of leaves and naming them.

● *How is the adult catching the child's attention?*

How language is linked to children's behaviour

One of the things that language helps children with is controlling their actions. Most people have a 'little voice' in their head that calms them down or gets them to think through the consequences of possible actions. It is interesting that once children's language becomes more fluent, they are able to control themselves more easily. This goes some way to explain why at 3 and 4 years, most children are finding it easier to wait, share and be reassured by adults. The link between language and behaviour means that some children with language delay may show aggressive behaviours. Working on their speech or finding alternative ways of helping them to communicate their needs is therefore helpful.

Children may need support with their communication

Some children need support in order to communicate. There can be a variety of reasons for this. Sometimes children find it hard to make sense of what is said, although they can hear. Some children may have physical difficulties in pronouncing words, while others may have a hearing impairment which means that they cannot fully hear the spoken word.

Makaton

Makaton is a visual system of communicating that uses signs. It is designed to support the spoken word, not to replace it. Children using Makaton learn signs that accompany words and this helps them to understand the meaning of the words. Children who use Makaton will not have a hearing impairment, but may have a learning difficulty. Some children who use Makaton will then be able to use language.

British Sign Language

This is a complete and recognised language. It is important not to confuse it with Makaton, which has a very different purpose. Sign language is used by deaf people as a complete way of communicating instead of relying on the spoken word.

Speech therapy

Speech therapy is a way of helping children to use spoken language. It is usually provided by the health service, but in many areas speech therapists work closely with education departments. A speech therapist will assess a child's speech and develop a programme to help them. Common reasons why children may be referred to speech therapy include difficulties with pronunciation, stammering and a reluctance to talk.

Visual aids

Some children need clues as to what is happening. Pictures can help children to understand the meaning of words and they can use the pictures to show what they want. Children with significant difficulties in communicating may be helped by using picture systems.

Personal, social and emotional development

Most people enjoy having friends. Children and young people are no different. People also like feeling good about themselves. Personal, social and emotional development is about the way in which children learn to be with others. This, like other areas of development, is a process that adults can help children with. These areas of development are interlinked. Children, for example, will find it hard to make friends if they have not learned to share or control their anger.

Early relationships (attachments)

Children's earliest and strongest relationships are usually with their parents. Babies will quickly recognise the smell of their parents and are soon comforted by hearing their voices. These special relationships are called 'attachments' and appear to be essential for children's later development.

What happens when children are separated from their parents?

Fifty years or so ago, people did not realise the importance of children's early attachments. It was only in the 1950s that research showed how important they were. One of the key figures in this work was John Bowlby. He noted that there was a link between later ability to form relationships and respect society's rules and children's early attachments. His work and that of others has had great influence in the way early years workers care for children when their parents leave them.

It is now known that young children who are left even for a few hours can become very stressed and anxious. This is called separation anxiety. The earliest signs of separation anxiety can be seen in babies from around 7 months. Babies start to dislike being held by anyone other than their parents and may start to swivel round to get back to them. From 8 months, babies will start to cry but will stop once they are back with their parents. Separation anxiety continues until children are around 3 years old. After this point, most children who are separated temporarily from their parents seem to cope more easily provided that they can understand what is happening.

Signs of separation anxiety

The earliest signs of separation anxiety are hard to miss. Babies and children will cry, scream and even kick. If they are mobile they will try to get to the door! This stage of separation anxiety is not surprisingly called protest. Once exhausted, children will then move to the next stage, which is called withdrawal. Children will be quieter, sorrowful and withdrawn. They are not interested in playing, joining in or being with the other children. They may wander round with thumbs in their mouths or clinging onto a comforter or an adult. It is important not to see this as progress! Children in the second stage are literally becoming depressed.

Settling in to avoid separation anxiety

Separation anxiety can be avoided if children have already got used to the setting and more importantly have developed an extra special relationship with the carer who will be looking after them. This person is often referred to as a key person or keyworker. It is important that children have a chance to meet and play with this person before their parents leave. Settling in policies should therefore be designed to help children adjust to their new carer.

It is also important that children who show any signs of separation anxiety are quickly reunited with their parents. The danger of leaving children to cry is that they will learn that they do not like being in the setting. This can lead to situations where children cry every time they come in.

Helping children to make smooth transitions

Moving from home to nursery, school or any new setting can be hard for children of all ages. It is important to recognise this and find ways of helping them.

Age	How to help children to settle
0–3 years	The aim is to make sure that children have made an attachment with a keyworker in the new setting before being left. Many settings encourage children to make several visits first to help them to become familiar with the environment. It is also important for settings to adapt their routine to the needs of babies, rather than the other way around.
4–7 years	Children are more able to understand what is happening. If they have had good experiences of being separated, they will adjust more easily. All children will need time to settle down. If possible children should be put with friends or children that they already know. If children go into a setting and do not know any adults or children, you will need to take extra care of them and to introduce them to children who will be happy to let them join in.
8–12 years	Children may start to express strong feelings about changing setting. It is important that they can see the positive aspects of any change. Avoid comments such as 'You won't be able to do that when you get there!' As friendships are important, efforts should be made to keep friends together or to structure activities so that children quickly get to know each other. While some children are naturally outgoing and sociable, others find it hard to make friends from scratch.
13–16 years	Young people will find it easier to move settings smoothly when they have had some input and feel in control of the process. Adults should try not to take over, but should listen to young people's thoughts and fears.

Self-concept and self-esteem

Children need to develop a sense of identity, to feel confident and to see themselves positively. Learning about themselves is a process that is hugely influenced by other people. From the time that babies are born, people will make comments about them. Hopefully, most of the time they are favourable!

From the reactions and comments of others, children learn about themselves. This can shape their behaviour. If a child begins to perceive himself or herself as 'difficult', the child looks for ways of living up to that image.

The chart below shows the stages that most children pass through as they develop a sense of identity.

Age range	How children develop a sense of self
2–3 months	Babies begin to realise that they are separate beings from their parents. They learn this by realising they can make things happen around themselves – e.g. if a child pushes a rattle, it moves.
9–12 months	Babies start to realise objects are still there even if they cannot see them. Piaget referred to this as 'object permanence'. Once babies have an understanding of object permanence, they gradually understand that objects and people continue to exist when they are out of sight.

continued on next page

Age range	How children develop a sense of self
	The next stage for children is to work out what they are like. In the same way that a wooden cube is hard and firm, the child needs to ask what his or her own properties are.
21 months	At around 21 months most children recognise themselves in a mirror. To test this, experimenters put a spot on a child's nose and then show the child a mirror. Do children touch their reflection or their own nose? Children who have self-recognition touch their own nose.
2 years	Most children know their names, their gender and whether they are little or large. By the age or two, most children have a feeling of identity and it is interesting that this coincides with their becoming more assertive and wanting to do things for themselves.
2.5 years omwards	Children use imaginative or role play – e.g. home corner onwards and dressing up. They play helpers, babies, mothers and 'baddies'. It is thought that this type of play helps children explore different roles.
5–7 years	Children are now aware of who they are and that they have their own qualities. They tend to be fairly positive about themselves and their skills.
8–12 years	In this period, children become more aware of what other people think about them. They also begin to compare themselves to others. Children might make comments such as 'I can draw a little, but not as well as my brother'.
13–16 years	The pressures and changes that affect young people can show in their self-esteem. Young people who as children had high self-esteem can 'wobble' during these years. They see that their body shape has changed and their role as a 'child' is also changing. This throws up issues that they need to resolve. The transition from child to adult may not be fully completed until a young person leaves home to become fully independent.

 Keys to good practice: How to develop children's self-esteem

✓ Make sure that children feel valued

✓ Do not talk negatively about children

✓ Praise and encourage children

✓ Observe children and notice their reactions

✓ Encourage children to try new skills and to be independent

✓ Provide opportunities for role play for all ages so that children can explore identity

Case study 5: Children learn about themselves from the reactions of adults

Michael has not had a good day at nursery. He became excited and boisterous. This led to him running into another child. He overhears one staff member saying to another, 'I will be pleased today when he goes home. I don't know what has got into him.'

1 *Consider why this comment might affect Michael's view of himself.*
2 *How might it affect Michael's future behaviour?*
3 *Explain why it is important that adults are very careful about what they say in the presence of children.*

Developing children's self-reliance and independence

A key way in which you can help children to gain confidence is by encouraging them to be independent. This process should start as early as possible and should carry on until children are ready to join the adult world. Developing children's self-reliance has added bonuses in terms of behaviour. It can prevent tantrums and other behaviours associated with frustration.

Age range	Examples of how self-reliance skills can be developed
0–1 years	• Independence can begin with babies! • Encourage babies to push their arms through clothes. • Give older babies something to hold while nappy changing. • Provide finger foods from 9 months. • Encourage toddlers to pull off their socks when undressing or their hats. • Put out a choice of toys for toddlers. • Encourage toddlers to help tidy away.
2–3 years	• Children need to learn about making decisions. Adults need to give children choices. With young children consider limiting the possibilities to avoid overwhelming the child. • Begin providing choices where appropriate, e.g. choice of coloured beakers, toys or activities. • Build choice into the routine. • Encourage children to take off coats and hats. • Play games to help children to learn to tidy up. • Encourage children to serve and feed themselves, and pour their own drinks. • Provide simple cooking activities. • Support children in their play, encouraging them to develop their own ideas. • Organise areas where children have free access to equipment and toys without. needing an adult's help.

continued on next page

Age range	Examples of how self-reliance skills can be developed
4–8 years	• Children need to set more of their own boundaries and be able to learn more about choice, decisions and consequences. • Provide open-ended activities which give children the scope to problem-solve. • Give children small areas of responsibility, e.g. plants to care for, wiping tables, playing with younger children. • Provide opportunities for children to learn everyday skills, e.g. using scissors and other tools, washing up. • Encourage children to evaluate risks, e.g. playing outdoors.
8–12 years	• Adults should increasingly be trusting children and expecting them to take increasing responsibility. • Encourage children to choose and prepare simple meals. • Provide opportunities for children to plan their own activities and to solve their own problems. • Praise and encourage independent behaviour. • Encourage children to ask for support, but avoid taking over. • Provide opportunities for children to organise themselves, e.g. thinking what they need to pack, put out, consider.
13–16 years	• Young people need to explore what independence means. • Provide a small budget for an event, e.g. a party. • Encourage young people to plan and organise. • Listen and use questions to help young people think things through rather than give. advice and solutions. • Provide opportunities for young people to demonstrate their skills, knowledge and achievements, e.g. asking young people if they wish to take part in fundraising.

The development of friendships

Friends are important in most people's lives. In children's lives they grow more important as they develop. By the time a young person reaches 12 or 13 years, the chances are that their friends are becoming as important as their family members.

Age	How friendships develop
0–3 years	Children's first friends are their parents and main carers. They will learn how to play with them and how to communicate. Babies and toddlers will notice other children and be fascinated by them. At around 2 years, they are likely to play alongside each other. From 3 years, you will see the beginnings of more co-operative play.
4–7 years	Children really enjoy being with other children. They will show some friendship preferences, but these are mainly based on play interests, especially until the age of about 5 or 6 years. It is likely that towards the end of this period, children will play mainly with the same sex.

Age	How friendships develop
8–12 years	Children's friendships are becoming more settled and children now spend time with the same groups of friends. These are often same sex, although some play activities will encourage boys and girls to play together. There is some evidence to suggest that boys' friendships are likely to be group based while girls prefer closer but fewer friendships.
13–16 years	Young people start to want to spend more time with each other than they do with their families. This is in preparation for leaving home and establishing themselves as independent people in the adult world. Young people can find themselves caught between wanting to remain in a group but not wanting to adopt the group's values and behaviour.

Helping children to make friends

You can help children to make friends by observing children as they play. From around the age of 4 years, you should look out for children who do not appear to be interested in other children or find it hard to play co-operatively. There can be several reasons why they may be spending time alone. They may, for example, have recently moved or they might not have developed the skills of playing.

You can help them by organising small activities with one or two other children. This could be anything that children find enjoyable including cooking, playing a simple board game or helping out an adult. The aim would be to guide the child, to encourage the child to take turns and to think about other children's needs, and to give the child confidence.

Helping children with 'fallouts'

The path of true friendship is generally a bit bumpy at times. Adults need to sense when children are unhappy and be skilful at deciding when to intervene. Sometimes children are able to sort out their friendships after they have had time to reflect. This means that a child who is upset in the morning, might be feeling differently in the afternoon. Fallouts can sometimes become serious and adults need to be on the look out for name-calling and any intimidating behaviour. Providing group activities that are new and interesting can sometimes help children to co-operate again. It is also important that children are praised for co-operative behaviour.

Best friends

Some children only want to play with one other child. This can be seen quite early on with some 7-year-olds having a specific preference for a friend. This can continue into the teenage years, especially among girls. The reliance on having a 'best friend' can cause problems. A best friend might be absent, decide not to join in or go and find a different friend. It can also cause great distress if children are separated to go to different schools.

For adults working with children, it is useful to encourage 'best friends' to also have times when they play and join in with other children. Look out for activities that require different size groups so that children are able to maintain their skill at talking to and playing alongside others while still staying with their 'best friend'.

Helping older children with peer pressure

Friendships are extremely important for young people. While this can be positive, it can also put pressure on young people. Some young people find that they do things because they are afraid of 'falling out' with a friendship group. This can be anything from playing on train lines to smoking and taking drugs. Young people need adults who can listen to them and can help them to feel confident enough to act independently. Talking through the issues that affect young people in a way that helps them to understand and explore them can be useful.

Children's behaviour

Children's behaviour is complex because it is linked to many areas of development. It is also a factor in children's social development as friendships and being with others requires being able to exercise some control.

Cognitive development
Children's behaviour becomes easier when they can understand the reason behind rules. This is why once children reach the age of 3 or 4 years, it becomes a little easier for them to be co-operative.

Emotional development
Children need to feel secure, valued and loved. Without this emotional support, children find it hard to show co-operative behaviour. Attention seeking behaviours can be a sign that a child needs more support.

Physical development
Children find it easier to manage and control their behaviour when they are responsible and independent. Physical skills mean that children can be more self-reliant. This can help children to become less frustrated. In older children, physical growth and the release of hormones play a significant role in their moods and ability to control their feelings.

Factors affecting children's behaviour

Social development
Children need to spend time being with other children as well as adults. This helps them to learn what is acceptable behaviour. This socialisation also teaches children as they 'model' from watching adults and other children.

Language development
Children have strong emotions. It is easier to control them when they are able to explain what they are feeling and what they want to happen. Children under the age of 3 years have more difficulty in controlling their feelings as a result. Children who have speech and language delay may find it harder to control their behaviour.

Keys to good practice: How to encourage appropriate behaviour

✓ Act as consistent role model for children.

✓ Recognise and praise examples of co-operative behaviour.

✓ Make sure that expectations of behaviour are fair for the age and stage of the child.

✓ Observe children and consider whether behaviour is a result of difficulty with a particular area of development.

✓ Consider whether activities, routines or expectations are meeting the needs of children.

✓ As soon as children are able to understand, give simple explanations.

✓ Encourage older children to set their own boundaries.

Moral development

At what age do children know right from wrong? This is a question that is difficult to answer, although two key theorists believe that it is much later than most people might think. The key question is whether children do something because they want to avoid getting into trouble or because it is the 'right' thing to do. Both theorists came to the conclusion that children don't start to make real moral decisions until quite late in childhood.

Keys to good practice: How to encourage children to learn about morality

✓ Remember that young children learn about morality from adults' behaviour and actions.

✓ Explain the reasons behind the rules wherever possible.

✓ Encourage older children to explore the necessity for rules.

The principles of supporting children's development

By using observations as a tool, you should be able to look at children's development and then work out how best to support children. This section outlines some of the ways in which adults working with the different age groups might support development. The section is subdivided into four broad age ranges:

- 0–3 years
- 4–7 years
- 8–12 years
- 13–16 years.

How to support the development of children aged 0–3

The early years of children's lives are known to be extremely important for their later development. This means that if you choose to work with this age range, you will need to be extremely good at observing children and attending to their needs. This is not an easy age range to work with. Babies and children under 3 years are completely reliant on the adults who work with them to keep them safe, but also to meet their physical and emotional needs. This is not always an easy task as children's ability to communicate and to understand is still developing.

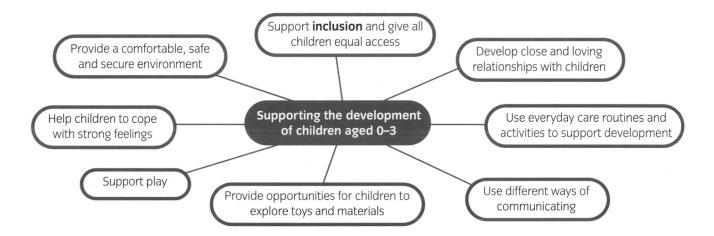

Support **inclusion** and give all children equal access

Provide a comfortable, safe and secure environment

Develop close and loving relationships with children

Help children to cope with strong feelings

Supporting the development of children aged 0–3

Use everyday care routines and activities to support development

Support play

Provide opportunities for children to explore toys and materials

Use different ways of communicating

Provide a comfortable, safe and secure environment

All children need to feel comfortable and safe in their setting. For very young children, this is critical. Babies and toddlers will respond according to the way that they are feeling. If they do not feel comfortable and safe, they will be unsettled and unhappy. This has short- and long-term effects. They may cry, refuse to eat or generally be unresponsive to activities. In the longer term, this can be a reason why children fail to thrive and also develop poor patterns of behaviour.

For babies and toddlers, you must also think about providing a varied environment. While older children are able to move easily and may change rooms or go outside, babies and toddlers may need more help. This is essential if babies and toddlers are to get enough stimulation.

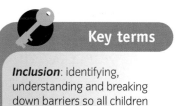

Key terms

Inclusion: identifying, understanding and breaking down barriers so all children can participate and belong.

Support inclusion and give all children equal access

Inclusion is about making sure that all children are valued and also that their needs are met. This means thinking hard about the way you care for children and also observing them. It means checking that what you are providing for them is working and changing the way you plan and work if necessary. This is important as you have seen that children's development can vary dramatically, so what you need to provide for one child may be very different to what another child of a similar age needs.

Develop close and loving relationships with children

When you care for babies and toddlers, you are providing them with a substitute for their primary carers. For babies and toddlers to thrive without their parents, they need you to provide close reassurance. To do this well means spending time with individual children so that they can develop a special relationship with you.

They also need physical contact from you. This acts as reassurance and helps the child to settle in and feel valued. Physical contact means hugs, sitting on knees and hand-holding when the child shows signs of wanting it.

This can happen early on when babies, for example, are able to indicate that they want picking up, while slightly older children may try to 'snuggle in' or may follow an adult closely. In the same way that children can signal that they need physical reassurance, they can also show you that they do not want it. They may put their hands behind their back or move away. These signals must not be ignored as otherwise the physical contact is not appropriate.

Use everyday care routines and activities to support development

H

While adults can find everyday routines dull, babies and toddlers can learn and be stimulated by them. This is because adults are fascinating for young children and most routine care activities allow babies and toddlers time with an individual adult. Physical care routines such as changing nappies, feeding and washing hands are therefore potential learning activities that will be hugely enjoyable for the child. The key is that the adults are able to talk, make eye contact and play little games as they carry them out.

In the same way, going out for a ride in a pushchair or holding an adult's hand during a walk around the garden can stimulate babies and toddlers. The change in environment means that they have new things to observe, smell and feel.

Use different ways of communicating

To support children's language development, adults must spend plenty of time with young children communicating with them. This means talking, singing, making eye contact and, crucially, listening and responding to children. It also means helping children to learn about gestures, facial expressions and simple signs. Most adults have the ability to support children in this way, but children do need adults to be physically close to them. For babies this means picking them up so that they can see the adult's face, while for older children, it means adults getting down to their level. As babies and toddlers make sounds and even say their first few words, it is important that adults show that they are interested and respond positively.

Did you know?

Research has shown that watching television, videos and DVDs is not good for children under 3 years. There are many reasons for this, but particularly important is the effect on language development. Children are not actively using their language while watching and are not learning how to communicate with people. Research is also emerging that suggests that children's brains might be affected by the rapid changes in light and images.

Unit 204

Use support systems to develop own practice in children's care, learning and development

Wherever you work or whatever stage you are at in your career you will always need to consider the importance of developing your skills and improving your performance at work.

This unit will help you to find out what sort of systems there are to help you progress and develop. You will discover the importance of:
- constructive feedback
- development of your practice
- using formal support systems
- using informal support systems
- professional development opportunities

What you must know and understand:
- How to recognise the strengths and weaknesses of your own practice (K2PS2)
- How your background and experience can affect your practice (K2PS3)
- How to identify and support your own learning style (K2PS4)
- The systems that are available for support and supervision (K2PS5)
- Why it is important to set performance goals and targets (K2PS6)
- Understanding the professional structure of the sector and your opportunities for career progression (K2PS7)
- How to undertake your professional development (K2PS8)

How to recognise the strengths and weaknesses of your own practice

When working with children you are pursuing a very responsible career. You have to show great sensitivity to the needs of children, parents and carers. In order to do this you need to be very honest with yourself about your strengths and weaknesses.

There are many ways that other people can give you **feedback**. This may be through:

- formal meetings such as appraisals
- supervision meetings
- observation of your practice
- team meetings.

Your strengths and weaknesses will affect your practice. Everybody has strengths and weaknesses but recognising them will help you to professionally **develop your practice**.

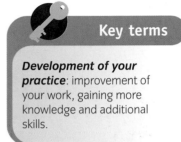

Key terms

Development of your practice: improvement of your work, gaining more knowledge and additional skills.

Test yourself

What are your own strengths and weaknesses? Try completing this checklist.

	Strength	Weakness
Good listening skills		
Good verbal skills		
Good written skills		
Co-operative team member		
Well organised		
Able to keep a confidence		
Show initiative		
Flexible		
Good at time keeping		
Aware of health and safety issues		
Respect other cultures		
Planning		
Observing		
Evaluating		
Able to follow instructions		
Acknowledge other's ideas and support		
Cheerful disposition		

You may want to add other things to your list.

Consider one area of weakness. How could you improve it? You may consider:

- asking your supervisor or tutor for advice or further training
- researching the subject
- observing a colleague who you think has a strength in this area
- giving yourself an action plan to develop this weakness
- discussing it in your next appraisal.

It is essential that you recognise your strengths. This is important for your own professional development and the benefit of your team and the children you work with. You could share your area of expertise or strengths in several ways.

- You could mention a strength at a team meeting, for example you may have excellent understanding of a particular culture. You could offer to do a presentation o your colleagues or plan a special activity for the children.
- You could discuss strengths at your appraisal and look at ways of using these in the workplace.
- You could use your strengths informally. For example, if you are a good team member you could offer support to your colleagues.

● *Sharing knowledge of a different culture*

How your background and experience can affect your practice

Where you come from, how you live and your experiences can have a positive or negative effect on the way you work. Look at the examples below.

Background/experience	Positive effect	Negative effect
English as an additional language	● You will be able to support parents and children. ● You will enrich children's experience of language.	● You may have some difficulty communicating but should feel able to seek support.
Different career before your current one	● You could transfer skills, bring another viewpoint.	● You may need specific support to settle down. ● It may be difficult to start in an inexperienced position.

continued on next page

Background/experience	Positive effect	Negative effect
Religious/cultural preferences	• You may be able to contribute to the curriculum, offering support to other children and colleagues.	• It may limit your involvement in some activities.
You are a parent or mature trainee	• You will be able to relate to parents. • You will have a mature outlook. • Your life skills will be useful.	• You may experience the stress of balancing work and family. You may feel too much is expected of you. • You may need support in taking instructions from someone younger.

Case study 1: Coping as a mature trainee

Jay has taken a position in an after-school club. She is a mature trainee who has a grown-up family and worked for ten years as a veterinary nurse. She is capable and calm, having learned a great deal in her previous job about dealing with difficult situations. Although she has had children, she has not experienced working with children in a professional capacity.

She is concerned that she is increasingly being asked by her supervisor to cope with difficult situations between staff, parents and children. While Jay has some natural ability, she feels she is not being given enough time to learn the new skills she needs.

1   *What do you think the advantages are of Jay's maturity and experience?*
2   *What do you think the disadvantages are to Jay of being a mature student?*
3   *How can Jay ensure she receives appropriate support?*

How to identify and support your own learning style

Everybody has different ways of learning. Although you are training at the moment you will still be required to learn when you are qualified. Whatever your learning style, your skills will improve with practice and some basic rules.

Check it out

There are many good training courses available on coaching and counselling. Ask your supervisor about courses that might suit you.

Test yourself

Carefully consider your own learning pattern and needs.

Are you someone who:
- is independent – likes to study alone
- requires support
- is practical – likes to learn actively
- is reflective – thinks carefully about things, researches widely
- finds work a challenge?
- enjoys working in a group
- has a limited attention span
- enjoys taking notes
- responds well to pressure
- has particular learning needs e.g. dyslexia
- asks lots of questions and enjoys learning from others
- finds work a challenge?

You will probably find that your learning style is a mixture of the above. By understanding how you learn you can choose the best training and learning programme.

The diagram below shows some of the basic skills that you will need to support any learning style.

Time management – using your time well

Organisation – making sure that you know where everything is

Keeping records – taking notes, recording or asking for handouts

Prioritising – making yourself lists of tasks you have to do in order of importance

● *Skills to support learning*

Remember that your learning style will be different from that of other people. There may be some things that you can understand in a short period of time while a colleague may take longer. The most important thing to do is to think carefully about the way that you learn. With support you can:

- make your own priorities
- set yourself goals
- work out your own strategies
- develop your own views and the ability to express them.

Keys to good practice: How to give and receive constructive feedback

Giving feedback

✓ Ensure you are in a confidential area.

✓ Clarify what you are discussing.

✓ Be supportive.

✓ Stress positives as well as negatives.

✓ Listen to the other person.

✓ Allow the other person time to ask questions.

Key terms

Constructive feedback: an honest opinion about what you need to improve on, with ideas about how to go about it.

Receiving feedback

✓ Listen carefully to what is being said.

✓ Retain eye contact.

✓ Ask for clarification if necessary.

✓ Accept responsibility for your actions.

Both parties should finish a feedback session feeling confident that they have listened to each other and can understand each other's point of view.

The systems that are available for support and supervision

While working in your setting you will need support and supervision. If you are supervised appropriately this will be a support to you. However, you may need to seek support yourself at times.

Support can be either **formal** or **informal**.

Study the chart below to see if you have this support available to you.

Type of support	How it can help you
Formal	
Manager	Your manager will usually hold an appraisal with you. Ideally this should happen twice a year.
Room leader/supervisor	The supervisor will help you to develop your professional role and support any concerns you might have.
Administrator	Your setting may have someone who can advise you over pay or other employment details.
Assessor	Your assessor will observe you, guide you through your training to ensure you gain an understanding of best practice, and assess you.
Tutor	Your tutor will teach you the theory you need for your course. A tutor will support you in writing assignments and gathering coursework as evidence.
Informal	
Mentor (or 'buddy')	You may be lucky enough to have a colleague who has been appointed to support you while you are training. A 'buddy' usually works at the same level as you and can answer your questions.
Colleagues in a similar job but another setting	You may find it helpful to share your ideas and experiences with people in similar jobs in other settings.

So that you can develop professionally you will need to:

- be clear that there are informal ways of being supported at work
- feel that you can ask for feedback at times other than formal appraisals and supervision meetings
- ensure that you are given the support you need to develop your practice.

It is sometimes your responsibility to seek support. Consider the case of Rashid in the following case study.

Case study 2: Seeking appropriate support

Rashid is working in a new Sure Start nursery. Everybody has been working hard to set up the nursery. Rashid has only just started his training at NVQ Level 2. He has been asked to mount a welcome display in a variety of languages in the entrance hall of the nursery. He is unsure about how to do this and is struggling to know where to start. He is aware of the fact that Tina, his supervisor, is extremely busy getting their room ready for the opening. Tina is very supportive of Rashid and always reminds him to ask for help if he needs it.

1   *How do you think Rashid could have avoided feeling awkward about asking for support?*
2   *Are there any other ways Tina could offer him support?*

It is important that you communicate your need for guidance and support.

Keys to good practice: How to communicate a need for support

✓ Carry out instructions willingly and promptly.

✓ Ask questions if you are not sure.

✓ Be alert to what is happening around you and listen to what you are told.

✓ Inform your supervisor about worries, concerns and potentially dangerous hazards.

Support can also come in the form of team meetings. This will give you the opportunity to benefit from other colleagues' experiences and ask for clarification. It can be very rewarding to work as a member of a team in this way. Sometimes it might be you giving the support! For example, if you see that your supervisor is worried about some paperwork, you might offer to do a display she was going to set up to relieve her. This would show your supervisor that you can take initiative and you will gain confidence in your ability to be supportive.

Test yourself

Think of a time when you needed support and didn't ask for it.

1 What did you feel like?
2 Did this affect your work?
3 How could you have handled the situation differently?

You can also seek support from a number of professional organisations. Some of the organisations ask you to pay an annual subscription to join.

- Disability Rights Commission
- Professional Association of Nursery Nurses
- UNISON
- 4 children, formerly Kid's Club Network.

Check it out

Find out about the systems of formal support available in your work setting.

Why it is important to set performance goals and targets

This section is all about you and is essentially about your willingness to accept and act on feedback, both verbal and non-verbal, about your working practice from others. It is vital you realise that you will need to learn and continue to learn all the time, building on your existing skills and knowledge and increasing your understanding of your work.

Working with children demands the highest standards and your willingness to learn will support you in this demanding role.

You will need to learn to:
- identify the gaps in your knowledge
- identify your objectives for your own development
- take responsibility to evaluate your own practice
- use both positive and negative feedback to improve your own work performance.

Identifying the gaps in your knowledge

This section identifies what you have to do within your work setting. Using this as your 'first base', you can then begin to identify what you need to learn regarding early years care and education and how you work as a member of your team. You might also need to improve your communication skills, IT skills or number skills.

When you are working towards an NVQ, it is recommended that you do a pre-assessment plan with the help of your assessor or mentor. A pre-assessment plan is another way of identifying what you need to know and what to do about it. It is often very useful to discuss these issues with someone else who is more experienced as he or she is able to 'map' what you already know against what you need to know.

While you are working with children, you will get informal feedback on a daily basis from comments from colleagues, parents and children. You will also be getting more formal feedback, such as in a session with your assessor, supervisor or senior colleague. Formal feedback may be written in the form of a report, or it may be given verbally. This feedback will help you to set objectives: the next step in developing yourself in your work role.

Case study 3: Identifying gaps in your knowledge

Sharmila has been working towards her NVQ in Children's Care, Learning and Development for several months. She is an assistant in a rising fives class. She is enjoying her work and is gaining in confidence. However, the class teacher does have some concerns, especially in the way that Sharmila uses story time. She does not read well, keeping her head down over the book, and forgets to show the children the pictures or involve them. The children consequently become fidgety and easily distracted during this time.

The teacher decides to speak to Sharmila about it. She sits down with her at the end of the session and asks Sharmila how she felt that day's storytelling went. Sharmila replies that she thinks it was 'all right', but confesses that she finds reading aloud 'nerve-racking'. The teacher and Sharmila begin to work out how Sharmila can improve her reading style and gain confidence.

1 *Why do you think Sharmila, having identified a gap in her knowledge (storytelling skills), did nothing about this until approached by the teacher?*
2 *What might Sharmila do to help improve her skills?*
3 *How might the teacher support her?*
4 *What formal and informal arrangements are there in your work setting to help you identify what you need to learn?*
5 *Identify what forms you may need to complete and obtain a copy of these.*

Identifying your objectives for your own development

An objective means what you need to take in order to achieve an aim. Your aims will be to improve what you have identified as the gaps in your knowledge or skills.

There is no 'right' method of developing skills and knowledge as each person will have individual needs. In the case study above, Sharmila's aim was to improve her storytelling skills. Her objectives might be:

- to tape herself reading a story and hear what it sounds like (very brave!)
- to practise reading out aloud to get used to hearing her own voice
- to make sure she chooses appropriate stories (with the support of the teacher)

- to make sure she reads them herself beforehand so she knows what is going to happen, then to think about possible questions to ask the children about the story
- to think about ways of making the stories more interesting, such as using puppets, using different voices for characters, etc.

Using all the above, Sharmila may find she is more confident and thereby may begin to enjoy the stories herself. Children respond very positively to enthusiasm in adults and the children will also respond to Sharmila's change in approach as well as her change in style.

Once you have identified your aims (i.e. what you need to achieve), you can then decide your objectives, as Sharmila and the teacher did. However, you do not always need to have someone with you. It is something you can do on your own as you break down what you need to do into small steps.

Setting objectives

Be very clear about what you want to achieve. For example, 'improving my work with children' is far too broad. You would need to decide what particularly you want to improve/develop and then set your objectives.

Make sure your objectives:
- are realistic
- are achievable
- develop your skills/understanding
- fit in with your work setting, role and responsibilities.

- *Using puppets can really make stories come alive*

Test yourself

Work out aims and objectives for the following situations:

1 Heather has twice planned activities which are not age appropriate for the children in her setting. Her supervisor has told her she is expecting far too much from the children and she needs to think more carefully about what they are able to do.

2 Darren is very enthusiastic. When tidying away activities he is inclined to take over and do it himself. The children are beginning to let him. This is causing problems for colleagues who insist on the children helping to clear away, seeing this as a way of supporting social and emotional development as well as care of the environment. His colleagues have asked his supervisor to approach him about it.

3 The supervisor has noticed that Peta is not talking to the babies when she is giving feeds but is much more inclined to talk to her colleague sitting next to her.

Discuss all of these with your supervisor.

Taking responsibility to evaluate your own practice

Working with children is a highly responsible career. You are required to show great sensitivity to the needs of children and their parents or carers. In order to do this, you must be able to be very honest with yourself and examine what you do and how you do it. You cannot always rely on other people to give you feedback about what you do and how you do it. It is up to you to be able to recognise where you need to improve or develop and to ask for help directly or do something about it yourself.

Using both positive and negative feedback to improve your own work performance

We all have to accept that occasionally we will get negative as well as positive feedback in our work. In addition, the way we receive feedback may not always be constructive. Positive feedback is, of course, always welcome and it can support you in identifying ways in which you can progress further. For example, positive feedback may lead to your supervisor saying that you have worked so well that perhaps you should consider doing a Level 3 NVQ in Children's Learning, Care and Development, or undertaking a full-time course of study to obtain a CACHE Level 3 in Child Care and Education. You may identify a particular skill – perhaps you have creative ideas that the children love in art or science. Perhaps you have a gift for bringing a story 'alive' or for being patient with children that others find 'difficult' or 'challenging'. These skills can be extended for your **professional development** and for the benefit of the children and your colleagues.

Key terms

Professional development opportunities: training programmes or courses, seminars, information days, conferences, exhibitions, study time, updating through reading

Negative feedback is more difficult to accept, but this does not detract from its usefulness. Negative feedback may not always be given in a constructive or positive way. For example, the teacher in the case study on page 150 might have told Sharmila about her lack of storytelling skills in an angry way. Sharmila might then have responded angrily or defensively herself. However, your colleagues and supervisors are human too and may not always give you feedback in ways that you will find easy to accept.

What is important is that you take time to think about the feedback you have been given. As you learn to take more responsibility for your own development, you may identify those areas in which you need to improve.

You should also receive a regular appraisal in your role as an employee. This will give you the opportunity to discuss your strengths and weaknesses in a confidential and supportive atmosphere. It is essential for you and your supervisor to be honest. You will have the chance to set targets and decide how these are going to be monitored. In some settings an appraisal is linked to your salary. The table below shows a professional development plan for an early years worker.

Objective	Measurement	Delivery date	Self-appraisal	Manager appraisal
Attend EYFS training	Attendance confirmed by training provider	December 09		
Update pediatric first aid certificate	Award of certificate	October 09		
Complete mentoring training	Attendance confirmed by training provider	October 09		
Use the web to update knowledge	Demonstrate new knowledge in the setting	December 09		
Start to lead room meetings	Write minutes of meeting	July 09		
Visit another setting	Write report on visit	December 09		

● *Example of a personal development plan for an early years worker*

Understanding the professional structure of the sector and your opportunities for career progression

There are different types of professional structure that vary according to the function and size of the organisation. An effective professional management structure will ensure:

- each member of staff can focus on certain tasks
- each member of staff will know whom he or she is responsible for and whom he or she is responsible to.

Look at the chart below of the Greenfield Day Nursery, a 30-place privately owned setting, and the roles of the professional team.

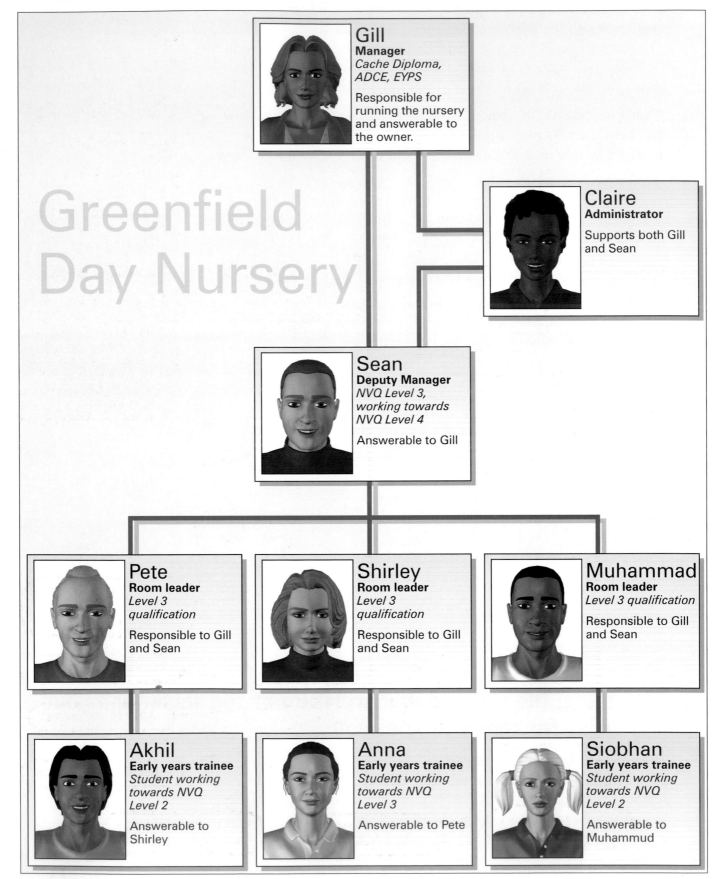

Greenfield Day Nursery

Gill
Manager
Cache Diploma, ADCE, EYPS

Responsible for running the nursery and answerable to the owner.

Claire
Administrator

Supports both Gill and Sean

Sean
Deputy Manager
NVQ Level 3, working towards NVQ Level 4

Answerable to Gill

Pete
Room leader
Level 3 qualification

Responsible to Gill and Sean

Shirley
Room leader
Level 3 qualification

Responsible to Gill and Sean

Muhammad
Room leader
Level 3 qualification

Responsible to Gill and Sean

Akhil
Early years trainee
Student working towards NVQ Level 2

Answerable to Shirley

Anna
Early years trainee
Student working towards NVQ Level 3

Answerable to Pete

Siobhan
Early years trainee
Student working towards NVQ Level 2

Answerable to Muhammud

● *How the Greenfield Day Nursery is organised*

The three trainees will have a variety of responsibility according to their level of qualification and experience. They will act as key persons in their setting. This means they will greet the child where possible and be the first point of contact for information exchange with parents.

Organisations need a structure so that:

- staff are properly supervised
- tasks are implemented
- children have high quality care and education
- parents are respected and valued
- the aims of the organisation are carried out
- national standards are maintained.

The childcare sector also has a professional structure, which consists of a framework of qualifications that are acceptable. A Level 2 qualification is part of that framework and enables you to work in a supervised capacity. Your next step could be to take a Level 3 qualification such as the Cache Level 3 in Childcare and Education or NVQ 3 in Early Years Care and Education. You could then eventually work in a supervisory capacity.

How to undertake your professional development

When you have gained your qualification you will have the opportunity to develop professionally in a variety of ways. Look at the chart below to find out what the opportunities are.

● *Opportunities for professional development*

The diagram below shows the variety of different ways you can study to suit your needs and learning style.

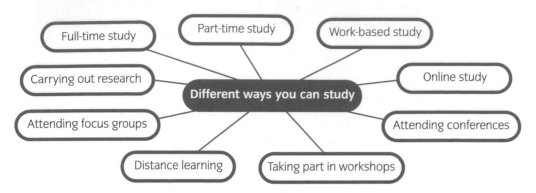

Check it out

To read more about the childcare sector's framework of qualification you can visit the CACHE website on www.cache.org.uk.

Evidence collector

This evidence collector supports elements
CCLD 203.1, 203.2, 203.3

Key Skills C AoN IT

Make notes about the management of your setting.

1 Use a computer to draw up an organisation chart for your placement.
2 Put yourself on the chart.
3 Make brief notes about each person's role within the organisation.
4 Identify areas of support you may need. With the help of your supervisor or mentor, identify how these needs could be met and which persons in the organisation might support you.
5 Make a professional development plan listing how you would like to develop your career and the support you will need to do that.

Check it out

Research your opportunities by visiting some websites associated with careers in the childcare sector, for example:
- CACHE website – www.cache.org.uk
- 4 children website – www.4children.org.uk
- NCMA website – www.ncma.org.uk
- your EYDCP website
- your local college or training provider websites
- the Open University website – www.open.ac.uk.[/BL]
- You could also read *Nursery World* and *Children Now* regularly.

End-of-unit knowledge check

1 Name two ways you can be given support.
2 Name two of your professional strengths.
3 Who would support you in strengthening your weaknesses?
4 How could speaking English as a second language affect your work?
5 What are the positive aspects of being a mature trainee?
6 Note one basic skill that will support your learning style.
7 What can an assessor do to support you?
8 How can you communicate your need for support?
9 What is Kid's Club Network now called?
10 Where could you find out about local professional development courses that might be available?

Check it out

Contact your local college or Early Years Care and Development Partnership (EYCDP) to find out what sort of professional development course will be available to you. To find more information about your local EYCDP contact your local Children's Information Centre or local borough offices.

Prepare and maintain environments to meet children's needs

This unit will help you to create a safe environment for the children in your care where they can develop to their full potential.

Before you start this unit consider the focus for standard 4 of the National Standards for Full Day Care and remember that the environment should be welcoming for children, staff and parents, safe and secure, with well organised space to promote children's development.

What you must know and understand:

- How to make the physical environment meet children's needs (K2D59)
- How to encourage children to participate in activities (K2D60)
- How to involve children in making decisions about their environment (K2D61)
- How to use the environment to promote positive images of people (K2D62)
- Why it is important to recognise achievements (K2D63)
- The relationship between self-esteem, confidence and resilience (K2D64)
- The importance of health and safety regulations and policies of the setting that relate to the environment (K2D65)
- How to stimulate each of the senses to support children's development (K2D66)
- How to understand the effects of change and to help children manage them (K2D67)
- How to make the environment appropriate to the ages and stages of children's development (K2D68)
- How security and reassurance affects children's confidence (K2D69)
- How to include children's additional or special needs in your setting (K2D70)
- How to recognise signs of insecurity and anxiety and provide children with reassurance (K2D71)
- How to display objects in a stimulating and interesting way (K2D72)
- How to maintain appropriate temperatures and levels of ventilation (K2D73)
- How the values and principles of the sector are reflected in the environment (K2D74)
- Why it is important for a child to have a consistent routine in order to develop (K2D75)
- Why physical play is important and how to help children who have limited physical play opportunities (K2D76 and K2D80)
- Why it is important for children to have quiet periods (K2D77)
- How to handle food safely (K2H78)
- The basic nutritional needs of children, the different food groups, and supporting children's food requirements (K2H79 and K2H81)
- How to care for children's skin and hair and teeth (K2H83 and K2H84)

You will discover that the environment has a huge role to play in a child's development and that there are many ways in which you can involve children of a variety of ages in maintaining their surroundings. They will even be able to make decisions about how to change things around them.

Through the activities and tasks in this unit you will have the opportunity to show that you understand how all children need a secure and familiar routine so that they can benefit from the different activities and experiences they will be offered.

Throughout the unit you will be encouraged to evaluate your own work setting and think about other settings and age ranges that you may not have experienced.

If your setting is part of your local early years partnership you might meet practitioners from other settings at training sessions. With the support of your manager, you might be able to arrange exchange visits to compare and contrast the way other settings maintain and develop the environment for children.

How to make the physical environment meet children's needs

Whatever age group or setting you are working with, you it is essential to plan an environment that encourages the development of the whole child. As this unit progresses you will study in more depth the different ways that your role in the physical environment can affect a child's development.

First of all, think about the different settings that **children** aged 0–16 years may experience.

These settings have both indoor and outdoor **physical spaces** that need to be considered:

- a day nursery for children aged 0–5 years
- a pre-school group for children aged 3–5 years
- a Foundation Stage or Key Stage 1 class in a primary school
- a crèche
- a home setting
- before and after care or holiday club for children aged 4–16 years
- a youth or activity club for children aged 11–16 years.

You may be lucky enough to work in a purpose-built setting, but not all settings are like this. For example, many groups may use a church hall that is a shared facility and will therefore have to set up and clear away at the end of each session.

The layout of the physical **environment** is the responsibility of the team of which you are a member. The available space will influence the way the **furniture and equipment** is set out. While it is important to create an attractive environment, everything should be safe, secure and have a purpose that supports each area of the children's development.

Keys to good practice: How to create a setting that supports children

- ✓ Divide the setting into areas so that children can experience a variety of activities.
- ✓ Provide space between the activities for children and adults to move freely.
- ✓ Carefully place activities to promote development.
- ✓ Ensure access areas are clear.
- ✓ Encourage independence.
- ✓ Ensure surfaces are safe and washable.

Key terms

Children: all children in the age groups 0–3, 4–7, 8–12, 13–16, including girls, boys, those with disabilities and those with special educational needs.

Physical space: the room, rooms or part of a room in which the children spend time. This could also be an outside area.

Did you know?

The 'Sure Start' initiative has been set up by the Government to ensure that Children's Centres are set up to provide loncal families with affordable provision that is of a good quality with age-appropriate learning experiences.

Key terms

Environment: the place, setting or service where you work with children.

Furniture and equipment: Any sort of physical object in the environment.

✓ Celebrate diversity.

✓ Ensure areas for display are visible and **accessible** to all the children.

✓ Provide opportunities for a link between home and the setting, i.e. a home corner.

✓ Ensure the outdoor environment is an extension of the indoors, i.e. painting, stories, etc. can be conducted outside.

✓ Ensure outdoor surfaces are safe and varied.

✓ Provide safe paths for bikes, etc. as well as visible areas for children to play quietly.

Key terms

Accessible: all children, regardless of any special needs, can use the environment. This means that a disability or special need does not prevent them from benefiting.

With this information in mind look at the two layouts below of an indoor and outdoor play area of a purpose-built day nursery.

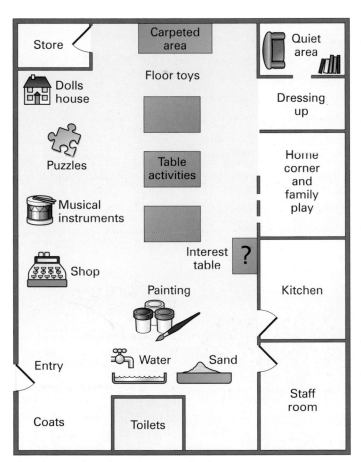

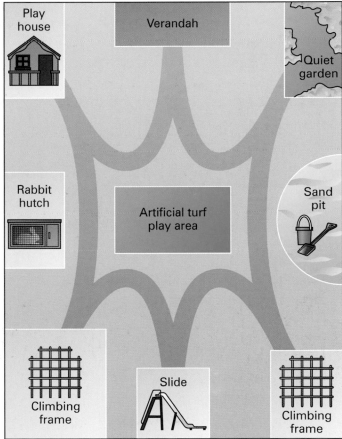

● *Indoor and outdoor play area of a day nursery*

Test yourself

Using the layouts above, make notes for discussion with your tutor or study group about whether the children could:

- play quietly in pairs
- move freely between activities both indoors and outdoors
- move easily in a wheelchair
- play safely on bikes outside
- listen to a story appropriately.

It will be useful to read about the ages and stages of development in Unit 203 before reading the next section.

By providing the right environment for the children in your care you will be able to promote their physical, intellectual, emotional, social and linguistic development. The table below shows ways in which the physical environment can meet the needs of the child you are working with.

Type of skills the environment should support	Examples of ways to make the environment suitable for specific needs
Physical development: Large and fine motor skills. Fine manipulative skills. Spatial awareness. Balance. Sensory awareness.	Clear spaces. Appropriate sized furniture. Tactile objects and surfaces. Outdoor spaces and varied equipment. Appropriate resources and equipment.
Social and emotional development: A sense of identity. Confidence. Socialising with other children and adults. Independence. Positive behaviour.	Positive images in visual displays. Appropriate play and group time areas. Accessible resources. Appropriately sized furniture. Secure and comfortable areas. Clear behavioural expectations shown in displays/notices.
Intellectual development: Exploratory play. Imitative play. An understanding of causes and consequences. Imaginary play. An understanding of time. Developing mathematical concepts. Use of language. Concentration. Curiosity.	Provision of age-appropriate resources. Provision of wide range of appropriate activities and experiences. Space to explore through play. Informative displays and labelling. Accessible book area. Displays and activities that invite exploration and discussion.
Language development: Communication between adults and children. Communication between children. One-to-one communication. Understanding of instructions. Listening and taking part in musical activities. Development of verbal and written communication. Participating in story activities and exploring books. Expression of feelings and wishes.	Provision of comfortable areas to have adult/child communication. Appropriate posters, notices and pictures. A wide range of appropriate experiences, activities and resources. Extensive and attractively presented reading resources Imaginative play opportunities. Provision of co-operative play opportunities.

● *How the environment can meet the needs of children*

Case study 1: Meeting children's emotional need to be independent

Following an Ofsted inspection, the team at The Maltings, a 20-place day-care nursery, had been asked to develop the independence of the 3–5-year-olds. Jo, the manager, held a team meeting to discuss how the environment could be developed to encourage the children's independence. The inspector had observed that the children's drawers were difficult for them to reach, and that resources such as building bricks and crayons were only labelled with words. She also observed that the children had a story time while the staff cleared away activities and set the tables for lunch. At lunchtime children were served by the staff and had their dishes cleared away for them.

1   *As a group, list ways in which the staff could develop the environment so that the children could:*
   ● *use their drawers throughout the day*
   ● *help to set up and clear away activities*
   ● *help to serve and clear away lunch*
   ● *Present this information in a clear way that could guide other staff. Ensure that your grammar and punctuation are accurate.*

How to encourage children to participate in activities

When considering approaches to encourage children to join in activities, it is essential to communicate at a level appropriate to their stage of development. You should ensure that they have choices and are involved in any decision-making by giving them as much responsibility as they are ready for.

If you encourage participation, children may become involved in preparing for an activity, such as by mixing paint or setting out a tabletop game.

Make sure that you are aware of the developmental needs of the children you are working with by reading Unit 203 on child development. You should also find out if any of the children in your setting have additional or special needs.

● *Adult and children sharing an activity*

Keys to good practice: How to encourage children to participate in activities in your setting

✓ Tell the children about the activities to be offered. For example, a group session before activity time could be an opportunity to explain the planned activities.

✓ Start to do the activity. For example, tapping a tin with a spoon may encourage a 9-month-old baby to imitate the activity.

✓ Explain to the children how to carry out the activity. A group of 8-year-olds cooking bread in an after-school club will need clear guidance and encouragement in order to succeed.

✓ Consider asking children to plan activities with you. A holiday club council is a good way of finding out what sort of activities children want.

✓ Ensure you are at the eye level of the children as eye contact is very important. Children can be intimidated by an adult standing over them.

✓ Make sure the activity is attractively laid out. A set of small world play toys can be set up as a town or farm, etc. as appropriate.

You may need to vary an activity to encourage participation, for example rolling a ball instead of throwing it as a child may not be ready to catch and throw. Perhaps you can remember the time when the ball fell through your fingers no matter how hard you tried to catch it!

How to involve children in making decisions about their environment

Decision-making and **active involvement** are an important part of children's social and emotional development as they will gain confidence in their own skills and abilities to make choices. If a child feels confident making choices he or she will grow into an independent adult who will take the initiative.

You should, wherever possible, ensure that children have an element of choice in most activities and experiences that you provide. This could include deciding where they may plant some sunflower seeds and where they may listen to a story in the outside environment.

The table below shows ways in which different age groups can be involved in making decisions about their environment.

Key terms

Active involvement: children having a say in what happens in their environment by saying what they want and by helping to make things happen (where this can be done safely).

Check it out

Observe how the children in your setting are encouraged to make decisions about their environment. Are there any more decisions that they could be involved in?

Age group	How children can be involved
0–3 years	• choosing play materials. • deciding where to play. • helping to put toys out, e.g. such as putting soft toys in an area of their choice. • selecting crayons to use.
4–7 years	• selecting activities. • helping to plan a display. • helping to decide agreements for the environment such as turning off taps. • choosing helpers. • choosing books for the book area from the library. • selecting paper, etc. to use. • designing a play area such as a wild garden.
8–12 years	• setting up activities. • helping to decide upon the curriculum. • designing areas such as a sensory area. • making agreements about the use of the environment, e.g. in the form of a poster or display. • making a display. • creating healthy menus for drinks and snacks.
13–16 years	• selecting and setting up activities. • designing different areas in the setting such as a 'chill-out room'. • making behavioural agreements. • making displays. • painting or cleaning areas, e.g. painting a mural on a wall.

● *Ways in which children can be involved in making decisions*

It is important to remember that children need guidance when making decisions, and that they should know that it is OK to make mistakes.

How to use the environment to promote positive images of people

When considering the environment that you are working in you will want to make all the children feel positive about themselves, their families and visitors to the setting. You have a responsibility to make children think positively about society and you should always challenge negative images.

The following list is essential for any environment and can probably be added to by you as you develop your experience.

- Provide a variety of skin-tone paper, crayons and paint.
- Present additional languages on labels, notices etc.

- Ensure a wide variety of people are presented in posters, books, etc. including those of both genders, from different cultures and of all ages.
- Include displays and projects about a variety of cultures.
- Ensure resources represent special needs, such as a doll with glasses.

Why it is important to recognise achievements

Everyone needs praise in order to feel confident and a child is no different. To develop into a confident adult children need to be praised when they have achieved something. You can do this by:

- praising and acknowledging the achievements of each child
- encouraging children to recognise their own achievements.

You have an important role to play in creating a positive emotional environment for children in your care. When children are praised and encouraged their self-esteem rise, and they take more responsibility for themselves and their environment. They relate better to other children and adults.

You can create a positive emotional environment in the following ways:

- Display children's work in a celebratory way, taking care to mount work carefully and label it appropriately. Do not be tempted to cut into the work to suit your display! To show respect for the work means to display it all.
- Draw attention to these displays in group times and by sharing them with parents. Children might even like to talk about their work to others.
- Give children stickers or badges for effort. This will be recognised by other adults and children as a sign of a positive achievement.
- Praise children appropriately without attaching any conditions. Do not say, for example, 'Well done, Sam, you have washed your hands. Now make sure you always do that.' This will make Sam will feel that some of the praise has been taken away. His self-esteem could be affected or he may feel it is not worth washing his hands properly again.
- Praise children for attempting a task even if they do not fully succeed. Children who try to pour their own drink but spill a little are more likely to develop the skill of pouring if they are praised for their effort and the spillage is ignored.

Did you know?

The Department for Children, Schools and Families (DCSF; formerly the DfES) has produced guidelines for working with children aged 0–5 years called the Early Years Foundation Stage. It states that children aged 40–60 months should 'gain an awareness of the cultures and beliefs of others' and 'begin to know about their own cultures and beliefs and those of other people'. They should do this by being introduced to 'a range of cultures and religions, telling stories, listening to music, dancing and eating foods from a range of cultures'. This information can be found in the Practical Guidance for the EYFS, page 88. You can find this document on the Every Child Matters website www.everychildmatters.gov.uk

Case study 2: Encouragement through praise

Tom is looked after in his home by Trishna, a qualified nanny. Tom is 4 years old and has had difficulty doing up the buttons on his coat. His grandmother is visiting and offers to accompany Tom and Trishna to the park. Tom puts on his coat and spends some time doing up the buttons. He remembers what Trishna has told him. Tom completes the task but has not matched the right buttons and holes. He grins with satisfaction. Trishna praises him and asks if he would like help to adjust the buttons. His grandmother laughs and says he must try to get it right next time! They go off to the park.

1   *How do you think Tom was affected by his grandmother's remarks?*
2   *What do you think about Trishna's reactions to Tom's efforts?*
3   *How would you advise Trishna to continue to encourage Tom to learn how to do up his buttons?*

The relationship between self-esteem, confidence and resilience

You can play an important role in developing a child's **self-esteem**, **confidence** and **resilience**.

If children are cared for in an environment where they are praised and made to feel worthwhile, they will gain the confidence to become independent and cope with things such as unforeseeable changes or criticism.

In the environment you can encourage children to cope with change by ensuring that they are confident.

The two examples below show how you can ensure that children are resilient in a variety of situations.

- A group of 10-year-olds from a holiday activity club are told they cannot have a football match as the visiting team's minibus has broken down. They have always been encouraged by their youth worker to plan their own matches and have been given the skills to do so. They are continually supported and encouraged to lead their own activities. As a result, they arrange a five-a-side match among themselves instead.
- A supply teacher is working in a Foundation Stage class nursery alongside two regular staff members. The children are welcoming and happy because the teacher has warned them about the change. The teacher encourages them to welcome visitors to their nursery and has told them how proud she is of the way they make visitors feel welcome.

You will note that the way the children cope with change is because of the way they have been praised and encouraged.

Did you know?

Self-esteem means feeling worthwhile and respected as an individual.

Confidence means feeling self-reliant enough to be able to carry out a task or activity.

Resilience means being able to cope with a variety of situations.

The importance of health and safety regulations and policies of the setting that relate to the environment

To make an environment a safe place to work a number of legal **health and safety requirements** are put in place. A list of policies and procedures guide the working practice of the staff whatever the setting and ensure the requirements are carried out.

All settings that have under-16-year-olds on site for more than two hours a day are likely to be inspected by OFSTED and will have to meet certain requirements. These can be found in detail in the OFSTED national standards.

The space used must meet basic requirements. These are highlighted in the boxes below.

Key terms

Health and safety requirements: the laws governing safety in your country.

Heating

Temperature at 15–18°C, or 20–22°C for babies

Fireguards in front of fire

Radiators and pipes covered

Smoke alarms and emergency equipment available

Doors and gates

All the external gates and doors locked and coded as appropriate

Handles and locks out of reach of children

Safety gates to BSI standard

Toughened glass where necessary

Lighting and electricity

All areas well lit so that there is full visibility

Current breakers for all electrical equipment

Plugs covered

Outdoor and indoor surfaces

Stable

Non-slippery

Soft under climbing equipment

Easily cleanable

Ventilation

Window open when necessary to circulate air

No draughts

Locks and toughened glass on windows

Access points

These must be kept clear, unlocked and made known to all children and adults, including visitors, in the case of an emergency evacuation

The policies and procedures of the setting should ensure:

- a welcoming environment
- a clean and well-maintained environment
- sole use of premises during the session
- clear telephone communication with emergency numbers, etc. available
- appropriate temperature
- adequate space and storage
- appropriate rest areas
- safe and appropriate toy and play equipment
- appropriate outdoor space with suitable equipment
- appropriate toilet facilities
- appropriate kitchen and laundry facilities
- safe and adequate supply of hot, cold and drinking water
- safe supply of gas and electricity
- adequate security
- appropriate supervision
- an awareness of fire safety
- safe outings and use of transport
- adequate insurance
- appropriate plants.

Outdoor areas should be checked each time they are used. The RoSPA (The Royal Society for the Prevention of Accidents) guidelines are a source of useful advice with regards to the security of boundaries.

Check it out

Ask your supervisor if you can carry out an audit of your setting to check if doors and gates comply with safety regulations and that access points meet required standards. You could produce a simple checklist.

Be careful to deal with any concerns in a sensitive and confidential manner.

How to stimulate each of the senses to support children's development

From birth children learn through the five senses of:

- touch
- taste
- sight
- sound
- smell.

The environment plays an important part in children's sensory development. From birth children use their senses to develop an understanding of their world.

Case study 3: Making a tactile display

Ted is working in the baby room of a neighbourhood nursery and he wants to encourage the children to develop their sense of touch. He is asked to mount a display that the babies can explore. He is told it has to be safe and secure. The setting's resources are limited.

1   *List ways in which Ted could mount a tactile display for the babies. Consider texture.*

There are many more ways that the environment can support sensory development. Children need a variety of colours, textures, sounds and smells to explore. The diagram below gives some ideas for supporting sensory development.

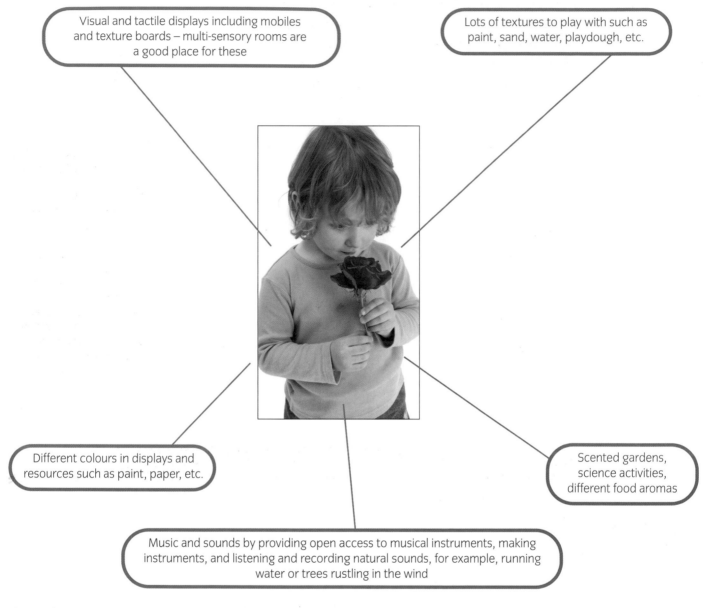

Visual and tactile displays including mobiles and texture boards – multi-sensory rooms are a good place for these

Lots of textures to play with such as paint, sand, water, playdough, etc.

Different colours in displays and resources such as paint, paper, etc.

Scented gardens, science activities, different food aromas

Music and sounds by providing open access to musical instruments, making instruments, and listening and recording natural sounds, for example, running water or trees rustling in the wind

● *How the environment can support sensory development*

Test yourself

1   List the five senses.
2   Write two ways that each sense can be developed for children in your nursery environment.

How to understand the effects of change and to help children manage them

Any changes to the children's environment can have a negative effect upon them if not managed properly. Examples of change could be:

- new staff at the setting
- moving from one setting to another
- leaving a parent for the first time
- death of a family member
- a new sibling
- moving house
- change to routine of the setting.

Children are often anxious when change occurs. It is therefore essential to maintain a calm and reassuring environment at times of change. Very young children are often the most anxious about separation and strangers.

Before the age of 2 most children are anxious about leaving their main carer or familiar environment. They have no concept of time and cannot understand that their carer will be returning soon. You can provide patience and a lot of reassurance.

Towards the end of their first year children may suddenly want to stay with their main carer. You must treat this in a sensitive manner.

Children older than 2 may react to change by:

- a change in sleep pattern
- eating or drinking less
- a reluctance to play
- subdued behaviour
- being disturbed when their parent leaves
- over-attachment to one carer
- becoming tearful.

Did you know?

John Bowlby (1907–90) developed what we know as the attachment theory. He suggested that children were emotionally affected by separation from their main carer. There has been much debate over this theory, but it has stressed the importance of a settling-in period for children who are being separated from their mothers for the first time.

Keys to good practice: How to support a child through change

- ✓ Work in partnership with parents.
- ✓ Provide verbal and physical reassurance.
- ✓ Be honest.
- ✓ Use play to explore the child's worries about change.
- ✓ Arrange visits to and from previous or future settings/carers.
- ✓ Liaise with the new setting or care about the child's needs.
- ✓ Warn the child about change where possible.

How to make the environment appropriate to the ages and stages of children's development

As children grow, their needs change. Whatever age children you work with you need to understand how environments have to be adapted as children grow.

The following table shows how environmental needs change as children grow.

Age and stage of development	Items required in environment
0–3 years	• Space to explore stable furniture. • Variety of textured and coloured objects. • Sounds. • Balls. • Crayons. • Appropriate mugs, spoons, etc. • Bright and bold books. • Tyres. • Small bikes. • Imaginative play equipment. • Paint, etc. • Water and sand.
4–7 years	• Beads. • Bricks, etc. • Small world play. • Scissors. • Pencils, paints, crayons. • Balls, ropes, bikes, large outdoor equipment. • Large and safe indoor and outdoor areas, i.e. obstacle courses. • Objects to classify. • Areas to read and relax in. • Interactive displays.
8–12 years	• Formal game areas. • Displays led by children. • Large indoor and outdoor spaces. • Varied appropriate curriculum opportunities. • Quiet areas to read and relax in. • IT areas. • Self-help snack and drink areas. • Source areas, i.e. library. • Separate toilet facilities.

continued on next page

Age and stage of development	Items required in environment
13–16 years	<ul><li>Formal game areas.</li><li>Displays led by children.</li><li>Large indoor and outdoor spaces.</li><li>Varied appropriate curriculum opportunities.</li><li>Quiet areas to read and relax in.</li><li>IT areas.</li><li>Self-help snack and drink areas.</li><li>Source areas, i.e. library.</li><li>Separate toilet facilities.</li><li>Area for meetings.</li><li>Socialising area.</li></ul>

 *How environmental needs change as children grow*

How security and reassurance affects children's confidence

When a child is lacking confidence you need to make them feel secure by reassuring them about what is affecting them. Try to remember times when your confidence was lacking and think how somebody made you feel more positive. If children lack confidence they may not want to participate in an activity for fear of failure. Children who lack confidence can sometimes display challenging behaviour.

 Did you know?

The theorist Erik Erikson (1902–94) believed that society was a strong influence on children's development and that children must have enough confidence to progress positively from child to adulthood. This emphasises the importance of your role in developing a confident child. Erikson also believed that people are naturally able to cope with crisis.

 Keys to good practice: How you can make a child feel confident

✓ Allow children to fail without criticism.

✓ Praise children when they are doing well, not just achieving the best.

✓ Celebrate work and behaviour.

✓ Praise children for helping, sharing or playing well.

✓ Provide children with tasks and activities that are age appropriate.

✓ Provide play resources that celebrate a variety of images and cultures.

✓ Make time to talk to a child who seems lacking in confidence.

✓ Ensure children have a personally labelled drawer and pegs.

✓ Make sure you welcome each child every time he or she enters the setting.

● *Welcome a child when entering a new setting*

● *Praise children for helping*

Test yourself

1   How should you manage children who are laughing at a child who falls over while playing a circle game?

2   Apart from writing signs, how could you encourage a child to remember where different areas of a setting are?

3   When you are talking to a group of children about previous group activities, how would you treat a new child who has not taken part in the activities?

4   How would you ensure a new child knew the rules of the setting such as hanging up aprons after activities?

5   If you had a new child at your setting who spoke a language other than English, how could you make the child feel at home?

How to include children's additional or special needs in your setting

A secure and comfortable environment is essential for a child with additional and special needs.

You will need to be aware of the additional or special needs of the children in your care in order to help to provide them with appropriate care and education.

The following diagram gives some examples of what you can provide to ensure a child with additional or special needs is included in the environment.

Did you know?

The DCSF (formerly the DfES) ensures that people working with children aged 0–16 years follow the Special Educational Needs Code of Practice. This was part of the 1996 Education Act.

Your setting will have a SENCO (Special Educational Needs Co-ordinator) who will support children who have special needs and their parents. The SENCO will also guide staff and identify appropriate training.

Hearing impairment
Quiet areas to work in pairs
Special audio equipment
Appropriate acoustics
Positive images of hearing-impaired people

Visual impairment
Space to move safely
Padded corners
Stable furniture
Tactile equipment and activities
Less frequent change to environment
Fluorescent tape on steps, etc.
Positive images of visually-impaired people

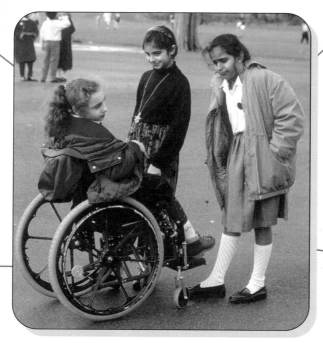

Wheelchair use
Ramps
Wide entrance and exits
Tables and surfaces at right height
Designated toilet facilities
Toys and equipment at right level
Positive images of wheelchair users

Dyslexia
Areas for quiet work
More time to complete certain activities
Support in reading and writing
Clear but brief instructions
Praise and reward
Coloured gels to highlight text sometimes needed to read print
Activities to promote co-ordination and spatial awareness
Positive images of people with dyslexia

These are only examples of additional or special needs that you may encounter. You should gain as much knowledge as possible about the needs.

How to recognise signs of insecurity and anxiety and provide children with reassurance

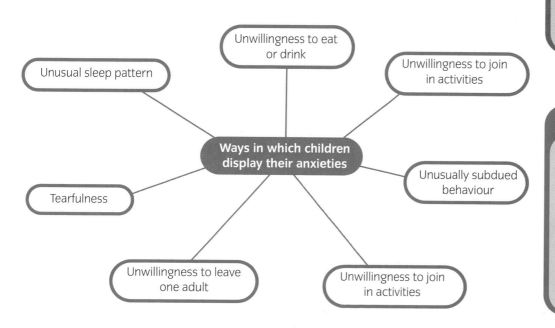

Unwillingness to eat or drink

Unusual sleep pattern

Unwillingness to join in activities

Ways in which children display their anxieties

Tearfulness

Unusually subdued behaviour

Unwillingness to leave one adult

Unwillingness to join in activities

Check it out

1 Find out who the SENCO is in your setting.
2 Talk to the SENCO about his or her role. Ask how he or she can support you in understanding children in your setting who might have additional or special needs.

Did you know?

People who have dyslexia sometimes find that coloured gels or coloured glass will help them to see the print on a page more clearly.

The colour of the gels will vary from person to person, but in general, a yellow background is helpful.

How to maintain appropriate temperatures and levels of ventilation

OFSTED requires settings working with children to meet certain standards in order to ensure that children can play in an environment that is appropriately heated and ventilated. Any appliances, such as heaters, must be regularly checked and maintained.

Remember it is your responsibility as a working member of your setting to help to ensure that policies covering temperature and ventilation are followed correctly for the sake of the children in your care. They will then be able to develop fully in a safe environment.

Check it out

In your work setting you will have **risk-assessment** procedures that are used for regular checks. Ask if you can see a risk-assessment form and identify what on the list relates to heating and ventilation.

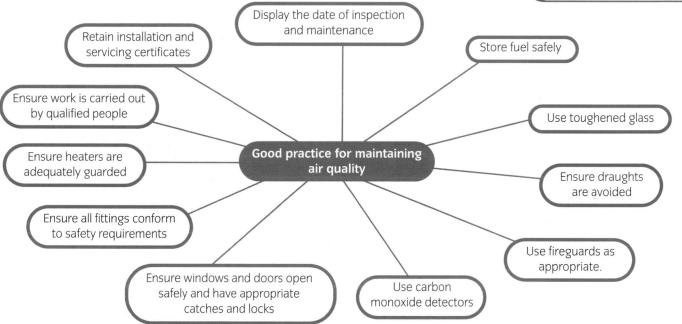

- Display the date of inspection and maintenance
- Retain installation and servicing certificates
- Store fuel safely
- Ensure work is carried out by qualified people
- Use toughened glass
- Ensure heaters are adequately guarded
- **Good practice for maintaining air quality**
- Ensure draughts are avoided
- Ensure all fittings conform to safety requirements
- Use fireguards as appropriate.
- Ensure windows and doors open safely and have appropriate catches and locks
- Use carbon monoxide detectors

How the values and principles of the sector can be reflected in the environment

Your environment must ensure that:
- you value the welfare of each child
- you contribute effectively to each child's care and learning
- you work with parents as partners.

The following table shows how the values of the childcare sector can be reflected in the environment of your setting.

Key terms

Risk assessments: the assessments that must be carried out in order to identify hazards and find out the safest way to carry out certain tasks and procedures.

Did you know?

The temperature of a setting should be 15–18°C for children and 20–22°C for babies.

Value	Examples in the environment
Ensure the needs, rights and views of each child are at the centre of your environment.	• Support for special needs. • Access for all children to activities, resources and materials. • Child-centred displays and activities.
Celebrate individuality, difference and diversity.	• Range of resources, activities, displays, posters. • Involvement of parents where possible.
Ensure equality of opportunity and anti-discriminatory practice.	• Clear policies. • Welcome posters in different languages. • Materials, resources and activities to celebrate different cultures and family styles.
Provide a safe environment that allows appropriate risks and challenges.	• Clear health and safety policies and standards. • Risk assessment. • Clear and appropriate supervision.
Promote children's health and well-being.	• Appropriate activities. • Healthy eating. • Outdoor provision. • Policies on illness and infectious diseases. • Clear hygiene procedure. • Qualified staff in first aid and food handling.
Promote children's self-esteem and resilience, and positive self image.	• Involvement of children. • Praise and reward. • Activities and resources relating to a range of cultures. • Encouraging respect of each other.
Respect confidentiality.	• Clear policy of recording, exchanging and sharing information. • Places to talk confidentially. • Information shared appropriately.
Share professional knowledge, skills and values for the benefit of the children.	• Range of resources and training opportunities for staff. • Time to share ideas and experiences.
Ensure best practice, which requires reflection and a continuous search for improvement.	• Opportunities to evaluate the curriculum and practice with colleagues and children. • Planning of activities and resources. • Team meetings.

• *How the values of the childcare sector can be reflected in the environment of your setting*

Why it is important for a child to have a consistent routine in order to develop

A routine is the regular things that occur throughout a child's day. This can range from nappy changing to mealtimes.

When carrying out routines you should:

- keep children informed in a way that is appropriate to their age and stage of development to ensure that they are certain of what is happening
- always inform new children and parents of routines or any changes
- ensure that children who have English as an additional language are supported
- ensure that children understand expected behaviour, for example during an emergency evacuation practice
- involve children in routine tasks, for example handing out drinks
- allow children to make mistakes
- help children to carry out routines, for example include footprints to the cloakroom
- turn routines into learning opportunities as they are part of the curriculum.

Check it out

Make a list of the routines for children that take place in your setting. What do you think would happen if some of the activities in a routine were neglected, for example washing hands before lunch? How do you think that the children might be affected?

Case study 5: Teaching children about routines

Frank works in a pre-school group and wants the children to learn the importance of washing their hands as part of their toileting routine. During a group time, Frank tells the children all about unfriendly bacteria. He tells them about the importance of washing their hands using soap and water, and how they must use paper towels to dry them. He shows them some colourful notices he has made to remind them what to do. He puts the notices up in the toilets at the children's height. Two children help him.

1   *Do you think that Frank made the information fun? If so, why is this important?*
2   *How will the children understand the importance of handwashing from this activity?*
3   *How will the children's confidence develop as a result of Frank's activity?*

> Turn on the tap
> Put some soap on your hands
> Rub the soap all over your hands
> Put your hands under the tap and take all the soap off your hands
> Turn the tap off
> Dry your hands very well with the paper towels
> Put the paper towels in the bin

Why physical play is important and how to help children who have limited physical play opportunities

Physical play encourages children to develop all their physical skills and to practise the skills that they already have. Your role in supporting a child's physical development will be to ensure that the child has a wide variety of experiences in a safe environment.

Any setting should offer a wide range of equipment that can be used both indoors and outdoors.

It is considered important that children are given opportunities to develop their gross motor skills indoors as well as outdoors. Such opportunities may be provided by designated areas such as a soft play area or by activities such as drama.

Some settings may be lucky enough to have designated areas for physical play or have the opportunity to use other facilities. These could include:

- a soft play area
- a swimming pool
- a sensory room
- a games pitch, for example for football, netball or tennis
- a cycle path or course
- a climbing area
- an obstacle course or exploring area using things such as tractor tyres.

Children with additional or special needs may have limited play opportunities. It is your role to ensure that they can do as many activities as possible. This support may be given by adapting equipment, for example:

- placing fluorescent strips on the steps of a slide for a child with a visual impairment
- ensuring that a child in a wheelchair has enough space to turn the chair in a game of catch.

You may also support children with special needs by:

- discussing their requirements with their parents, colleagues, SENCO and the child
- encouraging children to support and learn about their peers with special needs
- having a positive attitude towards exercise
- referring to role models such as stars in the Paralympics.

Did you know?

Some schools believe that games should be non-competitive and concentrate on the playing of the game rather than the result.

Test yourself

1 What do the letters SENCO stand for?
2 What is the role of the SENCO?

Why it is important for children to have quiet periods

Children lead busy lives. This is hard work, so periods of rest are important.

By resting all children will:
- allow muscles to recover
- allow the heart to settle to a normal rate
- have a chance to reflect upon experiences.

An area should always be set aside for children to relax in. Some examples of quiet areas are given in the table below.

Setting	Suggestions for quiet area
Private home for a baby aged 10 months	Carpeted area with subdued lighting, soft music and some gentle, tactile toys.
Foundation Stage classroom	Book corner with cushions and screens that can be seen by adults, or a listening corner with story tapes and headphones.
Holiday tennis club for children aged 11–16 years	Area in the shade with comfy chairs, snacks and magazines.

● *Quiet areas for different settings*

All children vary in the amount of rest they need and children require less rest as they get older. The wishes of the child's parents must be taken into consideration, as must the routine of the setting. The amount of rest a child needs may be affected by the following.

- If parents are working they may want their child to rest in the setting so they can have more time with them in the evening.
- In some cultures children go to bed at the same time as their parents and this may result in more rest during the day.
- A child living in accommodation with shared bathroom facilities may have to get up earlier than usual to wash and may need rest during the day to compensate.
- A child who is unwell may need more rest during the day.

Remember that children are individuals and that different children's needs must be met. For example it is good practice to allow children who do not want to sleep to undertake quiet activities. These activities will not disturb other children when resting. They could be:
- reading or looking at books, drawing
- listening to story tapes or gentle music.

How to handle food safely

All children in your care must be able to eat and drink safely so that food poisoning is avoided. Bacteria can grow very quickly on food and your role in handling food and drink appropriately is essential. You need to understand how to store, prepare and serve food.

By reading the information below you will understand the importance of basic food handling.

Storing food

- Regularly check 'use by' and 'sell by' dates and throw away anything out of date.
- Use a fridge thermometer to make sure that a fridge temperature is kept between 0°C and 5°C.
- Ensure the freezer is working and the temperature is below 18°C.
- Cool hot food quickly before placing it in the fridge.
- Do not leave food out at room temperature. Store food as soon as you can.
- Store raw meat and fish separately.
- Store raw foods at the bottom of the fridge to avoid juices dropping onto other foods.
- Never refreeze food that has begun to thaw.
- Date food you put in the fridge so that other members of staff can discard if you are not there.

Preparing food

- Wash hands thoroughly before preparing food.
- Remove watches, bracelets, rings and jewellery.
- Tie back hair and wear an apron.
- Cover cuts and wounds with a coloured waterproof dressing.
- Do not touch your nose or mouth, or cough and sneeze over food.
- Never smoke in a room where food is being prepared.
- Clean the floor, surfaces, sink, utensils, cloths and bins regularly.
- Cover waste bins.
- Disinfect work surfaces before preparing food.
- Wash tops of cans before opening.
- Wash equipment in hot soapy water before preparing raw food.
- Keep a separate cutting board and knife solely for poultry and wash them thoroughly after use.
- Use a separate cutting board for bread.
- Cook foods thoroughly according to instructions.
- Only reheat food once and ensure it is heated all the way through.
- Ensure that whites and yolks of eggs are cooked thoroughly and are firm.

Did you know?

National Day Care Standards require that all people working with children undergo a basic food-handling course. This usually lasts for one day. OFSTED inspectors will check that every member of staff has been on a course by looking at their certificates during their visit.

Serving food

- Only use clean crockery and utensils that are not cracked and chipped.
- Provide all children with their own cups and utensils.
- Ensure all children and adults wash their hands before serving and eating.
- Ensure children sit down and are able to reach their food safely.
- Do not give younger children sharp knives for cutting their food.
- Always supervise children when eating.
- Do not allow pets in the eating area or allow children to touch pets during mealtimes.
- Ensure meals and drinks are not too hot and never heat plates for young children.

The basic nutritional needs of children

Children need to be given a balance of certain foods in order to grow and function properly.

The diagram below will help you to understand the functions of food and drink.

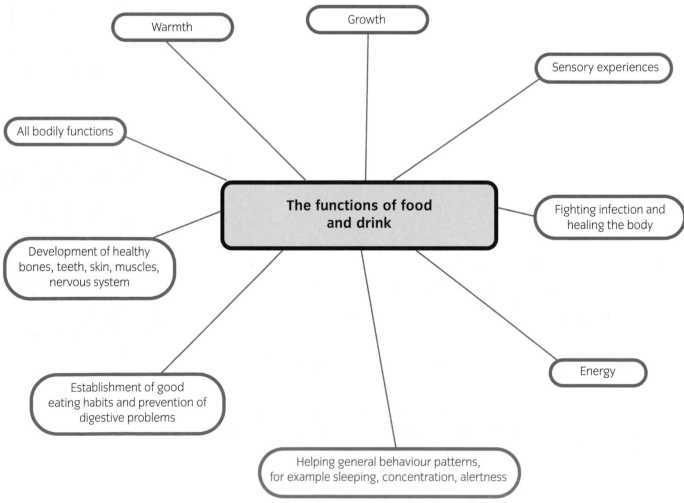

• The functions of food and drink

All food is made up of one or more of the following seven nutrients.

Proteins
- Build the body
- Are good for the brain, blood, skin and other tissues

Vitamins
- Help to maintain a healthy body
- Are made by plants and animals

Carbohydrates
- Give energy
- Are present in foods such as pulses, bread, oats

Fats
- Give energy
- Stored as body fat if too much is eaten

Fibre
- Maintains a healthy bowel
- Adds bulk to foods
- Is known as roughage
- Cannot be digested
- Is made of plant material
- Is present in foods such as bread, pulses, oats

Minerals
- Build bones and teeth
- Come from the earth
- Include calcium, iron, fluoride
- Are present in most foods

Water
- Makes up two-thirds of the body's weight
- Is essential for children to drink

A variety of these foods need to be eaten to maintain a healthy lifestyle. Water is continuously lost through sweating, breathing and urinating, so it needs to be replaced through food and drink.

How to understand different food groups and support children's food requirements

A balanced diet for any child requires a recommended portion from five different food groups.

Now study the following table and find out what children need to eat each day.

Each section represents one group of foods. By giving the recommended number of portions from each group you will know that the body is receiving all the nutrients it requires in the right amounts.

Did you know?

We all need energy to stay alive. We use it to breathe, grow, move and keep warm. It also helps to keep our blood circulating properly. The correct nutrients in food will give children the right energy.

Providing the right foods for a balanced diet

Potatoes and cereals (group 5)

This group includes the high-energy foods. These include bread, pasta, rice, breakfast cereals and potatoes. They provide the 'bulk' of the diet and provide energy as well as some protein, vitamins, minerals and fibre.

The fibre content of these foods can be raised by using whole-grain pastas, rice or chapattis, wholemeal breads and potatoes in their skins. Fibre provides bulk and helps digestion, and prevents constipation, as well as encouraging chewing and healthy gums. **Children need five portions from this group of foods per day – a portion should be included in each meal of the day. Examples of a portion are: one slice of bread, one small potato, one small bowl of cereal, two tablespoons of rice or pasta, a slice of pizza.**

Fruit and vegetables (group 4)

This group of foods provides rich sources of vitamins and minerals as well as fibre. Green vegetables contain iron, and citrus fruits and potatoes have high vitamin C content (essential for healing and healthy skin and blood formation). The orange-coloured fruits tend to contain more vitamin A (for healthy skin and good vision). Tinned or frozen vegetables and tinned or dried fruit can be used as a stand-by and will still provide the required nutrients – as long as they are stored and cooked correctly. Many vitamins are destroyed through poor storage and in cooking.

These tips will help you to keep the vitamin content of food high:
- eat food while it is as fresh as possible because sunlight destroys vitamins
- eat whole raw fruit and vegetables where possible, otherwise peel and chop them immediately before eating
- when vegetables and fruit are cooked, use the water for gravy or sauce because this will contain any vitamins which have dissolved into the water.

If children will not eat vegetables then give fruit, salad or fruit juice instead.

Children need five portions from this group of foods per day and at least one portion should be rich in vitamin C. Examples of a portion are: one glass of fruit juice, one piece of fruit, two tablespoons of cooked vegetables, one piece of salad fruit, e.g. slices of cucumber, or a tablespoon of dried fruit.

continued on next page

Milk and dairy products (group 3)

This food group includes milk, yogurt, hard and soft cheeses, including cottage cheese and fromage frais. These foods contain protein, vitamins A and B (for the healthy working of the nervous system) and are rich sources of calcium. One pint of milk or its equivalent each day will ensure a child gets enough calcium to form healthy bones and teeth, and if milk is not taken then more of the other foods from this group must be taken instead. Because of their lower energy and smaller fat-soluble vitamin content, reduced-fat dairy products should not be given to children under 5 years of age. **Children need three portions from this group of foods per day. Examples of a portion are: one glass of milk, or one yogurt or fromage frais, or a tablespoon of grated cheese.**

High-protein foods (group 2)

This group of food includes meat, fish, poultry, eggs, tofu, quorn and pulses (i.e. beans including baked beans and kidney beans, lentils, ground nuts and seeds, etc.) These foods, along with dairy foods, provide the main source of protein in the diet (essential for growth and repair in the body). Meat, eggs and pulses contain iron (needed for blood formation) and many of the B vitamins, and oily fish and liver contain vitamin A. The pulses provide an alternative source of protein for vegetarians.

Children need two portions from this group of foods per day. Examples of a portion are dependent on age for this group. For instance a portion of meat or fish fingers will vary from two slices/fingers for a young child to three or four for an older child.

Oils and fats (group 1)

These foods are a concentrated source of energy but research has shown that too many saturated fats (animal fats) may result in heart disease in later life. As processed foods contain hidden fats, for example in sausages, cheese, crisps, chips, pies and biscuits, etc., care must be taken to ensure that children do not eat their main diet from these foods. However, it is important that children do get some fats so that fat-soluble vitamins are taken. Use unsaturated fats where possible, grill instead of fry and use oven chips rather than deep frying.

Children under 2 years need a diet with more fat and less fibre than older children or adults. The fat provides the extra energy needed at this stage and too much fibre will fill young children up and other more important foods may be left out.

Oils and fats (group 1)
A concentrated source of energy, but too many saturated fats (animal fats) may cause heart disease in later life
Use unsaturated fats where possible
Found in sausages, cheese, chips, crisps, pies, biscuits

High-protein foods (group 2)
Essential for body growth and repair
Foods include meat, fish, poultry, eggs, tofu, quorn, pulses
Meat, eggs and pulses contain iron for healthy blood formation
Oily fish and liver contain vitamin A
Children need two portions per day

Potatoes and cereals (group 5)
Provide energy as well as some protein, vitamins, minerals and fibre
Foods include bread, pasta, rice, breakfast cereals, potatoes
Children need five portions per day

The five food groups in a balanced diet

Milk and dairy products (group 3)
Contain protein, vitamins A and B (for the healthy working of the nervous system)
A rich source of calcium for the formation of healthy bones and teeth
Foods include milk, yogurt, hard and soft cheeses
Children need three portions per day

Fruit and vegetables (group 4)
Provide rich sources of vitamins and minerals as well as fibre
Fibre helps digestion and prevents bowel problems such as constipation
Citrus fruits and potatoes have high vitamin C content for healing and healthy skin and blood formation
Green vegetables contain iron
Children need five portions per day

Test yourself

1   Consider the menu below. For each meal, fill in the number of portions of each food group.

Menu

		Group 5	Group 4	Group 3	Group 2	Group 1	Sugary foods
Breakfast	Cornflakes with milk, slice of toast, fruit juice						
Morning snack	Rice cake and glass of milk						
Lunch	Fish fingers, peas, boiled potatoes, yogurt, water						
Afternoon snack	Apple or banana, drink of water						
Teatime	Boiled egg, slice of toast, tinned papaya, water						

2   Do you think a balanced diet is being provided?
3   In your study group talk about ways of improving this menu.

Sugary foods, including sweets, chocolate, snack bars etc., are not essential for a balanced diet and so are not included in any of the food groups. They are a source of rapid, short-lived energy and have little or no other nutritional value. Too many sugary foods may cause a child to become overweight or suffer tooth decay. If they are offered to a child they should not replace foods from the other groups. Naturally occurring sugars, such as those found in fruit and fruit juices, are the only ones necessary for health.

Salt occurs naturally in many foods, so a well-balanced diet should contain all that is necessary. Too much salt such as adding salt when cooking or at the table, can cause ill health in later life and should be avoided with children. For babies and young children it can cause kidney problems.

Liquids are just as important as foods in a healthy diet. Many squashes and fizzy drinks have a very high sugar content and no other value. Water is a far better alternative, or natural fruit juices. However, a mixture of different drinks may be more realistic, including milk. Do not add sugar to drinks either as this will encourage a 'sweet tooth'.

Additives are substances added to food to preserve it or to improve its look or taste. All manufactured foods are required by law to list any additives in the food – these are all coded with E numbers so that they are recognisable. In general, try to offer fresh or frozen vegetables, or fresh fruit, as much as possible.

Snacks Children often require snacks at mid-morning and mid-afternoon to maintain their energy requirements. This is an ideal time to introduce new tastes and unfamiliar foods and should be included as a portion from the appropriate food group. Here are some suggestions:
- raw vegetables, such as carrots, celery, white cabbage, cucumber
- pieces of fresh fruit, e.g. apple, orange, mango, kiwi, banana, grapes
- dried fruit, e.g. apricots, sultanas, raisins, figs and apple rings
- natural yogurt with fresh fruit
- different sorts of bread and rolls, including wholegrain, with a healthy topping such as tuna, cheese, or houmous
- unsweetened biscuits or crackers (check the salt content), or plain breadsticks or popcorn (without added sugar or salt)
- unsweetened breakfast cereal,
- dips such as tomato, dahl, cucumber, yogurt and mint, etc.

Keys to good practice: How to ensure safety at mealtimes

✓ Ensure you know if any of the children have any food preferences or allergies.

✓ Supervise young children closely when eating raw foods such as carrots, apples, etc. in case they choke.

✓ Check that all stones and pips are removed from food to avoid choking.

✓ Encourage children to eat a healthy diet as this will help to ensure that they grow into healthy adults.

You will encounter children with different dietary needs and it is important that you understand what can affect a child's dietary requirements. The following can affect a child's diet:

- **medical conditions** such as diabetes: **Diabetes** means that the pancreas cannot regulate the body's sugar levels. Children need to avoid sugar but should have regular meals and snacks. Each child's needs will be different and you will have to work closely with your supervisor and parents to support a diabetic child. **Coeliac disease** is another medical condition which means that children cannot absorb their food normally. Coeliac children avoid gluten, which is found in cereals such as wheat, barley, etc. Coeliac disease is usually detected after a child has been weaned from breast milk.

- **religious or cultural beliefs**: It is important to respect the diets of a variety of different religions. Look at the table below, but remember that only some members of that religion may eat those foods.

Muslims	<ul><li>Eat halal meat, fish and shellfish, which is slaughtered and prepared in a certain way.</li><li>Do not eat pork or dairy products that contain rennet.</li><li>Fast during Ramadan.</li></ul>
Jews	<ul><li>Eat kosher lamb, beef and chicken, which is slaughtered and prepared in a certain way.</li><li>Dairy products are not eaten with meat.</li><li>Eggs must not have blood spots.</li><li>Fish should have fins, scales and backbones.</li><li>Fast during Yom Kippur.</li></ul>
Sikhs	<ul><li>Rarely eat pork.</li><li>Do not eat beef as the cow is a sacred animal.</li><li>Some Sikhs eat chicken, cheese, fish and shellfish.</li></ul>
Hindus	<ul><li>Usually vegetarian.</li><li>Do not eat beef as the cow is seen as a sacred animal.</li><li>Do not eat dairy products that contain rennet.</li><li>Some Sikhs eat eggs and shellfish.</li><li>Fish with fins and scales is eaten.</li></ul>
Rastafarians	<ul><li>Some Rastafarians do eat lamb, beef and chicken, but do not eat shellfish.</li></ul>

- The dietary requirements of some religions

- Vegetarians do not eat meat or fish.
- Vegans do not eat meat, fish or any other products that come from animals, such as milk, eggs and cheese.
- Some children may have food allergies. This means they cannot tolerate certain foods and may become very ill if they eat them. Common food intolerances are:
  - lactose – found in milk and dairy products
  - histamine – found in strawberries and ripe tomatoes
  - tartrazine – found in yellow food colouring and some drinks and sweets.

You will need to be aware that some children can go into anaphylactic shock if they eat certain foods. You will learn how to deal with this on your basic first aid course.

You must work closely with parents when a child has specific dietary needs. However, as children get older they will know their own requirements and will be able to make suggestions about their diet.

How to care for children's skin and hair

You will need to make sure that children's skin and hair is appropriately cared for. Babies have different needs to older children. As children grow up they become more independent in their skin and hair-care routines.

If a child has dirty skin or an infection, he or she will feel uncomfortable.

You must work with parents to find out about a child's skin and hair-care routine. Every family has different routines, needs and traditions. The parents will also be able to advise on the best products to use on their child's skin if their child has an allergy or irritation.

The information below will help you to provide the best skin and hair care for the children in your setting.

Skincare

Skin helps to stop infection to the rest of the body.

✔ Keys to good practice: Doing observations

✓ Change nappies carefully to avoid infection.

✓ Wash sweat off bodies regularly to avoid sore areas and inflammation.

✓ Moisturise skin as appropriate.

✓ If working in a child's home, find out if the family prefers showering to baths.

✓ Ensure water is not too hot – 63°C is a recommended temperature.

✓ Encourage older children to wash themselves.

✓ Show young children how to wash hands and praise them well.

✓ When washing a younger child's face ensure any flannels are only used once and are thoroughly washed.

✓ Use soap carefully as it can dry skin.

✓ Never leave young children alone by water.

✓ Use recommended products if children have allergies or skin conditions such as eczema.

✓ Ensure feet are washed and dried properly and that footwear fits to avoid blisters and sores.

Did you know?

Children who have nut allergies must not eat any food that contains nuts or has come into contact with nut products. Some children cannot even tolerate nut-free food that has been prepared in the same factory as a nut product. You can help to prevent allergic reactions by carefully reading the ingredients on food labels. Manufacturers must declare any traces of nuts. You will read warnings such as 'This product may contain some traces of nuts'.

● *Encourage the habit of washing hands*

Hair care

- Find out about children's needs by talking to them or their parents
- It is common for black children to have oil rubbed in hair, braids and less frequent hair washing.
- Allergies will require specific products.
- Head lice are common. The lice live on the scalp. Treatment varies and can include special combs and lotions.

● *Take part in grooming and hair care*

Case study 6: Head lice

One morning, 13-year-old Beth storms into the club and says she has caught head lice off Maria. Some of her friends tease Maria who asks to go home, although her hair has been treated. Two of the teenagers tell her she is dirty because she has lice.

In a group council session, Jim, the manager of the scheme, informs the young people about head lice. He tells them that head lice are often attracted to clean hair and that anybody can catch them. He emphasises that it is important to treat people with sensitivity and not name or blame them. He gives them informative leaflets about head lice. A discussion follows and the council agree on how they would support another outbreak. Beth apologises to Maria.

1 *Why do you think Beth was angry?*
2 *Do you think Maria should have been upest?*
3 *Do you think that Jim ensured that the reaction to a future outbreak of head lice would be more appropriate?*

Sun care

Skincare in the sun is essential. While you will have to do more for young children, you will have to ensure that older children understand why they must protect their skin from harmful rays.

Children have delicate skin and you need to observe the following guidelines during strong sunlight.

Did you know?

Exposure to the sun can cause skin cancer (melanoma). Skin cancer causes a large number of deaths per year.

Keys to good practice: How to protect children's skin against the sun

- ✓ Always keep babies under 6 months out of direct sunlight.
- ✓ Ensure children are kept out of the sun between 11 am and 3 pm.
- ✓ Cover up children using sun hats, T-shirts etc.
- ✓ Use a high-factor suncream with not less than 15SPF.
- ✓ Ensure faces are protected.
- ✓ Ensure older children understand the importance of protecting themselves against the sun.

How to care for children's teeth

Teeth develop in a particular order and the way they are cared for is important to ensure healthy adult teeth.

Look at the diagram of the jaw to find out how teeth usually develop.

Teeth facts

- Babies are born with teeth growing inside their gums.
- The average age when teeth start to appear is 6 months.
- There are 20 teeth in the first set of teeth. These are called the milk teeth.
- All milk teeth appear by the age of 2–3 years.
- From the age of 5 onwards milk teeth begin to fall out.
- Permanent teeth start to come through when children are about 6 years old.
- Milk teeth are replaced by teeth that are larger.
- The 12 extra molars make a set of 32 teeth.
- The first permanent teeth to come through are molars and incisors.
- Sometimes permanent teeth are crooked and teenagers may need braces to correct this.

Chewing is good for the teeth, but sweet and sticky foods can cause decay. Encouraging children to clean their teeth after every meal is important. You can make this fun. You could put a sequence of actions to music or make an attractive poster using pictures as well as words. By the time children are older thorough teeth cleaning should be an accepted part of their routine.

In the box below is an example of what you might put on a poster.

Check it out

Find out what the policies and procedures are in your setting for protecting children against the sun. Does your setting have any information for parents and children?

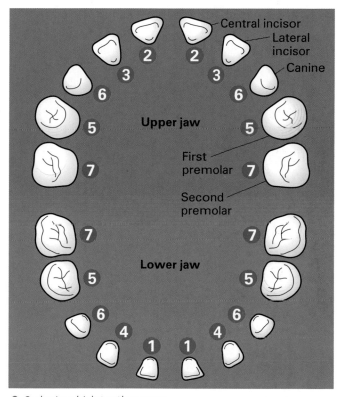

- *Order in which teeth appear*

Wash and dry your hands

Put water on your toothbrush

Place a little bit of toothpaste on your brush

Use a circular action to brush your teeth

Brush all teeth and inside edges

Rinse your mouth

Rinse your brush and place it in a clean place

Wipe your mouth

Did you know?

To build strong and healthy teeth the children in your care will need:
- calcium
- fluoride
- vitamin A
- vitamin C
- vitamin D.

In areas where water supplies do not have enough fluoride children should be given fluoride drops.

Evidence collector

This evidence collector supports elements CCLD 203.1, 203.2, 203.3

Key Skills

This activity will help you to evaluate the way in which you can prepare an environment to meet children's needs. Design one of the following settings by making a floor plan. You will need to use symbols.

- Nursery for a baby aged 3 months in a private home
- Foundation Stage classroom in a primary school
- Youth drop-in centre for children aged 13–16 years

1 Ensure that the physical space meets legal requirements and that you allow for the children to be involved.
2 Indicate how you will ensure access and adapt the environment for different activities such as changing a messy play area into a lunch area.
3 Show where you will have wall and object displays.
4 Ensure that your plan allows children to socialize.
5 Ensure there are areas for rest and sleep.
6 Indicate where water, snacks and meals are available.
7 Ensure that there are areas to allow the children to develop independence.
8 Consider the importance of outdoor play as appropriate.

If you want to you could present your diagram to scale. Indicate the scale you are using on your diagram.

● ●

End-of-unit knowledge check

1 Name three different environments for 0–16-year-olds.
2 Why should you celebrate diversity in the environment?
3 What is the Sure Start initiative?
4 How could a 4-year-old child be involved in making decisions about setting up a tabletop game?
5 How could you involve a 16-year-old in making a decision about his or her environment?
6 What have the DCSF produced as a framework for those working with 0–5 year olds?
7 Would you praise a child if they did not complete a task?
8 What does self-esteem mean?
9 Which settings would Ofsted inspect?
10 What does RoSPA stand for?
11 List the five senses.
12 What could a visual and tactile display include?
13 What was the name of the theory that John Bowlby developed?
14 What is a SENCO?
15 What is the temperature that you should maintain in a setting for babies?
16 How would you promote rest for 3–5-year-olds?
17 What are the seven nutrients that children need?
18 What are molars and incisors?

● ●

Support children's play and learning

This unit relates to children from birth to 7 years. However, the knowledge you gain could also be applied to children who are older but are perhaps in the early stages of learning.

You will discover the importance of the environment in learning and understand how important it is to work in partnership with parents when supporting their children's learning.

You will develop knowledge and understanding of supporting children's:
- communication and language
- imagination
- creativity
- physical play and exercise
- exploration and investigation.

What you must know and understand:
- How to understand and support the pattern of children's communication, intellectual development and learning (K2D85–7)
- How to plan for different curriculums (K2D88)
- Encouraging communication using music, movement, songs and games (K2D90)
- How to encourage children's communication and learning using appropriate language (K2D92)
- How imaginative play can be used to encourage children's learning (K2D89 and K2D93–94)
- that children will play out roles they see in the world around them (K2D95)
- How to encourage free flow imaginative play with minimal intervention (K2D96)
- How to encourage creativity through a variety of activities (K2D97 and K2D99)
- How to display children's work (K2D98)
- How to provide activities for the development of children's fine motor skills (K2D100)
- How physical play can help children to assess risk … (K2D101)
- How children can benefit from physical play and exercise (K2D102)
- How to provide objects that engage children's interest (K2D103)
- How children's learning can benefit from grouping similar objects (K2D104)
- How children's learning can benefit from knowing about their own background and community (K2D105)
- How to provide a stimulating environment to develop children's curiosity, problem solving and exploration (K2D106)
- Why it is important to understand the scope of practical daily activities to enhance children's learning (K2D107)
- How to ensure your practice is appropriate for the children in your setting (K2D108)
- How to set up activities to help children learn (K2D108–10)

How to understand and support the pattern of children's communication, intellectual development and learning

This is dealt with in detail in Unit 203. This chapter is particularly concerned with children from birth to 7 years, so remind yourself of children's physical, communication and intellectual development and the support they need by reference to the development section for this age range.

How to plan for different curriculums

When planning activities you will need to understand the curriculum that is required for the children in your care. Different curriculums are recommended for children from birth to 7 years:

- Early Years Foundation Stage (EYFS) has been designed to support children from birth to 5 years
- Key Stage 1 of the National Curriculum for children aged 6–7 years ensuring a clear transition from end of Foundation Stage to the first year of KS1.

Did you know?

The Foundation Stage Framework has been designed for all those practitioners in England working with children in their pre-school years. It aims to ensure a smooth transition from each stage of development. It has been created to encourage practitioners from all areas to work together to achieve similar outcomes. The guidance contains a wealth of advice and examples of best practice

Early Years Foundation Stage

In England, a new curriculum for children has been created for children from birth to 5 years from the existing Birth to Three Matters framework and the Foundation Stage curriculum. By September 2008, all early years settings will be expected to implement this new curriculum – the new Early Years Foundation Stage (EYFS).

The EYFS has four themes which show how you can help to support the care, learning and development of the children in your care. They are:

1. A unique child
2. Positive relationships
3. Enabling environments
4. Learning and development

The EYFS curriculum has six areas of learning and development:

1. Personal, social and emotional development
2. Communication, language and literacy
3. Problem solving, reasoning and numeracy
4. Knowledge and understanding of the world
5. Physical development
6. Creative development

● *Give opportunities to be imaginative*

Case study 1: Encouraging communication

Sanita, a Level 2 trainee in a day-care setting, is planning an activity that ensures that Billy and Rose, both aged 2, are encouraged to enjoy and achieve through learning by listening and responding.

Sanita collects a basket of objects that make different sounds for Billy and Rose to play with. Billy takes a shaker tin and makes noises that imitate the beans in the tin. Sanita gives Rose a bottle with coloured water in and takes one herself. Rose laughs when Sanita makes a 'whooshing' sound and joins in. Sanita, Rose and Billy spend a happy ten minutes listening and responding to the sounds of the objects in the basket.

1   *Why do you think it is important for children to enjoy their learning to achieve? How did Billy and Rose do this?*
2   *How are Billy and Rose encouraged to listen to the sounds of the objects? Why is listening an important part of communication?*
3   *List five other useful objects that could have been in the basket.*

Each area of learning is linked to the five outcomes of the Every Child Matters framework and key early learning goals – a statement of what most children should achieve in each area of learning by the end of the EYFS. The development stages outlined are broad and intended to show the different ways that children can achieve the early learning goals. The framework is intended to be holistic and centred upon the needs of the individual child, to enable children to progress through the areas of learning and development.

Check it out

Obtain a copy of the Early Years Foundation Stage and find out how the children's developmental stages are presented. You can order a copy by telephoning 0845 602 2260 (ref. 00013-2007BKT-EN) or download it from www.standards.dfes.gov.uk/eyfs.

● *Ensure there are opportunities for creative development*

The boxes below will show you pointers to good practice when supporting the older child within the EYFS.

Personal, social and emotional development

- Encourage sharing and taking turns.
- Give the children clear guidelines and ensure all staff interpret them in the same way.
- Set a good example in the way you talk to and treat others in the setting.
- Stress the children's positive aspects.
- Learn about other cultures and religions.
- Use positive language, e.g. say 'Please walk' not 'Don't run'.
- Always give the child a chance to avoid confrontation.
- Encourage children to sort out their own problems, e.g. sharing the bicycles.
- If the children cannot sort out their own problems, offer strategies, e.g. 'Have one more turn then let someone else have a turn'.

Check it out

How is the development of language through play for 3–5-year-olds promoted in your setting? Think of an example of an activity you have observed or taken part in recently. How did the activity encourage children to develop their language?

If you do not work with children of this age group, ask your manager or tutor if you can have the opportunity to observe a language activity for 3–5-year-olds.

Problem solving, reasoning and numeracy

- Talk to the children about age, buttons, pairs of gloves/socks, house numbers, car registration numbers (numeracy).
- Count the children at group time.
- Get the children to set places at the lunch table – 1:1 cutlery items.
- Offer children milk and a snack – 1:1 correspondence, e.g. child to milk.
- Line up the children in height order – relative size, ordering by size.
- Group the children by various criteria – sorting.
- Discuss whether there are more boys than girls, etc.
- Observe shapes in the environment.
- Conduct weighing activities, e.g. a see-saw is a simple weighing machine.

Knowledge and understanding of the world

- Provide well-planned activities in sand and water.
- Provide more structured activities, e.g. magnets, magnifiers, reflection, etc.
- Talk about healthy food at mealtimes and brushing teeth.
- Discuss personal hygiene, e.g. hand washing.
- Discuss the need for and carry out physical sense.
- Discuss the weather and the natural environment.
- Take walks around the area and talk about buildings, jobs and other features.
- Talk to the children about your own life and culture, providing examples of your home life and culture/language if appropriate.
- Talk about the sequence of the day or the week.
- Discuss events in the lives of the children.
- Language, communication and literacy.

Communication, language and literacy

- Talk to children at a level appropriate to their understanding.
- Extend the child's vocabulary.
- Listen to children and add to the conversation.
- Provide activities to promote language development, e.g. role play, stories, Lotto.
- Work on phonics, letter recognition and names.
- Ask the children to carry verbal messages and follow and issue instructions.
- Read to children and stress that print carries the meaning.
- Run a finger under the words as you read so that children can see the relationship between the word and the sound.
- Look for words and letters that match.
- Provide children with a variety of writing media e.g. pens, pencils, chalk.
- Provide sand, tea, rice, etc., so that children can experiment in it with their writing.
- Help with pencil control, e.g. correct size of pencil, correct pencil grip, and provide fingergrips if necessary.

Physical development

- Provide activities to develop manipulative skills, e.g. threading, cutting, small construction.
- Offer help with threading, cutting, pencil grip, dressing/undressing.
- Encourage children to perform physical activities in the appropriate place.
- Inside activities could include large construction, dancing, action songs or role play – but these need to be in a safe, large area.
- Play games, e.g. football, throwing and catching, rolling hoops.
- Help children to ride bicycles and tricycles.
- In PE, teach the children how to find a space that is safe to work in, e.g. unable to touch nearest child with arms outstretched.
- Stress the importance of fitness.
- Talk about the children's interests, e.g. football, ballet, swimming.

Creative development

- Encourage role play in the home corner and outside.
- Provide a variety of dressing-up clothes and role-play equipment.
- Provide a wide range of artistic media.
- Provide a balance of activities which do/do not involve paint.
- Observe sound in the environment.
- Display finished work attractively, using work by all the children.
- Do not take work from children if they do not want you to have it – ask them to do two: one for you and one for them.
- Play music – use instruments from a variety of cultures.
- Sing songs from different cultures, in different languages and with or without accompaniment.
- Ensure there are opportunities for: free expression, interpretation of moods, interpretation of action words, e.g. bang, crackle, float.

National Curriculum Key Stage 1

The National Curriculum Key Stage 1 starts in year 1 of primary education.

The core subjects of Key Stage 1 of the National Curriculum are:

- English – speaking, reading and writing, listening
- Mathematics – the concepts of number, number bonds and relationships between numbers, the development of mathematical language
- Science – knowledge and understanding of science through play, the importance of science in everyday life and its importance to health, computers, asking scientific questions and responding, and investigating familiar everyday objects.

The following table shows the skills you will need to help children develop when supporting delivery of the National Curriculum at Key Stage 1.

Check it out

It is good practice to ensure that children can move comfortably from the EYFS to Key Stage 1. This is called the transitional stage.

Ask your local primary school how they do this, or use the Internet to help you find out.

- *Give opportunities for children to read aloud*

Core subject	Skill
English Speaking	• Respond appropriately. • Have an awareness of standard English.
Reading and writing	• Read aloud with developing fluency. • Recognise familiar words accurately and easily. • Express opinions about events or ideas in stories or poems. • Communicate meaning through written words and phrases and an appropriate level.
Listening	• Develop and expand ideas. • Adapt to the needs of the listener.
Mathematics	• Understand the concepts of number. • Know number bonds and relationships between numbers. • Develop mathematical language.
Science	• Realise the importance of science in everyday life and its relevance to personal health. • Use computers in their work as and when appropriate. • Ask scientific questions and know how to respond. • Investigate familiar everyday objects.

- *Skills children will need to develop at Key Stage 1*

Encouraging communication using music, movement, songs and games

Music, movement, songs and games may seem daunting to you if you have only recently started to work with young children. However, even with a simple activity children can develop all areas of their learning. Activities can take place both indoors and outside. You might, for example, spend a half hour in the shade of a tree playing round and round the garden with a 6-month-old baby.

Music is simply another creative activity and you don't have to read music, sing well or play a musical instrument to lead a music session. You do need to understand:

- music in relation to language and other areas of development
- how to organise a musical activity
- the choice of songs and musical activities
- the importance of movement with music and singing.

Music in relation to language and other areas of development

Children will respond to music whatever their stage of development. It is necessary to choose the right activity for the age of the children you are working with. Remember that music is rhythmical, which is an important basis to language. It also encourages recall, repetition and listening skills.

● *Encourage activities involving music and movement*

Test yourself

Read Unit 203 on development. Carefully study the different stages of children's language development. Make sure you are aware of the needs of the age group you are planning musical activities for.

Read the information below to find out about activities that you can provide for children of different ages.

Birth to 1 year

You may have heard the theory that babies respond to music before they are born, for example that a newborn baby will respond positively to the theme tune of a TV soap opera which the mother watched regularly! From a few days old, babies will respond to the rhythm of being rocked gently or to a lullaby. A lullaby or a quiet piece of music (such as Mozart) can have a calming effect in a way that a loud or sudden noise will not. 'Rock-a-bye-baby' is often the first lullaby that springs to mind. Can you think of some others?

The stages of play

You need to be aware of the way children play and that these stages of play are closely linked to a child's development. The different stages are outlined below.

1. Exploratory play

Young babies will observe their surroundings. They may make movements to reach out, and will grasp fingers or rattles.

2. Solitary play – up to 15 months

Babies or children will play alone.

3. Parallel play – 2 years

Children play side by side and play separately with little interaction.

4. Association play (2–2½ years)

Children begin to interact and may be involved in the same activity. Play can remain solitary.

5. Taking turns/sharing (2¾–3 years)

Playing becomes more complex and simple rules are understood.

6. Co-operation play (over 3 years)

Children are able to play together. They can adopt a role within the group and take account of others' needs and actions.

Appropriate games to play with children in your care

Now that you have considered the variety of games that children can play, you must learn how to choose the right games for different age groups. You already know that some commercial games are labelled with suggested age suitability, but many games don't have this advantage. Study the table below to discover how you can choose appropriate games to play with children in your care.

Age of children	Types of games	Role of adult to develop
1–2 years	• Dominoes and simple matching • Ring o' Roses.	• Guided by adults, often on a one-to-one basis.
2–3 years	• Dominoes, matching, lotto. • Dominoes, matching lotto, dice.	• Need to be well supervised in small groups. • Avoid lengthy games.
3–5 years	• Small grouping games, e.g. Farmer's in his/her den, Five currant buns in a baker's shop. • Circle games – such as bean bag and ball throwing.	• Still needs to be led by adults in a sensitive way – try not to exclude children.
5–7 years 11 months	• Dominoes, lotto, dice, counters, draughts, chess. • Physical games with rules, e.g. 'Simon says' and 'Follow my leader'. • Recognition skills. • Hand–eye co-ordination. • Balance and gross motor skills. • Language repetition. • Hand–eye co-ordination. • Manipulative skills. • Understanding of simple rules – concentration. • Taking turns and co-operation. • Perception. • Discrimination. • Mathematical skills.	• Can begin to follow rules of games and organise some of their own physical games.

● *Games to play with children of different ages*

How to encourage children's communication and learning using appropriate language

When encouraging the children in your care to communicate through play you will need to know how to use:

- open-ended questions
- language to extend learning.

A very effective way for you to learn these skills is to observe how your more experienced colleagues use the right language to encourage communication.

The Practical Guidance for the EYFS states that adults should 'provide time and relaxed opportunities for children to develop spoken language through sustained conversations between children and adults' (page 40).

Open-ended questions

Open-ended questions encourage children to respond in their own way and develop their own ideas. Open-ended questions start with 'Why', 'How', 'Which', 'What', 'When'.

Consider the following questions:

- Do you like that hat?
- Do you have a favourite teddy?
- Are you coming to join us?

You will notice that all the questions can be answered with 'yes' or 'no', which makes it difficult to extend communication further.

Consider how the questions could be asked differently to encourage more conversation:

- Why do you like that hat?
- Which is your favourite teddy?
- When are you coming to join us?

When discussing a child's painting with the child a useful and respectful open-ended question to use is 'Tell me about your painting'. Sometimes a long and informative dialogue can follow and the child will feel valued that they are being listened to.

- Language to extend learning
- One of your main roles is to encourage children to explore and investigate in their play and really develop what they are learning. The opportunities you have will be sometimes planned and sometimes spontaneous. New vocabulary is often better used in context. When children absorb new words they will naturally extend the number of words they are able to use.

- When children hear a word in context they are more likely to use it appropriately.
- Children usually learn new words through play experiences rather than formal learning
- Books are a useful way to introduce new words to children
- Open-ended questions are a way of extending a child's vocabulary if not too heavy.
- Activities are also a useful way of extending children's language.
- Mathematical language can be extended through play activities.

Children love to question in order to learn. Group times are a great time to encourage children to ask questions, for example:
- talking about a musical instrument
- talking about a new story
- looking at an interesting photograph
- talking to an interesting visitor
- looking at an object such as a dead wasp's nest.

- *Encourage children to talk as they play*

Case study 3: Using play to develop mathematical language

Peter and Layla, both aged 4, have chosen to play with coloured plastic bears during free choice activity time in their pre-school. Janet, one of the supervisors, is observing them.

Peter: My line of bears is longer than yours.
Layla: I know because I don't have so many.
Peter: You can have four of my red ones.
Layla: OK, now my line is longer and I have lots more than you.
Peter: Let's play marching bears now and put them all together so that we have a lot.
Layla: We can have double.

1   *What is the mathematical language used by Layla and Peter?*
2   *Do they understand the concepts of 'more than' and 'less than'?*
3   *Think of other activities to encourage these concepts.*

How imaginative play can be used to encourage children's learning

Imaginative play can start at a very early age and it plays an important part in any child's development. You are going to consider:
- how children use their imagination to make one thing stand for another
- how children can play out different roles.

Key terms

Imaginative play: pretending or acting, either alone or in a group.

In role play children pretend to be other people. They will act out situations for enjoyment or to make sense of their own world. You will notice that children often lead in their own role play. They may, for example, use wrapped-up towels as dogs and climbing frames as space rockets.

There will be times when you will provide equipment to support role play but you should always ensure it is safe for imaginative play.

The role of the early years worker in providing a suitable environment

Study the spider diagram below so that you can begin to consider the key role of the early years worker in providing suitable **props** to stimulate role play.

Key terms

Props: objects and materials children use to support their imaginative play, for example dressing-up clothes, dolls, puppets, masks.

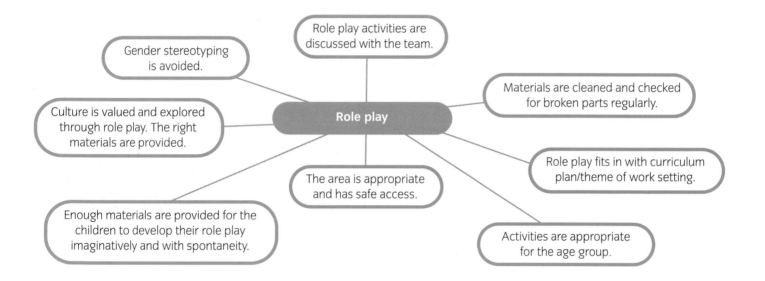

How to use role play to develop communication and language skills

Role play is an excellent way of developing children's skills in many ways. Children as young as 2 years old will use role play to develop their imaginations. They will also develop their language, communication and literacy skills through role play.

Before you think about planning suitable role play for the children you work with, think about how babies and very young children need to be encouraged to communicate. They need to learn to:

- listen
- look and understand what is being communicated through body language, such as the nod of a head or a smile
- talk – by being talked to and observing other people.

Children from 18 months upwards will respond to role play that is set up in a suitable area. First of all, let us consider role play that links in with a theme or curriculum plan in your work setting.

Ideas for role play

There are many ideas for imaginative play areas to encourage role play. Here are a few:

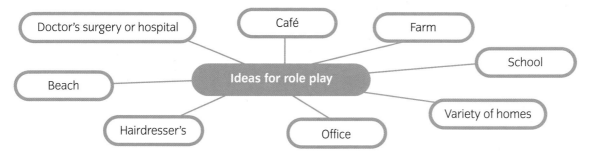

In fact most ideas can be adapted for a role play area and children will respond. Through their (usually vivid) imaginations children will be able to understand and experience the theme that is being explored.

Child-led role play can occur in a theme-led role play area or spontaneously in everyday play. Role play can be totally unplanned. One child may be playing under a climbing frame using it as a jungle and very soon two or three other children may be joining in this imaginary play.

Remember that role play does not occur only when children are dressing up. You may observe some interesting role play in the following activities:

- small world play, such as Duplo/Lego or Playmobil scenes
- puppets/dolls
- books and stories
- painting and drawing
- playdough.

Did you know?

Hats can be one of the most important visible elements in role play. By providing a box of different hats, early years workers can enable children to role play many different characters.

Case study 4: Using hats in imaginative role play

Beverley looks after 4-year-old twins, Holly and Ben, in their home. They have their cousins, Kate, who is 5, and Philippa, who is 3, over to play. Beverley has collected together a large number of hats for the children. The hats are freely accessible and kept in a large basket in the playroom. The children set up some chairs to represent a bus. Holly finds a flowery hat to put on and becomes one of the passengers. The other children are soon rummaging in the hat basket and sitting on the chairs imagining themselves as passengers on the bus. Kate finds herself a flat cap and decides she is the driver. A great deal of time is spent travelling to the seaside! Holly suddenly gets off the bus and swaps her flowery hat for a large net veil. Soon a wedding is taking place, very much like a family wedding they had all attended last month.

By collecting a variety of hats for the children to use, Beverley has enabled them to lead their own role play.

1 *What is this type of role play called?*
2 *How did the hats help to develop the children's play?*
3 *What particular ability or skill did the hats encourage?*

Why it is important to recognise that children will play out roles they see in the world around them

The home corner provides a great opportunity for children to explore their environment. Ideally the home corner should be separate to an imaginative play area.

Consider the shopping list for a home corner below.

○ Multicultural and gender dolls

Hats

Clothes

Bed

○ Washing up facilities

Cooking facilities

Telephone

Cleaning materials

Washing machine, etc.

Iron and board/pegs

Pots and utensils

Shoes and bags

Did you know?

Friedrich Froebel (1782–1852) founded the first kindergarten ('a garden of children'). He believed that symbolic behaviour should be encouraged. This is when children make one thing stand for something else, for example a yogurt pot is a teacup.

Test yourself

What activities could you encourage using items in the home corner shopping list? Think about the different roles the children could play.

Now look at the diagram below and think about how you can provide role play opportunities in your home corner.

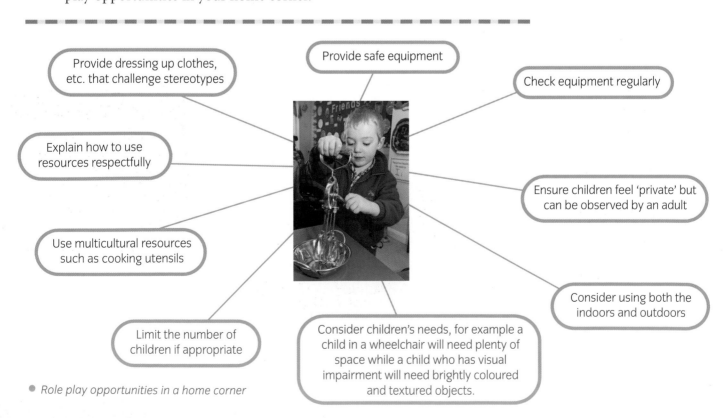

Provide dressing up clothes, etc. that challenge stereotypes

Provide safe equipment

Check equipment regularly

Explain how to use resources respectfully

Ensure children feel 'private' but can be observed by an adult

Use multicultural resources such as cooking utensils

Consider using both the indoors and outdoors

Limit the number of children if appropriate

Consider children's needs, for example a child in a wheelchair will need plenty of space while a child who has visual impairment will need brightly coloured and textured objects.

● *Role play opportunities in a home corner*

Test yourself

If you were welcoming a child from China into your setting how would you arrange the home corner to help to celebrate the child's culture? How could the other children share that experience? If you are not familiar with Chinese culture, consider how you would source the information you need without making assumptions.

How to encourage free flow imaginative play with minimal intervention

If you allow children to play freely, they will be building up a strong base for more structured learning at a later stage.

Free flow imaginative play is usually child led and sometimes unplanned. For example, a group of children may turn the outside shed into a cake shop and become completely absorbed in their imaginative game.

To encourage free flow imaginative play you will need to:
- allow time
- allow space
- ensure other children are involved as appropriate
- ensure that the play is calm
- ensure the children can return to their imaginative world at another time
- occasionally intervene if play becomes too boisterous or could be added to in some way.

Free-flow imaginative play can occur using:
- small world play such as Lego
- dolls/puppets
- sand and water
- playdough
- dressing up clothes
- large equipment.

Remember that hats are one of the most important imaginative play resources for all age groups.

● *Dressing up acts as a catalyst to free-flow imaginative play*

Did you know?

A child with an emotional need may benefit from adult support during role play. For example, a child who has a new sibling may be able to work through the new experience using a doll or teddy.

Did you know?

Margaret Macmillan (1860–1931) was a teacher in a London school who was one of the first people to introduce nursery schools. She believed it was important to work with parents. In her schools great emphasis was given to good nutrition and medical support. She believed in free play to encourage imagination and felt that a child could develop to his or her full potential through active learning.

Check it out

Find out how your setting encourages children to play imaginatively without interference from adults. You might consider where in the setting such activities are presented.

How to encourage creativity through a variety of activities

Through **creative play** you can encourage children to create and explore.

Children can:

- explore the properties of different materials through their senses
- develop physical, social, emotional and intellectual skills
- gain satisfaction and develop confidence and self-esteem.

Key terms

Creativity/creative play: opportunities for children to develop their own ideas using art, design, making things, music, dance and movement. Children can express their creativity in every area of learning.

 Keys to good practice: How to support creative play

✓ Never stress the end product – children often enjoy the process rather than the end product.

✓ Ensure there is no competition.

✓ Praise children for their efforts.

✓ Value the results but do not compare.

✓ Remember that children, unlike adults, will not always visualise an end product.

Your role is to provide the right materials for the creative activity and not over-direct the end result.

The range of materials and choosing an appropriate activity

A wide range of creative materials is available for children. Once you have studied the range, and probably added your own ideas to the list, you will be able to consider how these materials can be used in activities to encourage different stages.

Sand and alternative materials

If you are working in a nursery or school setting you will probably have a sand tray. However, sand can also be provided in a baby's bath, a washing bowl or a sandpit in the garden. Special play (silver) sand is available which is soft and does not stain hands. Sand can be used in a wet or dry form and can be used by children to create an imaginary environment for diggers, animals and other toys. With simple containers sand can be dug, raked, scooped, patted and moulded. A sand tray is also an area where children can learn to play creatively together, sharing their imaginative experience.

In addition, sand can be used as part of a collage picture or to provide an interesting sound in a shaker made from a clear plastic bottle. Sawdust, beans or peat can also be used in collage activities.

Water

From an early age water plays an important part in **creative play** – starting in the bath! It is an inexpensive material and can encourage creativity in endless ways. Children will play at a water tray, washing bowl, paddling pool or bath for a long time – simply enjoying playing with water. Water can be transformed in creative play by adding ice, colouring, bubbles and even a variety of smells, such as lavender or lemon. Children can be given a range of equipment to stimulate their imaginations, from buckets and bottles to sophisticated water wheels. If your funds are limited, children will display as much creativity from different sized yogurt pots and an empty washing-up liquid bottle.

Did you know?

Creative play does not have to result in an end product. Sand and water play are excellent examples of this. The children can simply enjoy using their imaginations to play creatively.

Painting and drawing materials

A wide variety of drawing materials are available including:

- pencils
- coloured crayons
- felt-tipped pens
- wax crayons
- chalks.

They can be used as a medium on their own or mixed together. Drawing can be 'free' or topic related. Drawing materials such as wax crayons can be used to explore and to do rubbings on a variety of textures, such as bark and walls. The medium provided to draw on will also encourage children to explore their imaginations. Papers can range from thin tissue to thick paper they may have made themselves.

Check it out

Look at the resources in your work setting and discuss ideas with your colleagues. See how long you can make the list of paint ideas. It will probably be very long!

Painting can be done with a variety of brushes, depending upon the manipulative stage of the child involved. Household brushes can be used on large areas. Paint can be applied in many other ways including the following:

- potato printing
- scrubbing pads and nail brush painting
- blowing paint with straws
- painting with rags or scrunched up newspaper
- printing with a roller that is commercially made or made from a kitchen roll
- sponge painting
- drawing with wax and painting over with coloured paint
- roller painting using an old deodorant bottle
- finger painting.

Paint can be bought ready mixed or in a powder form. The type of paint you provide for a creative activity will depend upon the consistency of paint required. You can make your own inexpensive thick paint from powdered glue and powdered paint. Other materials, such as glitter and sand, can be mixed with paint to give it a different texture. Glues, such as PVA, will give a shiny finish.

Malleable materials

Malleable materials can be bought ready-made in forms such as clay or plasticine, whereas materials such as playdough can be made at home or in the work setting.

Dough or clay can be used in a raw form or cooked to make it more permanent – it may then be glazed or painted and varnished. Dough used in cooking is also creative and children can create their own shapes or use commercial cutters. Children will enjoy rolling, shaping, moulding and cutting dough or clay.

Papier mâché can also be provided – either as strips of paper dipped in glue or soaked pulp that can be moulded and dried out ready for painting.

Cornflour and 'gloop' activities can be provided in shallow trays. Very young children enjoy pushing this medium, holding their hands in the air and observing it fall slowly from their fingers.

Collage

Collage can be an imaginative and creative experience for children from a very young age. Your role as the facilitator is to provide the children with a variety of materials, such as:

- different textured and patterned papers and cards
- a variety of ribbons, wool and textured thread
- pasta and beans.

(*Note*: there is some controversy about using food for creative activities as some people are concerned that food is being 'wasted' in this way. Be sensitive to such views.) Remember to make sure that a strong glue is provided as there is nothing more frustrating for a child than watching all the pieces fall off a collage picture on the way home!

Construction

This is often referred to as modelling from recycled materials and can be an excellent form of creative play if a variety of materials are provided. Your modelling collection could include:

- kitchen roll centres (avoid toilet rolls as they can harbour bacteria)
- cereal and food boxes
- circular cheese boxes (good for wheels!)
- large and small cardboard boxes such as egg boxes
- a variety of packaging waste such as cellophane, tissue, etc.
- Many manufacturers will provide offcuts of materials to schools, nurseries and playgroups at no charge.

Case study 5: Supporting a child in a construction activity

Catherine, aged 4, has decided to make a police car. She is inspired by a visit to the nursery from a policeman the day before. Jean, her keyworker, discusses the visit and encourages Catherine to describe the police car she sat in. Catherine picks up a tissue box and then proceeds to look for some wheels. Jean sees that she is having difficulty finding anything she wants in the 'junk' box. She finds some empty circular cheese boxes in the store room and gives them to Catherine; she also finds some large paper fasteners and shows Catherine how she could fix them onto the tissue box so that the wheels move around. Catherine then paints the car in white and blue. She places a piece of red cellophane on the top of the car to represent the light. Jean praises Catherine, who proudly shows the car to her father when he collects her from nursery.

Because of Jean's support, Catherine gains a great deal from this construction activity.

1   *How does Jean stimulate Catherine's imagination?*
2   *How are the materials chosen?*
3   *How does Jean support Catherine without dominating the activity?*
4   *What effect do you think Jean's encouragement and praise has on Catherine?*
5   *Which early learning goals are involved in this activity?*

0–3 years
Activities and experiences linked to a child's overall development.
A child learns through senses and movement.

A child can enjoy:
- finger paint
- crayons and non-toxic felt pens
- playdough
- water play (carefully supervised)
- sand.

A child will become easily frustrated if a task is too difficult. Manipulative skills are developing.

3–5 years
The curriculum is based on the early learning goals – this is known as the Foundation Stage.

A child can enjoy activities using:
- Wet and dry sand
- Water – to encourage investigation
- A variety of pens and paints for painting activities, cutting and sticking
- Construction materials clay and dough.

A child will enjoy exploring different materials. Manipulative skills are developing.

6–7 years 11 months
Creative activities will be influenced by Key Stage 1 requirements of the National Curriculum. This starts at the end of the Foundation Stage.
A child will use creativity to learn about other topics.
A child is able to learn specific creative skills and follow instructions.
A child's concentration span and manipulative skills are developed.

● *The role of creative play in a child's development*

Test yourself

What are the two main activities that children are encouraged to do through creative play experiences?

How to display children's work

When displaying children's artwork you should be celebrating and respecting the child. It is all too easy to over-direct the end product. It is worth remembering that children enjoy the process and are often unconcerned about the final result.

Consider the many ways that you can present displays:

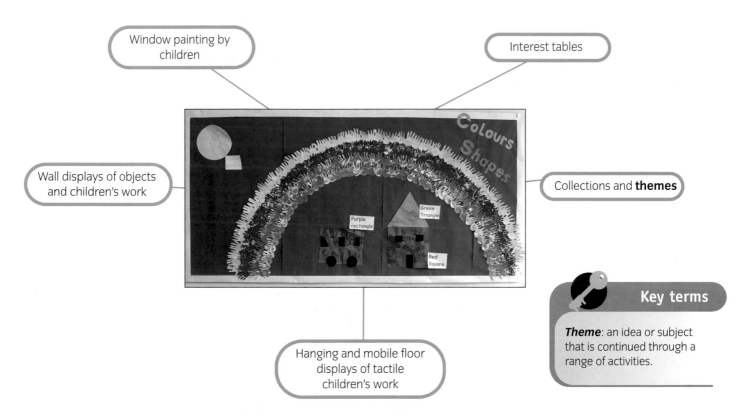

Window painting by children

Interest tables

Wall displays of objects and children's work

Collections and **themes**

Hanging and mobile floor displays of tactile children's work

It is always useful to have a resource box when displaying children's artwork. The box should contain:

- a good quality staple gun and staples
- drawing pins and ordinary pins
- small pointed scissors
- a large pair of scissors
- fibre tipped pens
- a pencil and rubber
- a ruler and tape measure
- a glue gun and sticks
- a craft knife with a safety cap
- Blu-tack or similar
- Blu-tack or similar
- safe glue.

All these items must be kept out of reach of children at all times.

Materials and colours needed for displays

The materials and colours that you choose to use in a display must complement, not dominate, the children's art work involved and must help to celebrate the work displayed. If backgrounds are too dominant the topic for the display can be overshadowed.

There are many types of paper available on the market to use as a backing on a display board. One of the best choices is 'talkie' paper that is coloured on one side and white on the other. This type of paper is strong, clearly coloured and does not fade – it is also available in a variety of widths.

Border paper can also be used and is supplied on large rolls in a variety of patterns, textures and colours. However, many wallpaper shops sell odd border rolls cheaply and they can make ideal borders for your display.

Sometimes plain wallpaper lining can be used on a board, particularly if children are going to decorate the background in some way. Even newspaper can be effective if it is a background for plain coloured work, such as cut-out paper shapes – perhaps of animals or imaginary monsters.

A store of fabric is always important for an early years setting. The following could be usefully collected:
- lengths of dress and lining fabrics
- old sheets
- curtains – a variety of textures and fabric
- quilts
- blankets
- fish netting.

Fabric can be draped on a display board to add depth or cover a box or table. Children can also be involved in decorating fabric used in a display, such as making autumn leaf prints for an autumn display.

Test yourself

Many other materials can be used as a background for displays. Collect a list of at least ten different 'free' materials that you could use as a backing for a display in your work setting.

Tables and cardboard boxes are useful to add a third dimension to your display. Boxes placed securely at different heights, and then covered with paper or material, are excellent bases for displaying solid objects or books. Remember that perspex holders can be useful if you want to incorporate leaflets or books in a display.

There are many ways to mount work and you can only learn and progress through experience!

How to mount and arrange work:

- Clearly cut paper on to a coloured background
- Double mounting – second background may be a different colour or texture
- Shape mounting – follow the shape of a child's shaped paper

When possible use a cutting machine to cut the mounts, as they have perspex rulers that can be used as a guide. If you are unsure, lightly stick the work onto the background paper and draw lines with a ruler – although this is more time consuming. Shape mounting is not easy and you need plenty of practice to follow the shape of the work evenly using scissors!

Remember that some artwork does not need to be mounted and some may be effective with a simple line drawn around the edge of the paper.

Once the work is prepared for a display, time must be taken to consider:

- the area you are going to use
- how to arrange it to the best advantage
- how to vary spacing
- the importance of selecting pictures of different sizes
- how work can be angled – but always try to make it parallel.

Organising work on a table is different as you have to consider the angle at which it will be viewed. Consider creating different secure levels and allowing the display to be touched by the children!

Hang work from the ceiling in front of the display board – this encourages interest and makes the children look up in their environment! For example, a line could be strung across a room (out of reach) and double-sided paintings attached with pegs!

You must make sure that all work is securely positioned. Avoid any visible drawing pins and use staples sparingly.

Labelling children's artwork, displays and printed notices

The labelling of displays must always be very clear and easy to read. You must take into account the language spoken by parents and any learning needs of older children. Therefore labels and notes may have to be in a dual language or incorporate the use of symbols.

Fibre-tipped pens are easy to use and you can vary the thickness according to the size of the letters required. When printing captions on children's work always write unobtrusively and ask their permission. Their words can be written in quotation marks such as:

'This is me eating an ice cream'

'This is my daddy in the kitchen'.

Check it out

Does your work setting have a specific printing policy? For example, early years workers may follow a certain printed alphabet or loop all their lower case letters. If there is a policy you must follow it or the children will become confused. Ask for a copy to refer to.

Where possible, print children's names on the left-hand side as we usually read from left to right!

If you have difficulty spelling always ask a colleague to check your printing. Respect is a very important element of your work with children. When displaying their work remember the following:

- Never misspell their names, however unusual, as this can offend young readers and parents
- Do not cut into a children's work without asking them.

Computer printing is widely used for display purposes but should not always replace handwriting. It is also important to find out if your setting uses a particular style of handwriting. This is often the case in an infant school.

Natural materials

Nature tables are a valuable resource that you must consider and plan very carefully. Such displays can be a positive way of involving both parents and children and there are a number of ways to do this:

- take the children for a walk to collect items
- encourage the children to bring items from home, when they have been on holiday, etc.
- invite parents to look at displays
- encourage the children to provide observational art work and photographs for the display.

Health and safety of natural displays

It is important that you, as an early years worker, are aware of the safe display of natural materials. Read the following guidelines:

- Don't allow water to become stale – change it daily
- Change food regularly – avoid it becoming stale or mouldy
- Avoid poisonous berries and plants and sharp leaves, e.g. holly.

How to involve parents and children

We have discussed ways of involving parents and children in nature tables but this can be extended to all display work by:

- discussing displays in group time
- carrying out other activities related to the display
- encouraging the children to help mount and provide work for the display
- asking children and parents to bring items from home
- asking children to help keep related activity tables tidy
- inviting parents to look at the display.

In some early years settings, a short monthly 'newsletter', perhaps illustrated with children's drawings, can be a good way to keep in touch with parents – especially those who work and who have carers to take and collect the children every day.

Case study 6: Diversity of culture

Aysha is a playgroup worker and has planned a display at the beginning of term based on the theme of 'Ourselves'. She has decided to encourage the children to look in mirrors and paint pictures of themselves. Many of the children are of Asian and Afro-Caribbean origin and Aysha wants to celebrate this diversity of culture. All the children involved are between 3–5 years.

Aysha and her team will need to:
- provide safe mirrors
- give the children time to look at and enjoy discussing their features, perhaps in pairs
- mix and make available a variety of skin-tone paints
- encourage the children to paint their own pictures
- mount the children's work carefully
- clearly label the children's work and make sure all names and titles are correctly spelt
- encourage the parents to look at and enjoy the results.

As Aysha is working with 3–5-year-olds in her playgroup she is expected to consider the early learning goals when planning her display.

1 *Which early learning goals have been developed in Aysha's display?*
2 *How has Aysha captured the children's interest?*
3 *Write down two ways in which Aysha shows respect for children's different social origins and backgrounds.*
4 *Why is the involvement of parents important?*

Celebrating diversity of culture and promoting positive images

It is essential to avoid stereotypes when making displays and make sure they encourage children to feel positive about themselves and their families. Consider these guidelines:
- provide a variety of skin-tone paints and crayons
- make sure various people are presented, e.g. an Asian woman doctor, a black teacher
- projects can incorporate other cultures, such as bread from around the world
- make sure that special needs are represented and that children with varied needs can participate in all aspects of displays
- use more than one language where necessary.

Look again at case study 6 and consider what Aysha was doing.

Safety

It is always important that displays are safe. Consider the following:

- use non-toxic materials
- staples and pins and all objects must be firmly placed
- no poisonous natural materials should be displayed
- items such as scissors and craft knives used to mount displays must be firmly locked away
- displays in children's reach and hanging from ceilings must be secure
- objects that could be swallowed must not be displayed
- displays must have easy access.

Keys to good practice

✓ Displays can be mounted in many different locations in an early years setting, using all sorts of themes.

✓ A variety of resources are needed to make the best use of displays.

✓ The appropriate curriculum should be considered carefully when planning displays.

✓ Cross-cultural displays can be used to promote positive images.

✓ Safety considerations are very important when organising natural displays.

How to provide suitable activities for the development of children's fine and gross motor skills

Did you know?

Children can develop at different rates. Think about the children in your setting. Do they all learn to walk, crawl, use scissors or run at the same time? The answer is 'no', but the sequence of movement remains the same, i.e. a child has to learn balance (standing) before he or she can walk.

When supporting the learning of the children in your care you will already be aware that you need to consider the whole development of each child. One important area of development is a child's physical skills. If you provide the appropriate curriculum children will have the opportunity to develop their muscles.

The development of muscles enable children to develop large and small movements. These movements are called:

- gross motor skills, for example jumping, climbing, walking
- fine motor skills, for example picking up pencils, doing up buttons.

If you look back to Unit 203 on children's development you can remind yourself of the expected stages of physical development.

Test yourself

In your study group consider the following.

1 Provide a suitable activity to stimulate the fine manipulative skills of a 9-month-old baby looked after in the home. Consider using objects found in the home.

2 Provide a suitable group activity using a ball for a group of eight 6 year olds in the playground. Consider which skills you will be developing.

3 Provide an activity to encourage a 14 month old to walk without an adult.

How physical play can help children to assess risk in a safe and controlled environment

If children are gradually encouraged to take responsibility for their own safety in **physical play**, they will become more able to foresee the possible risks and learn how to minimise them. Remember that children are naturally curious and need you to anticipate risks and accidents when they are unable to.

Key terms

Physical play: play focusing on movement of the body.

Case study 7: Encouraging safe play

Harry, aged 4, has gone to the park with his nursery. He has been warned of the dangers of going down the slide backwards. Harry climbs to the top of the slide and looks around to see if he can go down the slide backwards. Gina, the room supervisor, calmly asks him to remember why she had warned him it was dangerous and suggests that he turns round and slides down frontwards. Harry does this. And each time he takes a turn he goes down the right way and twice tells Gina what a good boy he is.

1 *Why do you think that Gina reacted to Harry's behaviour in the way she did?*

2 *Do you think Gina should talk to Harry again about safety on the slide?*

3 *How could Gina lead a group time that encouraged children to think about safety in the playground?*

During physical play your role should be to:
- ensure children are appropriately supervised
- give children freedom
- ensure children understand their limitations
- ensure children understand the consequences of their actions
- set clear rules and boundaries
- talk to children if they are putting their peers at risk.

Children who are too cautious may need individual supervision.

Keys to good practice: How to give overcautious children confidence to take appropriate risks

✓ Give them time.

✓ Encourage them without making them go too far.

✓ Build up their skills and confidence step by step.

✓ Ensure activities are relevant and enjoyable to them.

✓ Hold a child's hand if you need to.

Balancing is a crucial part of children's development through physical play. Children can sometimes be wary of balancing and may need your support so that they are prepared to take risks. If you give them a variety of activities to do in a safe indoor or outdoor environment, children will develop these skills through physical play. Appropriate equipment includes:

- bikes and tricycles to ride on grass or safe paths with enough space
- scooters to ride on safe surfaces with enough space
- Beams, climbing frames, logs to walk along
- Swings with space around and safety surfaces underneath
- Seesaws that have safety surfaces underneath
- Stilts that can be used on grass or safe surfaces
- Tightropes as part of a climbing structure.

Boundaries and behavioural expectations

If you involve children in assessing the risk of their own play by setting boundaries they will begin to understand the importance of safety. They will see how their own behaviour affects others and how safe they are when they play. You may invite people to talk to children about their safety, for example a judo or football coach. Another idea is to ask children to help create a behaviour agreement to do with their physical play.

Here is an example of an agreement made by a group of 6-year-olds to do with their outdoor play area.

● *Development of balance comes through physical play*

Our Outdoor Play Agreement

Let everyone take turns with the football

Only go down the slide one at a time

Only go down the slide sitting up facing forwards

Make sure there are no people too near you when skipping

Only ride the bikes and scooters on the special path

Always wear a helmet when riding a bike or scooter

Wear shoes with rubber grip soles on the climbing frame

Did you know?

Many local authorities are encouraging children and their parents to walk to school. Sometimes a group of parents act as volunteers and start 'walking buses'. Both adults and children wear luminous jackets so that they can be clearly seen by passing motorists. Walking is a very healthy form of exercise. Health experts worry that children spend too much time in cars.

How children can benefit from physical play and exercise

Physical play and exercise will promote good health in children. It will help them to turn into healthy adults. Physical play and exercise can also increase self-esteem and social skills.

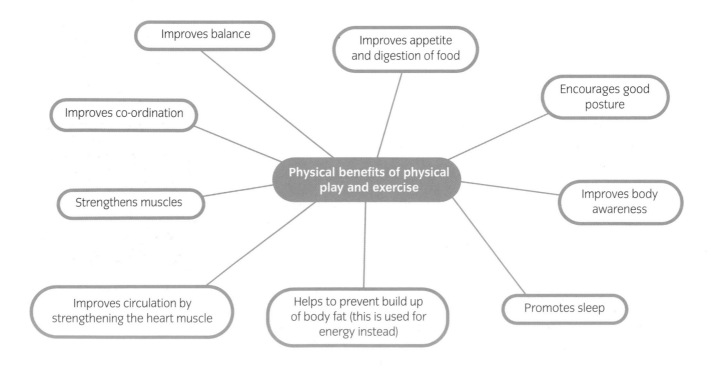

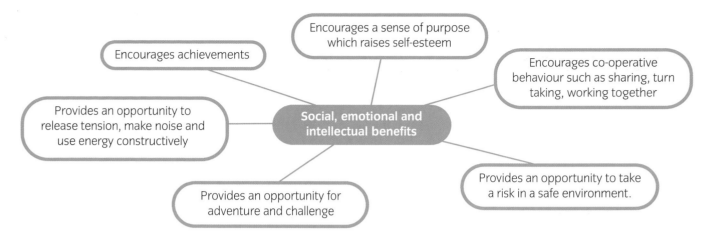

Those children who may find it difficult to participate may need individual support and a great deal of understanding. It may sometimes be worth pairing them up with a more confident child.

Children with special or additional needs will need to be supported according to their needs. Your SENCO will guide you as to the support you will need to give.

How to provide the kind of objects that engage children's interest

Children are naturally curious and often challenge their carers by examining objects they should not touch. You role is to ensure that you provide children in your care with **objects of interest** that are suitable for their age. There are many different objects that children can be safely encouraged to explore. Objects will often stimulate more than one of the five senses.

You will remember that the five senses are touch, hearing, sight, smell and taste. Children who are encouraged to explore objects using their senses will soon interact with the environment. If their surroundings are safe they will soon develop:

● an understanding and interest in new areas
● an awareness of the differences, similarities and relationships between objects
● an ability to discuss objects with adults and peers.

How examination of objects can promote development

Interest tables and thematic displays are an essential part of encouraging children's sensory and intellectual development. If appropriately presented, an interest table or display will encourage a child to ask questions.

Check it out

Observe a group of children engaging in physical play in your setting. Make a checklist of the things that you would like to see which show a child is benefiting emotionally from the play. If you tick an area on your checklist, make notes about what you saw.

Did you know?

Early Years Partnerships often sponsor Topstart training for their members. The Topstart scheme provides a large bag of PE equipment for different age groups that can be used to promote children's physical development. Special trainers will show people in your setting how to use the equipment.

Key terms

Objects of interest: any objects that interest children and that can extend their learning, for example fossils, stones, food or living things such as insects.

Carefully study the different types of display described below. You might well be able to add to the ideas. Interest tables will probably be part of the early years curriculum in your setting.

Display tables can encourage children to consider the environment they live in and the world around them. Children can be involved in collecting materials for displays, either during the time they spend with you or with their family. Interest tables can include 'taste and touch' tables, displays of natural objects and musical instruments.

Taste and touch tables could include food such as fruit with contrasting taste and flavours, or strongly scented liquids. Such interest tables may need careful supervision. This will give the children the chance to explore the objects safely and gain the most from the sensory experiences available.

Case study 8: Using the senses to examine fruit

Philip has brought a variety of fruit into the playgroup where he works. He shows some of the fruit and at group time displays it on brightly coloured plates on a low table. The eight 4-year-olds involved sit around the table and have great fun touching the different shapes and textures, smelling the fruit and tasting apple, watermelon, mango, kiwi, banana, star fruit and dates.

1   *Which of the five senses do the children use during this activity?*
2   *How does Philip encourage the children to examine the fruit?*
3   *What kind of follow-up work do you think such an activity would lead to?*

Displays of natural objects encourage children to consider items such as shells, pebbles, fir cones, fabric and safe plants. A mixture of common and unusual objects can be displayed. If you prefer the children to look at the objects rather than touch them, they can be part of a wall display or perhaps even hung somewhere in your setting. Displays can even be successfully presented outside. Here are two examples of natural displays:
- a large tray of sand placed in the garden, with a variety of shells of different colours and shapes displayed
- a basket full of brightly coloured, textured, natural fabrics placed on the floor of a baby nursery. The children can be encouraged to take fabrics from the basket and feel, touch and smell them.

Musical instruments are a wonderful way of encouraging children to explore different sounds and other cultures. Avoid displaying too many instruments at once as this may confuse the children.

Thematic displays will help children to relate more closely to their surroundings, giving them an opportunity to interact with their environment. They will also extend their learning by asking questions.

Ways of displaying objects for children

Displays and interest tables should:
- be within easy sight and reach of the children
- stimulate the senses
- extend children's understanding
- make best use of available space
- be safe and secure
- involve the children in collection and display.

The following are ideas to make themed displays more interesting:
- draped cloths as backgrounds
- varied textures as backgrounds
- cardboard boxes to create different levels
- photographs and pictures
- children's work labelled with their names.

When the display is set up you can encourage the children to:
- add to the display
- examine and question its contents
- learn to care for objects.

● *Children examining the contents of a display table*

 Keys to good practice: How to create a healthy and safe display that is part of the curriculum

✓ Ensure the display is at an appropriate height.

✓ Secure any drapes and clothes.

✓ Supervise the use of small objects.

✓ Avoid poisonous objects.

Case study 9: Creating an effective display

The reception class in Holly Primary School are studying different colours during the term. Brendan, a nursery nurse, prepares a wall and table display based on the colour red. He drapes the wall with red textured fabric and mounts photographs of interesting red objects on top of this including a section of a tomato, a red hot-air balloon, etc. All the children are asked to bring in an interesting red object for the table. Brendan displays these on different levels and labels them. On the floor in front of the display is a large red box full of red construction toys for the children to explore. Two group sessions are spent around the display, discussing and exploring the objects children have brought in. Objects vary from a red embroidered Muslim waistcoat to a red patterned wooden spoon from Hungary.

1   *How does Brendan manage to create an effective 'red' display?*
2   *How do the children get involved with the collection?*
3   *Such an activity would probably lead to work in other areas of development. Which other areas can you think of?*
4   *Consider which areas of learning this activity covers.*

Encouraging questions

When you share objects of interest with children in an appropriate manner they will inevitably ask questions. If these questions are answered in a thoughtful way children will be able to extend their knowledge.

Listed below are some objects that may provoke interesting discussion:

- an object photographed in an unusual way
- a piece of clothing from another country
- an unusual food
- a dead beehive or some dried seaweed
- a bucket of frogspawn
- an unusual musical instrument.

How children's learning can benefit from grouping together objects with similar characteristics

By displaying objects with similar characteristics together children can learn to sort and classify them.

There are many activities to encourage children to develop sorting skills. Even a 6-month-old baby can start to develop sorting skills by posting shapes into a sorting box. The following are some of the items that can be used for sorting:

- jigsaws
- shells and stones
- washing
- wooden pegs or bricks
- buttons
- feathers, plastic or wooden shapes.

Did you know?

Sorting and classifying means a way of comparing objects and then deciding what they have in common to link them together.

Case study 10: Grouping

Danny has been asked by his team to plan a sorting activity for the 3–4-year-olds in his care. The team have decided to concentrate on sorting in numeracy-focused activities. Danny plans an activity using small multicultural figures. He reads page 69 of 'Curriculum Guidance to the Foundation Stage' to remind himself that children should match the numbers of objects counted.

Danny lays out the figures randomly in the centre of a low round table and asks four children at a time to join him. He asks the children to do the following, giving them time and support.

- Make a group of four boys.
- Make a group of six girls.
- Make a group of seven boys and girls.
- Make a group of three boys and girls with blond hair.

1 *How do you think Danny prepared the activity?*
2 *How are the children given the opportunity to develop their sorting skills?*
3 *Can you think of three more sorting ideas using the multicultural figures?*

How children's learning can benefit from knowing about their own background and community

By exploring their own background and immediate community children will gain confidence in their learning. They will feel valued and at the same time will learn to value their local environment.

Children can learn and value their own culture in a variety of ways, for example by:

- playing in the home corner where they can experience their home culture
- making homemade books about 'me'
- bringing in photos connected with family activities
- drawing pictures such as 'the house I live in'
- sharing foods from their culture
- dressing up in relevant clothes.

Parents can come in and talk to children or lead activities such as cooking.

To learn about their community you can encourage children to:

- share books about the community
- take instant photos of the local environment
- carry out surveys on the local environment, for example how many cars go past the nursery door
- go on walks and outings to parks, shops, etc.
- go on visits using local transport.

Check it out

Take time to walk around the environment outside your setting. Think of ways to encourage children in your care to learn more about their local surroundings using the following checklist.

- Note special features, for example trees.
- Are there places to walk to?
- Could you safely carry out an activity there, for example take rubbings of different textures?
- Is there something that you could link in with a project, for example posting letters?
- Is there a bus or train journey you could take?
- Is there a local park, pond, etc.?

You could also use **community resources** and invite visitors from the local environment to come into the setting to talk to the children, for example a local community policeman.

Key terms

Community resources: Resources found in the local community such as parks, allotments, libraries, people and organisations.

How to provide a stimulating environment to develop children's curiosity, problem-solving and exploration

To encourage children to be curious, to problem-solve and to explore you will need to make sure that your setting is exciting and challenging. You have already discovered the importance of making sure that children are safe and that you meet their individual needs. You will also need to be aware of the developmental needs of the children you are working with.

Test yourself

Read Unit 203 on children's development and find out what stage the children you are caring for are at in their intellectual development. Carefully read the three diagrams below to find out how you can encourage children to:

- be curious
- problem-solve
- explore.

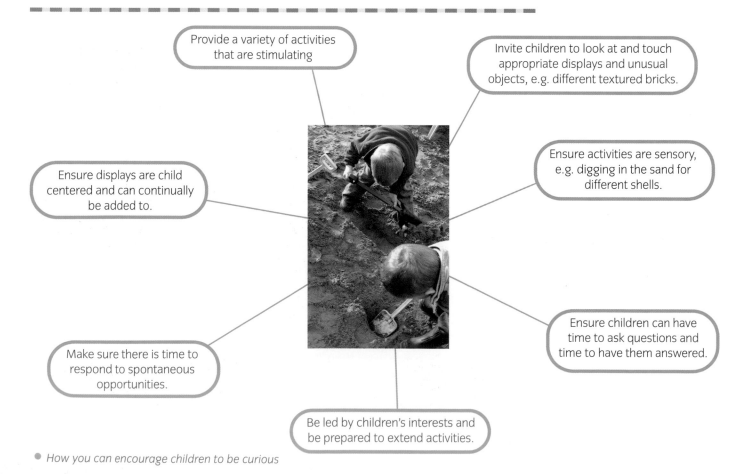

Provide a variety of activities that are stimulating

Invite children to look at and touch appropriate displays and unusual objects, e.g. different textured bricks.

Ensure displays are child centered and can continually be added to.

Ensure activities are sensory, e.g. digging in the sand for different shells.

Make sure there is time to respond to spontaneous opportunities.

Ensure children can have time to ask questions and time to have them answered.

Be led by children's interests and be prepared to extend activities.

● *How you can encourage children to be curious*

Give them praise when they achieve something, e.g. finding out that heavy objects sink such as stones. Remember that you may already know the answer but it is new for them.

Present activities that allow the children to solve problems such as floating and sinking in a water play activity.

Allow them to ask questions.

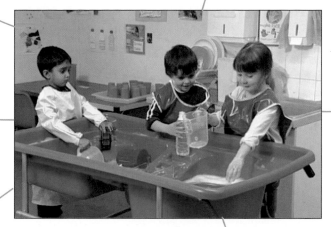

Give children time to investigate.

Allow them to make mistakes.

Give them time to work together, e.g. in group times, perhaps deciding where to put something such as a new piece of furniture or deciding how to encourage everyone to keep the book corner tidy.

● *How you can encourage children to problem-solve*

Invite activities that encourage exploration.

Include a variety of activities.

Encourage exploration of their own bodies through movement and drama.

Encourage children to observe, e.g. by producing a weather chart or exploring their local environment.

Plan activities that relate to children's experiences, e.g. playing in the snow.

Encourage children to listen as well as look, e.g. listening to familiar noises.

Encourage living areas such as gardens where children can plant and watch things grow.

● *How you can encourage children to explore*

Why it is important to understand the scope of practical daily activities to enhance children's learning

The activities that you provide for the children in your care, whatever the stage of their development, can be varied and exciting. There are a variety of examples of daily activities that reflect children's everyday lives. These can take place in the home corner or can be specific activities. Two important activities are gardening and cooking.

Gardening

Gardening can develop children's knowledge and understanding of the world and can be carried out in a relatively small space.

The following table will help you to understand the scope of gardening activities.

Where	• Small garden patch. • Tubs on a balcon.y • Pots indoors. • Old containers such as baby baths. • Small food trays.
What	• Planting and growing seeds, e.g. sunflowers and beans. • Digging and preparing ground. • Watering. • Weeding. • Measuring and observing growth. • Creating wildlife gardens. • Growing food to eat and cook.
How	• Give children daily tasks. • Involve children in planning. • Involve children in recording. • Encourage children to take photos of what they are recording. • Encourage children to watch how plants change as they grow. • Encourage children to care and maintain the gardening area. • Ask parents or grandparents to help and share their expertise. • Visit different gardens to get ideas.

• *Raking leaves*

• *The scope of gardening activities*

When developing a gardening area, you will need to consider:
- the available space
- the age of the children
- how the children can be involved
- the cost
- which areas of the children's development you will encourage.

Check it out

Does your setting give children, however young, the opportunity to garden? If not, make notes as to how you could develop a gardening area and discuss your ideas with your supervisor.

Keys to good practice: How to ensure gardening activities are safe

✓ Check that tools are safe and age appropriate.

✓ Ensure soil, etc. is free of chemicals.

✓ Make sure plants are not poisonous.

✓ Supervise activities.

✓ Make sure children wear gloves as appropriate and wash hands after each gardening session.

✓ Ensure children's needs are considered.

Cooking

Like gardening, cooking can be a very enjoyable experience and can enhance children's learning. You can even cook the food you have grown.

You do not have to be an expert chef to assist children with a cooking activity. Cooking can introduce them to healthy eating and foods from other cultures, while encouraging many areas of their development. Cooking activities can be an important part of the early years curriculum, sometimes involving all six areas of learning. The table below shows how mealtimes can be used to plan for the delivery of the early years curriculum.

Activity	Area of Learning (Foundation Stage curriculum)
• Wash hands before preparing and eating food.	• Personal, social and emotional development.
• Lay the table and count out beakers, plates, etc.	• Personal, social and emotional development. • Problem solving, reasoning and numeracy.
• Learn the names of different foods.	• Communication, language and literacy.
• Talk about favourite foods.	• Communication, language and literacy.
• Recognise name cards.	• Communication, language and literacy.
• Make their own pretend menus, e.g. for a cafe.	• Communication, language and literacy.
• Clear away at the end of the snack or meal (with adult help).	• Personal, social and emotional development.
• Notice the texture and properties. of food while preparing or eating it.	• Knowledge and understanding of the world.
• Pour out drinks, serve food, e.g. using tongs.	• Physical development.
• Lay a table with a pattern, e.g. orange plate, blue plate, orange plate, blue plat.e	• Problem solving, reasoning and numeracy.

● *How mealtimes can deliver areas of learning of the Foundation Stage curriculum*

Whatever the environment, all cooking activities should allow children to join in as much as possible. You will find that older children may be able to help choose a recipe to cook, while you will have to make the choice for younger children.

Remember the following rules when choosing a cooking activity.

- Cooking activities should always be suitable and safe for the age of the children.
- Cooking activities should always encourage healthy eating.

The promotion of children's development

Carefully study the diagram below and consider how children can develop their skills in the different areas of learning when participating in a cooking activity.

Creative development
Choosing colour and shape to create individual results and expressing own ideas

Problem solving, reasoning and numeracy
Counting, weighing and dividing ingredients
Costing and buying ingredients
Looking at shapes and size

Personal, social and emotional development
Working in a group, sharing during the activity
Understanding other cultures
Thinking about personal safety and hygiene
Taking turns

Communication, language and literacy
Naming foods and utensils
Discussing the cooking process
Reading labels and recipes
New words:
whisking, creaming, rolling

Knowledge and understanding of the world
Understanding of other cultures through recipes from around the world
Visiting various shops to buy ingredients
Observing what happens when ingredients react with each other, to heat, to cold, etc.
Asking questions and predicting outcomes

Physical development
Developing manipulative skills and hand–eye co-ordination through stirring, pouring, beating, cleaning, etc.
Developing sensory awareness through taste, feel, touch and smell throughout the activity
Developing gross manipulative skills through clearing away the activity, sweeping, etc.

● Benefits of cooking activities

Health, safety and hygiene procedures

First of all we will consider the importance of providing a hygienic and safe area for children to cook in. Whether you are working in a home, a temporary area or a specifically designed cooking area, hygiene procedures should always be followed.

Keys to good practice: How to ensure safety during a cooking activity

✓ Always wash both adults' and children's hands thoroughly before cooking to avoid cross infection.

✓ Clean all surfaces and equipment thoroughly using a clean cloth to avoid infection.

✓ Ensure that the floor surface is non-slip to avoid accidents.

✓ Use cooker guards and make children continually aware of heat, even after the cooker has been turned off (this is called residual heat).

✓ Keep sharp knives and utensils out of reach of children. Make sure all utensils are safe to use with children. Supervise the use of knives very carefully when used by older children.

✓ Always make sure electrical flexes are safe and kept away from water.

✓ Turn saucepan handles inwards.

✓ Make children aware of utensils that have hot liquid or ingredients in them.

✓ Use aprons. Tie back hair.

How to provide and store ingredients appropriately

Ingredients for cooking and food that is already cooked should always be stored hygienically. This usually means in separate containers. Store perishable ingredients, such as flour, in boxes and containers with tightly fitting lids to keep vermin and insects out. Make sure that food cupboards and shelves are cleaned at intervals.

Keys to good practice: How to store foods safely in a refrigerator

✓ Keep dairy products and meat separate and store them at a low temperature. Keep other foods separate until they are cooked to eliminate bacteria passing from one food to another.

✓ Cover all foods.

✓ Look at 'sell by' dates on foods and do not exceed them.

✓ Make sure that your refrigerator is kept clean and is defrosted regularly.

Contribute to the effectiveness of teams

Wherever you are working you will be a member of a **team**. This might be in the formality of a day care setting or the more informal structure of a private home. The way you work as a team member is crucial to the provision of quality childcare for the children in your setting. In this unit you will discover the importance of your role and the way you treat and support your colleagues. You will also find out that there are many legal and organisational requirements that ensure you provide appropriate care and are protected as an employee.

What you must know and understand:

- The values of your organisation (K207H01)
- Legislation and policy (K207H02–03)
- The organisation of your team (K207H04)
- Principles and theories of teamwork (K207H05–10)
- Contribute to the development of good practice (K207H05)

The values of your organisation

The values of any childcare setting are based on a number of legal requirements. Your organisation will have policies and procedures that will help to ensure that this legal framework is at the heart of your **team's** practice.

Everyone in your setting has a right to the following.

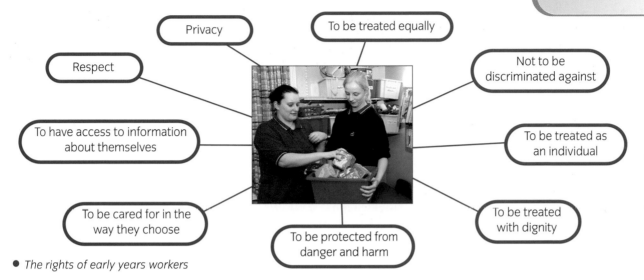

Privacy

To be treated equally

Respect

Not to be discriminated against

To have access to information about themselves

To be treated as an individual

To be cared for in the way they choose

To be treated with dignity

To be protected from danger and harm

- *The rights of early years workers*

Test yourself

In your study group consider the following statements. How might the speakers be showing a lack of respect for the **individuals** concerned?

1. 'I think that Tom better not read that story to the children as he is dyslexic.'
2. 'Amy and Debbie can lay the tables for tea while Ben clears up the garden with the children!'
3. 'Josh, I am really fed up with your excuses for being late even though you are having problems at home.' (Josh is being told off by his manager in front of children in the after-school club for being late.)
4. 'We can't afford to put a safe surface on those steps, you'll just have to be careful when you go down them!'

Legislation and policy

Listed below are the main laws that are the basis to the good practice of your team. These laws will be in very long and detailed language and are only briefly outlined for you here.

Your team will apply these laws through the way that you provide the care and education for the children in your setting.

United Nations Convention on the Rights of the Child

This was signed by the United Kingdom in 1991 and is a formal statement drawn up by a number of nations worldwide to protect the rights of children. This important charter has influenced much current law and public policy. In fact, if you read the charter you will see that the policies and procedures of your setting include these principles.

The charter is split into articles, each one emphasising children's individual rights, for example:

Article 2   All rights apply to all children whatever their background and the State has an obligation to protect children against discrimination.

The Children Act 1989

This Act protects the individual rights of children regardless of race, culture, language and religion. All early years workers in registered settings are expected to treat each child as an individual. This has an influence on all areas of practice from planning the curriculum to providing food that meets the dietary needs of each child.

Childcare Act 2006

OFSTED standards used for inspection have become part of the framework for the EYFS. All providers have to conform to this framework.

Every Child Matters 2004

Since 2004, all children's services in England that work with children and their families are operating within a framework of shared outcomes. These five outcomes were made law in the Children Act 2004. These outcomes are listed below and should form the basis of all early years curriculum planning in England:

- Be healthy
- Stay safe
- Enjoy and achieve through learning
- Make a positive contribution to society
- Achieve economic well being

Special Educational Needs and Disability Act 2001

The first part of this Act gives parents of children with special educational needs more rights to access mainstream education for their children. The second part is a development of the 1995 Disability Discrimination Act.

As a result of this Act, a *Code of Practice For Special Educational Needs* has been produced by the DfES. This clearly outlines how children with special educational needs should be supported. If an early years setting is following the Foundation Stage, this code of practice should also be used. For example, if you have a child with special educational needs in your setting, you will be expected to provide him or her with the same play opportunities as other children. This might mean adapting an outside ball game so that a child who uses a wheelchair can be included. You may come across the term 'inclusion', which means including all children in the activities and play in settings. Early Years Partnerships provide training for practitioners in this area and each setting has an appointed Special Educational Needs Co-ordinator (SENCO) to ensure that the Code of Practice is implemented. The Special Needs Code of Practice is available from the DCSF.

Education Act 1996

This Act influenced the approach early years settings now take towards children with special educational needs. A code of practice must now be followed and parents have the right to full information about their child's progress and attainment. In 2002 this code of practice was revised.

Human Rights Act 1998

This Act gives the individual even more right to privacy and attempts to even further ensure that people are not discriminated against. For example, this Act enforces the fact that each child has a right to education. If your setting is receiving Government funding for children in the Foundation Stage then you are helping to ensure that all 3- to 5-year-olds are receiving an education that is rightfully theirs.

While legislation and policy can be very complicated, it is your responsibility to ensure that you are aware of the rights of all members of your team. It is important that your work setting is free of discrimination. You and the other members of your team have the same rights with regard to discrimination as the children in your setting.

It is your duty to challenge any form of discrimination against yourself or any member of your team. If the discrimination is direct, such as offensive comments, you might be able to challenge the remark immediately. However, indirect discrimination, such as a member of staff feeling their religion is not respected, may take longer to notice and may need to be managed by a supervisor.

Check it out

Find out more about these laws by visiting www.hmso.gov.uk/acts.

Understanding policies that are important to you in your work setting

You have read about the laws that support you and your team in your setting. Your setting will have a range of policies and procedures that will ensure that members of your team conduct themselves appropriately.

Possible area of discrimination	How discrimination can be avoided
Age	People should not be discriminated against because they are either too young or too old. For example, a manager might feel that someone who is in his or her 50s is too old to start training!
Gender	People should not be excluded from any aspect of employment or treated differently because of their gender. For example, a male early years worker should change nappies.
Social status	Employees' accents or backgrounds should not affect their employment and career prospects.
Cultural and racial needs	Individuals' cultural and racial needs must be supported, e.g. Muslims should be allowed time to pray during Ramadan and employers and colleagues should be aware that Muslims will fast during this period.
Health/learning needs	If a person is deemed fit to work with children any need that they have must be supported. For example, an employee with a hearing impairment may have to sit in a certain position during a meeting so that he or she can clearly watch everybody's facial expressions.
Sexual orientation	A person's sexual orientation should not mean that they are excluded from any aspect of employment, e.g. a man who is a homosexual (gay) should be given the opportunity to lead an after-school club.

● *How your work setting should be free of discrimination*

Test yourself

Which act will ensure that you are not discriminated against because of your gender?

Some policies and procedures will protect you as an employee and others will ensure the best possible care and education for the children in your setting. The only way a team can work effectively is by having clear guidance about how each team member should carry out his or her role.

Did you know?

When Ofsted inspect your work setting they will expect effective policies and procedures to be in place. They will also expect individual employees to be familiar with all the policies and procedures of the setting.

The following policies and procedures will be in place in your setting for your team:

- equal opportunities – ensuring that each member of staff has equal rights irrespective of race, gender, religion or culture
- diversity awareness – ensuring that the differences between team members are supported and celebrated

- health and safety – ensuring that the environment and the way staff act in that environment complies with legislation so that each person is safe and healthy.
- dress code – ensuring that team members dress in a professional and appropriate way
- confidentiality – ensuring that all information is treated sensitively and is exchanged appropriately
- disciplinary and grievance – ensuring that team members have a clear and fair way of being treated and making complaints.
- sickness/absence – ensuring that team members have fair sickness benefit and clear procedures to follow
- emergency – ensuring that each team member knows how to proceed in an emergency situation
- security – ensuring the safety of each team member and each team member's responsibility for this
- appraisal – ensuring that each employee's work is regularly and fairly reviewed.

Case study 1: Finding out about the dress code policy

Petra is starting work at a neighbourhood nursery. She is concerned about whether or not she will have to buy a new pair of shoes as she only has a pair of trainers that are comfortable enough to wear all day. Petra also has limited funds and does not want to waste her money on something unsuitable. Petra reads through the staff handbook again and is able to gain the information from the dress code policy that she is required to wear black leather loafers with a low heel. She also discovers that she will have to remove some of her jewellery, as she will only be able to wear a discreet pair of earrings. Petra feels relieved, as she wants to make a good impression on her first day of work.

1 *Is there any other way that Petra could have been made aware of the dress code policy?*
2 *Why do you think the neighbourhood nursery needed a dress code?*
3 *Why do you think the dress code required staff to wear minimal jewellery?*

You will also have to follow policies and procedures that will ensure the best care and education for the children in your setting:
- admissions policy
- curriculum policy
- parents as partners policy
- equal opportunities policy
- behaviour management policy and procedure
- meals, snacks and dietary needs policy and procedure
- rest and sleep policy and procedure

- child protection policy and procedure
- special educational needs policy and procedure
- complaints procedure
- transition procedure
- health and safety policy and procedure
- lost child policy and procedure
- late collection policy and procedure.

In order to implement any policies and procedures you will have to make sure that you always:

- are reliable and flexible
- use your initiative
- are organised
- learn the setting's routines
- get to know the staff
- get to know the parents
- get to know the children.

You will need to read the policies and procedures regularly to ensure that you work with them all the time. If you are unclear about anything you should consult with your supervisor. In your induction your supervisor should:

- discuss the policies with you
- help you to understand your role in implementing the policies
- help you to understand how the policies and procedures should influence your practice in the nursery.

You now know that every setting is required by law to follow health and safety legislation. You must ensure that you are familiar with your setting's health and safety manual and that you are aware of your particular responsibilities in following the health and safety procedures. This will include evacuation, accident and emergency procedures. Below are three important responsibilities that you will have.

> Be aware of any potential hazards and risks and report them immediately to a senior member of staff.

> Always behave in a safe and responsible manner and ensure that your actions do not put yourself or others at risk.

> Be a good role model for the children.

In your work you will have to deal with confidential information and exchange this information in an appropriate way.

Check it out

Ask your supervisor if you can look at your setting's policy and procedures. Carefully note those that affect the children and see how the list compares to the one above. Can you add to the list?

Are there any policies and procedures that are only relevant to your setting or the part of the childcare sector that you work in?

- *Make a note of your setting's policies*

Check it out

Consider the curriculum policy of your setting.

1 What is your role in delivering the curriculum?
2 Who has overall responsibility for the curriculum?
3 How do you know what your responsibilities are?

✓ Keys to good practice: How to deal with confidential information

✓ Only pass information on if you have permission of the person involved.

✓ Only pass information on if you feel it will affect the welfare of the adult or child.

✓ Discuss concerns with your supervisor initially.

✓ Ensure information is exchanged in an appropriate environment.

✓ Ensure you cannot be overheard or written information cannot be seen.

● *Discuss sensitive issues in confidence with your manager*

Recording, reporting and sharing information

Your setting will have ways of recording, reporting and sharing information (see also Unit 204,). The following are basic guidelines for all settings.

- Remember that confidentiality is always essential.
- Understand who information should be shared with.
- Inform people that some information must be shared.
- Avoid gossip at all costs.
- Never discuss situations with people who have no right to know.
- Keep written records in a secure place.

The organisation of your team

The most effective team is one where everybody is aware of their role within the team and what the lines of reporting are. All the team members will feel valued and able to express their views, and will know that they will be listened to. Becoming part of an established team can be difficult and it is therefore important that you are aware of your role and the structure of your setting. The flow chart below shows the typical structure of a setting.

Keys to good practice: How to contribute to good practice

✓ Manage your time effectively.

✓ Listen to instructions and carry them out promptly and accurately.

✓ Think about situations and suggest ways of improving existing practice.

✓ Be confident in your role.

✓ Explain what the objectives of your setting might be (i.e. what your setting wants to achieve).

✓ Suggest where the use of outside resources may be helpful.

✓ Identify poor practice.

✓ Give feedback as appropriate and as requested.

✓ Accept feedback, recognising where further guidance and training could be needed.

Supporting colleagues

To be an effective team member, your colleagues need to feel that you support them in a professional way, i.e. that you undertake your own role and responsibilities seriously.

As well as knowing your role and responsibilities and appreciating that you need to communicate effectively with colleagues, you will need to consider that your own **behaviour** will contribute to positive teamwork.

 Key terms

Behaviour: actions and communications in the work setting.

 Keys to good practice: How your behaviour can contribute to positive teamwork

✓ Carry out all instructions promptly and accurately.

✓ Ensure that you are a good timekeeper and are reliable.

✓ Show a willingness to listen to others and to learn.

✓ Show a willingness to seek help and advice.

✓ Try to offer constructive suggestions and ideas.

✓ Try to work on your own initiative.

✓ Always be pleasant in your manner.

✓ Ensure that you are always polite and courteous to others.

✓ Treat senior colleagues, parents and visiting professionals with respect.

✓ Ensure that your behaviour and dress is appropriate for working with children.

Negative behaviours irritate and upset other staff members and cause problems for them and for the particular person – as well as being unprofessional. A team can feel let down by early years workers who are unwilling to share in all the tasks associated with working with children or who do not 'pull their weight'.

Of course, the opposite can also happen when a team member feels particularly unsupported by others or is given tasks and duties inappropriate to his or her role, perhaps supervising children alone or being asked to speak to parents who are difficult and/or abusive (because nobody else will).

Individuals need to ensure that they are not 'put on' by other members of the team or by senior staff who may abuse a team member's willingness and enthusiasm. In a training situation, a tutor or peripatetic assessor (i.e. one who visits the setting) may be an appropriate person to talk over any difficulties.

Test yourself

Devise a code of conduct for a new member of staff entitled 'How to be an effective team member'. Discuss your code with your supervisor.

Evidence collector
This evidence collector supports elements CCLD 203.1, 203.2, 203.3

Key Skills

Imagine that you are a manager of a childcare setting. You are about to employ a new trainee. Plan an induction programme for the trainee.
The programme will include:

- policies
- procedures
- trainee's role
- code of practice
- lines of reporting
- job description.

You might like to produce this programme on the computer and use it as evidence for this unit.

End-of-unit knowledge check

1 Why are laws made?
2 When was the Children Act passed?
3 Which is the role of a SENCO?
4 Name two policies that your setting might have.
5 Name two policies that will protect the children in your setting.
6 Name two procedures that your setting might have.
7 List three ways of ensuring good practice when dealing with confidential information.
8 What is the role of a manager?
9 What is a job description?
10 Who would you expect to explain your job description to you?
11 List three areas of your work that you feel you do well.

Support the development of babies and children under three

This unit will support your work with babies and very young children. You will be finding out just how much babies can do and, at the same time, how much care they will need from you.

The huge developmental changes that take place within this period make this age range one of the most exciting and interesting to work with. The apparently 'helpless' baby develops into a young child who is highly active, can talk, and is able to explore, think about the world and play imaginatively.

What you must know and understand:

- Why it is important to carry out observations on babies (K2D112 and K2D119)
- How to observe children under 3 (K2D112–113 and K2D118)
- Key theories of child development and current frameworks of effective practice (K2D116)
- The main areas of development and how to support learning and development through play (K2D115, K2D117, K2M120 and K2D121)
- Why it is important to follow the risk assessment and safety policy of your setting (K2H123–124)
- How to encourage babies and young children to try out new and challenging activities (K2D122 and K2D125)
- How to give praise, encouragement and support to babies (K2D126)
- How and why babies communicate and develop language (K2C127)
- How to support the development of communication (K2C128)
- Why it is important to use recognised non-verbal language (K2C129)
- How to bottle feed babies safely (K2H131–133)
- How to wean babies (K2H134–135)
- How to spot signs of illness in babies and young children (K2H136)
- How to care for skin, hair and teeth (K2H137)
- How to change nappies, and wash and dress young children (K2H138–139)
- How to help children with their toilet training (K2D140)

Why it is important to carry out observations on babies

One of the most important requirements of your work with children will be to carry out observations. It is only through careful observation that you are able to really learn about the children in your care and so best meet their needs.

You will find that observations are 'part and parcel' of the everyday routines of day-care settings. They are a requirement of the Foundation Stage guidance for children aged 3 to school age and are also included in the 'Birth to Three Matters' framework. All the early year workers in your setting will need to carry out observations and it is therefore necessary that you become confident in their use.

Observations are also essential and required practice in the new Early Years Foundation Stage (EYFS). You should read the section in Unit 203 on observations (pages 00–00). This will give you the general information you need on how to carry out observations including issues on confidentiality and obtaining permission to carry them out.

 Carrying out observations on children is an important part of your work

How to observe babies and very young children

The method of observing children under 3 is very similar to that of observing older children. The same rules of confidentiality, respect, care and sensitivity apply. You should always ask permission of **parents** before carrying out observations. Much of the information in Unit 203 is applicable for this age range.

You might think that there is not much to 'see' when you are observing younger **babies**. However, the opposite is true. Even observing babies when they are asleep can tell you a great deal about how they may still be attending to the outside world. For example, a practitioner noticed that a baby, who was asleep when her father came to collect her, stirred at hearing her name. You could watch how arm and hand movements change and how babies move their whole bodies, how they watch and follow objects, and how this changes over time. Facial expression, their gurgles, coos, smiles and cries all relate to how babies are feeling and interacting with adults. Observing babies is a rich and rewarding experience.

Check it out

Find out about the Data Protection Act. This sets out what information is available to other people and who has access to information about people, including what we write about children. Parents do have access to such documents and your supervisors will explain the policies and procedures in your setting for recording, storage and access to observations.

Look up the Data Protection Act on the Internet. This will also support you in familiarising yourself with using the internet for research.

How to give praise, encouragement and support to babies

Babies and young children, unless actively discouraged by adults or not given appropriate opportunities to explore their surroundings, experience 'conversations', play and care, are curious about everything. Motivation is therefore not a problem! However, the role of adults is to provide safe opportunities for babies and young children and to give praise and encouragement so that their positive attitude remains. They will then continue to grow and develop in the best way they can. For example, showing a baby how to pat a ball and then praising the baby when he or she pats the ball and it moves a little way encourages the baby to repeat the activity. The baby will learn that his or her actions have a consequence on other things. Babies need to learn that they have choice and some control over their environment with gentle, appropriate encouragement.

How and why babies communicate and develop language

Babies need to communicate with their carers to:
- survive
- make relationships
- find out about the world and everything in it.

Babies need their carers to help them survive – without carers to feed them, change them, keep them warm and safe and provide them with bodily contact, babies would not survive very long. Babies' first vocal communication is crying. The pitch seems to be particularly useful for attracting the attention of adults who (usually) quickly go to find out what is wrong, soothe and comfort. Because of this, babies begin to make relationships with their carers. Babies learn about the world through what their carers do and the opportunities they give to babies to look at and feel objects.

All babies are born with the ability to learn any language in the world. However, by the time they are about 8 months old, they begin to babble using the pace and rhythm of the language they have heard the most. In other words, they are beginning to sort out their own 'home' language. In addition, from the day they are born, babies like faces, especially eyes and mouths. What babies don't like is if the sounds people make don't match up to lip movements. If you have ever watched a 'dubbed' film you will know what that feels like! So, when you are holding a baby and talking to him or her, you will notice how carefully the baby is watching you and learning.

● *Baby communicating visually with carer*

Babies communicate by crying, smiling, making little sounds (which become louder and more 'babbling' by about 8 months), body movements, arm waving and leg movements. They also watch, listen and respond.

How communication develops

The key factors in the development of communication are:

- social interest
- adult interaction
- shared attention
- everyday situations and routines
- baby talk (Motherese or Infant Directed Speech).

Language development from birth to 12 months

General development includes the baby:

- turning to familiar sounds
- varying emotional responses
- taking an interest in faces, especially when the person is talking
- vocalising in response to speech
- producing first sounds – open mouth vowel sounds.

Age	Communication
0–1 month	• Open mouth sounds.
2–3 months	• Cooing, laughing, smiling.
4–6 months	• 'Raspberries', squealing, growling.
6–12 months	• Range of sounds in babbling increases – at 7–10 months 'babbling' is in full flow and has the rhythms of speech. • Shows signs of understanding words at around 7–8 months. • Initiates vocalising to another person. • Shouts to get attention. • Produces lots of non-verbal communicative gestures and some words. • Shared attention and pointing. • Babies use much more rhythmic hand movements at around 6 months, although this can be observed sooner.

● *How communication develops between birth and 12 months*

The emphasis in the first year is on language comprehension, i.e. beginning to understand that the sounds have meaning. Between 10 and 12 months, babies are becoming interested in language production and they start building on the 'babbling' so common at 8 months.

Another reason that talking and interacting with babies is so important is because it helps babies to socialise, to get to know other people and to learn

Check it out

Watch a parent or a colleague talking to a young baby. Notice how the adult gives the baby time to 'reply' and so keep up a conversation.

about themselves. Babies learn from the way other people behave. It is very upsetting for babies if the adult they are with does not talk to them, turns away from them, or pays attention to someone else. They don't know the reasons and work very hard to try to get the adult's attention.

Test yourself

Observe three babies of different ages under a year in your setting. Write down how mobile each of these babies is for his or her age and usual stage of development. Check what sounds they make and how they communicate. You could make your notes in a folder or on a computer as a Development Journal. You could then track these babies as they develop.

Language development from 1 to 3 years

Age	Communication
By 18 months	• Some children have only a few words (if any), while others have around 200! • Comprehension (understanding) usually greater than ability for words.
By 2 years	• Children need fewer cues to understand what someone says. • Vocabulary increases greatly.

2–3 years	• Children begin to use sentences with simple grammar, word and sentence organisation.
	• The following are common:
	  • 'who', 'what', 'where' questions
	  • use of pronouns and possessives
	  • commentary – telling you what is happening and talking to themselves
	  • use of basic categories, concepts and adjectives
	  • 'why' questions
	  • development of attention skills leading to interest in stories.

● *How communication develops between 18 months and 3 years*

How to support the development of communication

The following can support the development of communication in babies:
- Talk and sing to the baby.
- Watch, listen and respond to the baby.
- Use self talk as well as talking to the baby, i.e. talk aloud as you are doing something.
- Use simple gestures to support what you are saying.
- Babies can hear the tone of your voice, the rhythm (how 'up and down' your voice goes), the pitch (how high or low) and the tempo (how quickly or slowly you speak). This makes you interesting and helps the baby work out sounds.

- Babies will look at your face and see a smile or a frown or a blank expression and they will sense your mood and respond to it. Research has shown that babies show distress or worry when their normally responsive carer suddenly shows a very still or blank face.
- Babies can feel what it is like to be with you – how you hold them and whether you are rough or gentle, firm or hesitant – and again will react to the sensations they have with feelings of pleasure, worry or distress.
- Babies will 'tell' you when they need a break, by closing their eyes, turning their heads or simply looking away. Pay attention and allow the baby space.
- Babies learn about turn taking in the two-way 'talking' and listening that they will do with a partner. Take time to let the baby respond to you.
- Babies like to imitate and be imitated. Copying what a baby does helps to establish a 'dialogue'.

If English is not the first language, find out some phrases in the child's home language to encourage continuity between home and the setting. This will illustrate that the home language is valued and will support bilingual learning. Parents' views must also be taken into account.

With older children you could:
- talk about pictures in books
- talk about what you are doing
- talk and sing alongside the older child
- repeat the child's phrases without correcting the child to both check out that you understand and to help the child hear the usual way of sentence construction, tenses, etc.
- help the child learn about the names of objects, colours, etc. by naming them in a *natural* way, for example 'oh look at the yellow flower/the red van,' 'you've got the blue crayon,' and so on.

For children who are visually impaired, opportunities to touch as well as listen are particularly important. It is vital that all practitioners respond to the child's cues which signal a need for interaction or to explore. Deaf children will use visual cues even more than 'normally' hearing children. Careful positioning of the head and body so that the baby or child can clearly see mouth movements, eye direction, etc. will be very important.

Early years workers must note that they may need to be more proactive, for example making sure that lighting supports the child's vision, using exaggerated facial expressions to support meaning and making sure noise levels in the room are not disruptive. 'Ritualised' games, such as peek-a-boo, or 'round and round the garden' where the same actions are repeated, are excellent for all children and also help the deaf child. Such routines provide consistent opportunities for simple language input.

Did you know?

Some researchers have shown that babies as young as 42 minutes can imitate someone sticking out their tongue. These babies watch and then, with a bit of effort, stick out their tongues too!

Parents will need to be consulted regarding any intervention programmes, and specialist help via speech and language therapists will most probably be sought. If parents would like their child to use sign language, carers will also need to learn basic signs to support the child.

Why it is important to use recognised non-verbal language

As well as through the spoken word, people communicate through facial expressions and body language. You do not have to say anything for someone to correctly identify that you are feeling sad, angry, happy, surprised, fearful or disgusted. These feelings are common to all people and are recognised across cultures. This sharing of emotions gives a good starting point for all types of communication. However, it remains that speech is the most common way of interacting and sharing information with others, and verbal speech has to be heard – so what about hearing impaired children for example?

Locke (1995) tells us that research indicates that hearing impaired children babble later than hearing children – for example between 11 and 25 months. Although they do babble eventually, they do not have the hearing 'feedback' that allows them to hear the sounds accurately. The development of their own ability to speak is therefore delayed and has different sound patterns. Hearing impaired children are often taught sign language instead. Again research shows that the earlier sign language is taught, the more 'natural' and fluent the signing.

There are different sign languages such as:
- BSL – British Sign Language
- ASL – American Sign Language.

Different countries have their own sign language but some movements are common to many, such as a headshake meaning no. Men and women may use different signs and there are regional variations in signing for the same objects.

A signing method known as Makaton is often used instead of BSL with people with learning difficulties. Makaton also uses speech alongside signing. This method helps children to link a word to an action or object and is an aid to communication.

BSL is a language with its own grammar and is used fluently by deaf people. In the UK, Makaton signing is based on BSL. As with spoken languages, where there are regional variations of dialect and accent, there are also variations in the signs that are used throughout the UK. The signs from BSL matched to Makaton have been standardised to those used in the South East/London region. This standardisation is to avoid confusion for Makaton users if they move around the UK. (This information is taken from http://www.makaton.org/about/faq.htm.)

Did you know?

In Greek Sign Language a backwards head tilt rather than a headshake means no!

We also know that language is learned not only through hearing but also through watching and matching mouth movements. Recent research seems to indicate that blind babies do 'not necessarily experience a slower development of spoken language' (Locke, 1995), although it is obviously more difficult for blind babies to work out what someone may be talking about. Giving blind babies cues by matching routines with sounds helps them orientate themselves and organise experiences.

Locke, J.L. (1995) The Child's Path to Spoken Language, *London, Harvard University Press*

Care routines

How to prepare bottle feeds

If you are feeling anxious when carrying out any part of physical care, you need to remember that you are not alone – ask any new parent how they felt! The other thing to remember is that feeling a bit nervous is actually a good thing because this means that you care about what you are doing and want to do it right.

Formula feeds are milks that are made especially to be as near to human breast milk as possible. Most feeds are based on cow's milk, which is specially treated, although some are made from soya beans for babies who cannot digest cow's milk.

Soya milk should *only* be given to babies following medical advice to the parents. You should never experiment with babies' milk feeds or substitute what the parent has recommended or provided with another type of milk.

If breast milk is not given to a baby, *only* formula milk feeds should be used. Formula milk itself is not without its dangers. If it is made up incorrectly, it can also cause problems for babies. For example, if it is made up too strongly it can lead to excessive weight gain, whereas if it is not strong enough, it can lead to poor weight gain, constipation and a hungry distressed baby.

For this reason all formula milks have precise instructions as to how they should be measured and made up. All makes will include their own measuring scoops which are specifically designed for that particular milk, so you must not swap them around – no matter how tempting this might be when you are busy and making up many feeds. There is a range of starter milks for young babies and 'follow-on' milks for older babies, so you need to read the packet or tin carefully and make sure that the milk is suitable for the age of baby you are going to feed. The packet or tin of milk powder will often state the recommended amount according to weight as well as age, because weight is a much safer guide in the first 12 months.

Check it out

Babies of varying ages will require different quantities of feed. You must make absolutely sure of the amount of feed each baby in your care will require – never guess.

in a microwave oven – it may cause isolated 'hot spots' and the milk continues to heat after you have removed the bottle, even though the bottle might feel cool.

Shake the bottle of milk well so that the warmth is evenly distributed throughout. You can then safely test the temperature by dropping a small amount of milk on the inside of your wrist. The milk should feel 'comfortable' on your skin.

How to wash and sterilise equipment

All babies' bottles, teats, cover tops and plastic utensils should be washed thoroughly using washing-up liquid in hot water. Make sure every trace of milk is removed, squirting water through the teats and using a bottle brush for the bottles. This may take some time and appear to be a chore but it is vital to avoid sickness in young babies. Rinse everything in clean water – tap water is fine here.

There are a number of ways of sterilising all feeding equipment for babies:
- chemical sterilisers – this is the most common method of sterilisation
- steam sterilisers –these are specially designed for sterilising bottles and are both quick and efficient
- microwave bottle sterilisers – these are designed specifically for sterilising bottles – an ordinary microwave does *not* sterilise bottles
- boiling – the cheapest method of sterilising, used to be the most common method.

Sterilisation is important for any equipment that is involved in feeding a baby or that is going into a baby's mouth. Plastic jugs, drinking cups, spoons, dummies and all equipment used for expressing breast milk should be washed and sterilised in the same way.

How to store feeds

Newly made-up formula milk can be stored in the fridge for 24 hours. It must then be thrown away if unused to reduce the risk of germs being transferred from other foods in the fridge. This also avoids confusion as to when feeds were made up.

Breast milk can also be stored in the fridge for 24 hours after expressing but then must be discarded for the same reasons. Expressed milk can be frozen for up to three months and, once defrosted, needs to be used within 24 hours.

Any milk left after the baby has finished feeding should be thrown away immediately. Never re-warm the feed or put back into the fridge as a partly finished feed is an ideal home for germs.

Check it out

Do the following exercise to see why it is important to measure feeds correctly.

1 Borrow or buy a small tin of formula milk and practise measuring using the scoop and three plates.
2 Press the milk down into the scoop and then empty it on to a plate.
3 Scoop the milk against the side of the tin and empty it on to a plate.
4 Scoop the milk gently and level it with the back of a knife (as in good practice) and empty it on to a plate.

You may be surprised at the difference in the amount of milk powder on each plate.

Check it out

In your setting, what methods are used for sterilising equipment? What are the policies and procedures in your setting for preparing feeds?

Write these down or make a photocopy to put into your portfolio.

Make sure you replace the lid on the milk powder firmly and store it in a cool dry place. If milk powder gets damp, it becomes lumpy and difficult to measure accurately.

How to bottle feed babies safely

When you care for a baby it is important that you are familiar with the routine already established by the parents. This means that either your supervisor or the baby's key worker will have discussed the best way of incorporating the baby's needs and the parents' wishes into the daily running of the early years setting. The routine agreed to should be recorded so that as feeding patterns change with the baby's needs, parents can be kept informed and vice versa.

As you know from Unit 203, a baby is born with two important reflexes. These are the rooting reflex and the sucking reflex. The rooting reflex makes the baby turn its head towards a touch on one side of the mouth to find something to suck. It immediately begins to suck vigorously – the sucking reflex. In other words, as soon as the baby is born it is ready to feed.

A baby has a powerful need for food to enable it to grow rapidly in the first year of life and particularly in the first few months. Birth weight is usually doubled by 6 months and trebled by 12 months. In addition to this, the brain itself grows very rapidly in this time so it is very important that sufficient food is given to enable this development to take place. (It is said that we learn more in the first year of life than at any other time and so plenty of food is needed to support this learning.)

Babies will usually wake from a sleep when they are ready for a feed. It is neither necessary nor good practice (unless on medical advice) to wake babies to fit into a routine specified by the setting rather than the child's needs. Sleepy babies will not usually feed well, while babies who are made to wait until 'feed time' are often too upset and distressed by then to enjoy it. Sometimes it may be necessary to establish a routine which also fits in with the demands of the setting, but flexibility must be maintained to meet the needs of individual babies.

A healthy baby who is feeding well should show certain signs, for example:
- shows consistent weight gain of approximately 130–170g per week (6–8oz) for the first four months
- skin is warm and silky, and firm and elastic to touch
- mucus membranes (the inside of the mouth and nose) are pink and moist no matter what the skin colour
- is alert when awake, moving and kicking well
- is eager for feeds or attention
- may cry if feed is delayed but settles quickly
- is calm and relaxed when fed

Check it out

What are the guidelines in your setting for recording times and amounts of feeds? Is there a form to include in your portfolio? If not, you may like to make up one of your own. You could use a computer to make up a basic chart and then alter it if you want to add more information. Information must include:
- the date
- the time
- the amount of feed taken.

Can you think what other information might be included on your chart?

- sleeps well between feeds
- passes urine and stools (faeces) easily without discomfort.

Preparing for a bottle feed

- Wash your hands before starting and then collect all the equipment needed for feeding.
- Have everything ready so the baby does not have to wait too long!
- Put the already prepared bottle of milk into a jug of hot water to warm and stand it on a tray. The teat and the teat cover should be in place.
- You may also need a bib to protect the baby's clothes, and some tissues or muslin squares.
- If appropriate, change the baby's nappy before starting to feed. However, some babies cannot wait this long and want to feed immediately on waking. In these circumstances, a nappy change can be done halfway through the feed or at the end, depending on the needs of the baby.
- Before settling down to feed the baby, find a calm relaxed area with a safe place to put the bottle during breaks. Look for a comfortable chair which will support your back. Allow plenty of time to feed so that you and the baby can enjoy the experience.
- Check the temperature of the milk and its flow from the teat by turning the bottle upside down and allowing a few drops to fall on the inside of your wrist. It should flow freely – a few drops per second – and feel warm (not hot or cold).
- Stimulate the 'rooting reflex' by gently touching the side of the baby's mouth with the teat. Place the teat in the baby's mouth over the tongue.

● *Adopting a comfortable feeding position*

- Tilt the bottle so that the hole in the teat is always covered with milk. This avoids the baby becoming frustrated and sucking and swallowing air instead of milk.
- Keep good eye contact (this is very important) and hold the baby firmly so that the baby feels secure.
- Relax and talk to the baby to give reassurance. A baby will sense if you are tense or rushed and will not feed as well.

Giving a bottle feed

- Remember that feeding time is important for the baby socially and emotionally – not just physically.
- Maintain eye contact and talk to the baby during the feed.
- Never leave a baby propped up with a bottle no matter how busy you are. It is unsafe because choking could occur. In addition, the baby is deprived of a very important time for social contact and emotional interaction with adult carers.

- Do not rush. The baby does not know or understand that you are in a hurry and often will become distressed and difficult to feed – actually taking longer than if you had accepted the fact that babies need time.
- Don't chat to others while feeding and ignore the baby.
- Break from feeding after 10 minutes, or approximately halfway through the feed, to give the baby a 'breather' or to 'wind' the baby. 'Wind' is caused by the baby swallowing air with the milk, which can be very uncomfortable. Note that 'winding' a baby is not practised by all cultures.
- Continue to feed until the baby appears to have had enough milk by pushing out the bottle with his or her tongue and/or turning away from the bottle. 'Wind' again if necessary and change the nappy, if required.
- Don't worry if the baby brings back small amounts of milk during or after feeds, but is otherwise happy and healthy and gains weight. This is caused by a weakness in the muscles at the opening of the stomach. Eventually the muscles become stronger and the baby will grow out of it. This is known as 'possetting'.

Settling the baby after a feed

- Gently clean the baby's face with dampened cotton wool to ensure that milk is not left on the skin. Never 'scrub' around the mouth.
- If necessary, check the nappy again and change it if required.
- Some babies will want to sit in a baby chair or play for a little while after a feed, while others (especially very young babies) will want to return to sleep. Whatever the needs, you should make sure the baby is safe while you clear away. If you put the baby into a baby chair make sure the straps are securely fastened and it will support the baby sufficiently. Always choose a chair appropriate for the age of the baby. Position the chair so that the baby can see you or other adults within the room.
- Provide one or two objects of interest, such as a rattle, mobile, natural sponge, hand whisk, piece of shiny material or paper, etc., depending on the age and stage of development of the baby.
- If a baby appears sleepy, settle the baby safely into a cot or pram.

Some common problems associated with feeding

Colic

This is an attack of abdominal pain (stomach ache) in which the baby may draw the knees up and cry desperately. It is sometimes called 'three-month colic' as it usually disappears by the age of three months. There is no known cause and no effective cure. Attacks can last from 15 minutes to several hours and often occur at the same time of day, frequently early evening.

What to do

The baby should be cuddled, rocked and comforted as far as possible. Your supervisor may seek advice from a doctor or health visitor if the parents have not already done so.

Vomiting (being sick)

When a baby returns some or all of its feed, and is not just 'possetting', this is known as vomiting. It is a sign that the stomach cannot tolerate the feed. You must report vomiting *immediately*. You will be asked to observe the baby closely while in the setting, as the baby can lose a lot of fluids quickly if vomiting persists.

What to do

Your supervisor will probably advise the parents to seek medical advice promptly or medical help will be sought, depending on the circumstances. It will help the parents and the doctor if you can judge the amount vomited and what it looks like. You should record the information on the feeding record every time the baby is sick.

Constipation

This can be quite a common problem and some babies seem to suffer constipation with different types of baby milks. Signs of constipation are very small, hard or infrequent stools, and the baby is often uncomfortable and strains. It can be caused by underfeeding, making the feed with too much powdered milk (i.e. too concentrated), dehydration (low fluid intake) or a change in type of milk.

What to do

If the feeds are being made correctly and records show that the baby is not underfeeding, then extra fluids should be given. Cooled boiled water can be given in a sterile bottle. Never add laxatives to milk feeds or water. Parents will be advised to speak to a health visitor or doctor if it persists.

Diarrhoea

This is caused by feeds rushing through the digestive system too quickly and resulting in watery loose stools being passed frequently. It may be caused by poor food hygiene or bottle preparation or an infection. Diarrhoea is a serious condition as the baby may lose a lot of fluid very quickly, particularly if vomiting occurs as well.

What to do

Medical advice should be sought quickly to avoid dehydration (low levels of fluid) and medical treatment obtained. If you notice that a baby has diarrhoea, report it to your supervisor *immediately*.

Overfeeding

If feeds are correctly made up and accurate records are kept, overfeeding should not be a problem. However, a baby may enjoy food too much and demand more and more, or the parents may feed the baby excessively as a solution to stop the baby from crying. The signs and symptoms of overfeeding are that the baby may vomit (be sick), pass large stools and gain excessive weight. The baby may become very unsettled and may develop sore areas around the anus.

If you are worried that a baby may be overfed, you should inform your supervisor, who may seek advice from a doctor or health visitor following discussion with the parents.

Underfeeding

Again, accurate record keeping and feeds made correctly according to the instructions should avoid this condition. If a baby comes to the setting underfed it is advisable to increase the frequency of feeds (i.e. give more feeds), before increasing the quantity (giving larger amounts) – although any feeds you give an underfed baby will be under supervision. The signs and symptoms are that the baby will be hungry, waking and crying for feeds frequently. There will be poor weight gain. The stools may be small, dark and hard. The baby may vomit (be sick) because of swallowing air when crying and may be difficult to feed.

Allergies and milk intolerance

You may wonder why a baby in your setting is on a soya-based milk feed instead of the more usual cow's milk-based formula milks. Some babies develop an intolerance to cow's milk protein. This means that normal formula milk will cause the baby to have diarrhoea, sickness (vomiting) and show a failure to thrive (not showing the usual pattern of weight gain and growth). Medical advice will have been sought in order to establish whether a change to a soya-based formula feed would be advisable. If there is a strong history of allergies in the family and breast feeding is not possible, the family may have been referred to a paediatrician (a doctor who is a child specialist) or an immunologist (a doctor who specialises in allergies) before the baby is born for advice on feeding.

Pyloric stenosis

You may have heard about pyloric stenosis, which is a condition seen usually about three to six weeks after birth. The baby feeds hungrily but then will vomit (be sick) in a way that shoots the feed several feet away. It is often called 'projectile vomiting'. The baby becomes constipated and dehydrated (lacking in fluids) and stops gaining weight. It is more common in boys than girls, but is easily diagnosed by a doctor. Pyloric stenosis is usually cured by a simple operation to widen the outlet of the stomach and allow food to pass through into the gut.

Check it out

What are the policies and procedures in your setting for reporting and recording problems with feeding or signs of illness in a baby? Obtain or make a copy and keep it for your portfolio.

How to wean babies

For the first four months after birth, babies cannot properly digest any foods other than breast or formula milk. Weaning is the term used for the gradual introduction of solid food to the baby's diet and people often refer to 'solids' when talking about weaning foods. The process of weaning usually begins when a baby reaches about 4–6 months of age. However, all babies are individuals and some may start a little earlier and some later, although most babies are ready for solids by 6 months of age. Babies who are premature will be ready at different times and the parents should seek medical advice from a doctor or health visitor before starting the weaning process.

Introducing solids too early will put a strain on the baby's digestive system, which is not yet ready to deal with solid food. It may also increase the likelihood of allergies or obesity (overweight). However, it is generally wise to introduce some solids by the time the baby reaches 6 months. The solids can be gradually built up so that by the end of the first year solid food becomes the main part of the diet with breast or formula milk to drink.

An important question is how parents and carers can know if a baby is ready to start this exciting new phase in life. Fortunately, babies are likely to exhibit some tell-tale signs which show when they may be ready to start the weaning process. Some of these signs are that the baby might:

- seem hungry after finishing a feed but does not want any more milk
- become unusually unsettled or unhappy
- require more frequent feeds than before
- wake during the night, having previously slept straight through.

Staff and parents should agree about how to manage the process of weaning and whether there are any foods that the baby should not have for medical, cultural or religious reasons.

Some parents want to start their babies on solid foods very early, as they feel pressure from others to move on to the next stage. They may also think it will help the baby sleep through the night. If the parents talk to you, you should understand these feelings but suggest that they discuss their ideas with a senior colleague, seek advice from their health visitor or visit their local baby clinic. You could tell them that (unfortunately) a baby who has never slept through the night is unlikely to change this habit simply by taking solids. On the other hand, some parents are very anxious about weaning and want to wait as long as possible. If the baby is showing clear signs of needing to start the process of weaning you should report it to your supervisor, who could explain to the parents why it will be beneficial or suggest sources of advice.

Why babies need to start taking solid foods

- From about 6 months of age, milk will not satisfy a baby's nutritional needs. The body will require more of the different nutrients, especially

Check it out

What information is provided in your setting regarding different cultural or religious requirements for any of the babies in your care?

iron, in order to maintain healthy growth and development.

- Babies need to develop the chewing action. Chewing develops the muscles around the mouth and jaw, which will also help the development of speech.
- Solid foods give more bulk to the diet and so satisfy a hungry baby's appetite.
- By introducing new tastes and textures the baby can begin to join in family meals.
- Eating solid foods will give a baby the chance to develop new skills that will encourage independence. These include feeding with finger foods and using a beaker or cup and cutlery.

No one should feel under any pressure to wean a baby at a certain time. All babies are individuals and develop at their own pace. All parents have different views and their wishes should be respected at all times. However, if these wishes seem to be detrimental in some way, then either direct advice or sources of specialist advice should be made available.

How to start the weaning process

- Do not rush.
- Give babies time to adjust to the change from receiving food simply from a bottle or breast. They have only known food as a fluid and solid food has a different taste and texture (feel). When they spit food out it is more likely to be because it is not familiar to them than because they dislike it. Babies need to progress at their own pace, discovering this new experience.
- Make it an enjoyable process for the baby.
- Relax and take time for feeding during the weaning process. The baby may still want to be cuddled while being spoon fed at the beginning. Talking softly and maintaining eye contact are ways of reassuring the baby and have a calming effect. As you introduce new foods remember that the baby may like foods that you detest, so try to be positive when introducing all new tastes.
- Do not 'force' the baby to feed – babies usually know when they have had enough to eat.
- Make sure the baby experiences a variety of foods.

Healthy eating

It is never too early to think about establishing healthy eating patterns, especially in view of the current concerns over obesity. Healthy eating means that the baby is offered plenty of fruit, vegetables and pulses as well as meat, fish, eggs and cereals at the appropriate times. In addition, parents and early years workers must remember that many babies need snacks between meals to ensure that their energy levels remain high (remember all that brain and body growth). Such snacks should mainly consist of pieces of fruit, raw vegetables or fingers of bread (or breadsticks) as appropriate. Sweet foods such as biscuits should be kept to a minimum.

Feeding as learning

Babies like to feed themselves! Babies soon start to investigate their food and will put their fingers in it to feel it. This is a great learning opportunity to investigate through feeling temperature and texture and is the start of independence in feeding – as well as being huge fun for babies! When they are able to hold a spoon, babies can be given their own spoon to 'help' feed themselves.

Babies will make a mess and, whatever the setting, staff should anticipate this. Rather than trying to avoid it, it is necessary to prepare for it (and parents will be advised to do the same). Any carpets could be covered with plastic sheeting and your own clothes can be protected with an apron. Babies' clothes will need covering with a bib and any soft furnishings should be covered or removed.

Eating is a social activity and eating alongside other people helps the development of positive social skills and emotional well-being. The opportunity for babies to interact with carers during feeding is very important. As they get older and more independent, during mealtimes children learn to share, to help others, to use eating implements and to talk to one another. Other aspects of development are also supported, for example:

- learning concepts such as 'more' or 'less', 'a bit of', 'a piece', 'a slice', quarters, halves, spoonfuls, etc.
- counting out knives and forks or other implements
- different sizes of plates and mugs
- different colours of implements.

Different types of weaning foods

Parents may provide food they have cooked themselves or be happy to use commercial baby foods. If you are using dried food in packets, the food

Keys to good practice: How to ensure good hygiene

✓ Always use a separate plate and spoon for the baby and wash them thoroughly after use.

✓ Clean and disinfect all food preparation thoroughly.

✓ Wash your hands and nails carefully prior to feeding a baby and tie back your hair if necessary.

✓ Wash the baby carefully after a meal of solid foods – the baby may manage to spread food to many areas of his or her hands, face, neck, ears and hair!

will need to be made up with formula milk, breast milk or cool, boiled water depending on the age of the baby, the parents' wishes and manufacturer's instructions.

Stages in weaning

Stage 1

The first food a baby eats will be puréed. This means the food will be made into a smooth paste just a little thicker than milk and with no lumps. Some foods will need extra fluids to purée successfully. Cooled boiled water, expressed breast milk or formula milk should be used.

Examples of 'starter' foods are fruits or vegetables such as pears, apples or carrots, or a little baby rice. The temperature of the food should be lukewarm.

In the first few weeks the baby will still be having milk as the main 'food' with just one or two teaspoons of weaning food.

To avoid a hungry baby becoming frustrated it is wise to give some of the bottle feed first until the solids become more familiar. Eventually you will be able to give solids first and top up with a milk feed.

Weaning foods should be introduced as follows:
- Together with the parents, establish a time when the baby is most hungry.
- Do not rush these first attempts at solid food.

Keys to good practice: How to maintain good hygiene

- ✓ Never leave prepared food uncovered at room temperature before or after preparation, as this can be a breeding ground for germs and germs can cause infection.
- ✓ Throw away any food that has been warmed ready for a meal and left uneaten – do not put it back into the fridge for later.

- Ensure the baby is sitting well supported on your lap.
- Put a little puréed food onto a plastic spoon – a plastic spoon is advisable because it is softer than metal, can be sterilised and has no sharp edges.
- Place the spoon gently between the lips and allow the baby to suck the food off.
- Introduce only one food at a time and let the baby get used to it before changing to another taste.

The baby may roll the food around in the mouth and not swallow any. Many early years workers or parents can be worried about this and think

Young babies pass urine very frequently, but the number of times they open their bowels (pass faeces or stools) varies greatly. As a guide, bottle-fed babies pass stools less often than breast-fed babies. A normal stool from a bottle-fed baby is likely to be firm, well formed and slightly smelly. A stool from a breast-fed baby is likely to be more fluid and yellowish-mustard in colour. It does not smell unpleasant and is passed frequently, sometimes at every feed. As babies become older and begin to take solid food, their bowel habits will alter and will usually become more predictable and regular.

Babies or toddlers should never be left in a wet or dirty nappy just because a particular time in the daily routine has not been reached. If you are looking after babies and you are not very sure about the type of 'signal' any individual baby might give to show that they are wet or uncomfortable, then there is no harm in having a quick check from time to time.

Individual settings may have particular procedures for getting rid of wet and/or dirty nappies (such as lidded buckets or specially designed disposal units). They may also like to use particular cleaning agents and have a preference for when you put on disposable gloves and so on. You must always follow the procedures of your setting. Your supervisor will help you by answering any queries you might have, especially if there are any differences between what we set out here and what they suggest.

Check it out

What are the safety and hygiene policies and procedures within your early years setting for washing babies and very young children?

The procedure for changing nappies

● *Always wash your hands thoroughly with hot water and soap before you start – a quick rub under the tap will not do! Dry your hands carefully.*

Make sure you have all the equipment you will need:
1 wipes **2** cream (if using) **3** cotton wool **4** changing mat
5 disposable gloves and apron **6** nappy of right size for child
7 nappy disposal bags if using* **8** spare clothes if necessary
9 bowl of warm water

*If the setting has a specially designed disposal unit such as a 'sangenic', make sure you know how to use this correctly.

Clean the mat using the setting's preferred method. Don't assume other people have remembered to clean the mat after using it.

After washing your hands, put on an apron (but check the setting's procedure in case they want you to wait until you have collected the baby)

Make sure any waste disposal bins are not full. If they are full, you must empty them following the setting's procedures. Then wash your hands.

Give the changing area and your equipment a final check before you go to collect the child. Check, for example, that there are enough disposable gloves in case you need a fresh pair during the nappy change.

● Talk to the baby or young child while you are changing the nappy. If the baby seems a bit upset, be gentle and soothing – not every baby likes being 'changed'.

● Lie the baby or toddler on the mat. Make sure the baby is in a safe position and comfortable. Make sure your bowl of warm water is not cold!

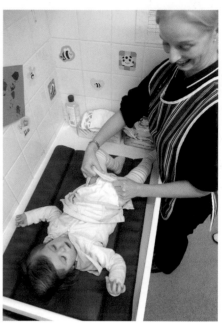

● Remove the baby's clothing as necessary

Never leave the baby or toddler alone. If you have forgotten something and it is in another room, take the baby with you or call for another member of staff to get it for you. Also make sure that you are always close to the child – keep all your equipment close to hand and any bins or disposal units within easy reach.

Put on your disposable gloves. If the baby's or toddler's clothes are soiled, you should put on your gloves before you start removing any of the baby's clothing.

Do not make faces or comment about a dirty nappy however unpleasant it may be (unless in a playful way with a smile, such as saying 'my goodness, someone had a full tummy'). If you show disgust, the baby won't know why you are pulling a face but may get upset because of the feelings he or she can sense, and the toddler might feel that something about him or her is 'bad'.

If your gloves have got dirty, change them for a fresh pair before you start to dry the baby. Dispose of the dirty ones safely.

Check it out

If the baby is in Terry nappies or re-usable nappies of any sort, make sure you know what to do with these by checking with your supervisor.

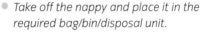
- Take off the nappy and place it in the required bag/bin/disposal unit.

- Gently (don't 'scrub'!) clean the baby or toddler's front and bottom area with either the parents' preferred wipes, or soft disposable cloth or cotton wool and warm water. Always remember to clean from front to back – never from the bottom forwards.
- Carefully dispose of soiled wipes, etc. in the bin or disposal unit.
- Dry the area carefully but thoroughly. Damp in skin creases can become very sore. Apply cream if this is the parents' preference or has been medically advised. Put on a clean nappy.

Before you put on the clean nappy, some babies enjoy the chance to move their legs and have a kick without the restriction of a nappy. Take the time to talk to the baby, play tickle games, sing, tell a rhyme or use a toy if you are more comfortable with this to share a playful time together. Follow the baby's lead! The section on development will have emphasised that babies and very young children need people to talk to and play with so that they learn many important things. So nappy changing, washing and dressing is not just about keeping a baby or toddler clean and dry, it is also a time for you and the child in your care to have some precious time together. You can make the experience the child has pleasant, rewarding and even fun!

If a work colleague is in the same room with you, try hard not to get involved in a conversation with your colleague as this will take your mind off the baby and babies find this upsetting. Mistakes may also be made when you are not concentrating.

You may need to put clean clothing on the baby or young child, so make sure that any dirty clothing is put into the correct laundry bag if washed on the premises. Alternatively, follow the setting's instructions for the safe storing of dirty clothing if it is to be sent home. When clothing and linen are washed and dried, they should be aired properly, stored in a dry place such as an airing cupboard and carefully labelled.

- Dress the baby taking your time and telling the baby what you are doing. Have a conversation! Take off your gloves and dispose of them in the bin or bag provided but you may still leave on your apron as you have to return to clean and tidy the area. You must change your apron if it has got dirty in any way before you pick up the baby again.

Take the baby back to the group room. Spend a few moments making sure that the baby is comfortable and settled. Tell the baby that you are going to tidy up and will be back. Don't just put the baby down and leave!

Return to the changing area and wipe the changing mat in the way preferred by your setting. Dispose of the cloths you have used in the correct bags or bins. Remove your apron once you have completely finished your tasks and put it in the correct bin.

Update the nappy changing chart and the individual baby's record as appropriate according to the procedures of the setting.

If the bins or disposal units are now full, follow the setting's instructions for emptying this type of 'waste'.

Before you leave the nappy-changing area, have a quick look round to make sure that everything is clean and tidy. You may have noticed, for example, that the box of disposable gloves was running low and it would be helpful to put out a new box or report the fact that additional equipment is required. Try not to leave such things to someone else – it is your responsibility too.

Make sure you both write down *and* report to your supervisor as soon as possible if you notice anything out of the ordinary such as the following.

- You may notice a rash.
- The stool or urine may be unusual in some way, such as having a different colour or smell. For example, the urine may smell 'fishy' or look very dark. Some changes would be cause for serious concern and must be reported. These include:
  - small, hard, greenish-brown stools (may cause pain for the baby to pass) – this could be constipation
  - very frequent unpleasant-smelling frothy green stools – may indicate an infection
  - a normal stool streaked with blood – may indicate an injury or an open crack around the anus (back passage)

- a sudden decrease in the amount of urine passed over several nappy changes – may be a sign of illness
  - very frequent passing of watery stools (diarrhoea) – a sign that food is not being absorbed properly. This condition also means that the baby loses a lot of fluid and can become ill very quickly, especially if they are being sick too. Any signs must be reported immediately.
- Unusual marks or bruises, which are usually frequent when a baby is learning to walk, should always be reported and recorded in case abuse (deliberate harm by someone) is suspected.
- You may notice signs of illness, for example a 'floppy' baby, a very hot, flushed baby or child, a baby or child who is unusually quiet or irritable.
- You must always report any signs of a change in behaviour, changes in skin tone, marks, bruises and so on. Very young babies cannot tell you how they are feeling and therefore you must bring to the attention of your supervisors anything, no matter how minor it may seem, that may cause concern.

Case study 3: Changing nappies

Sue and Jane are nursery nurses in a day-care setting looking after young babies. They are each changing a baby's nappy in the same room. They are very careful how they handle their babies – they change the nappies correctly and dispose of the dirty ones hygienically and safely. While they are changing the nappies, washing the babies and dressing them again, they are discussing a film they had both watched the previous evening. When nappy changing is finished the babies are returned to their cots for a sleep.

1   *Have Sue and Jane shown 'good practice'?*
2   *What might they have done differently?*
3   *How might the babies have reacted to this type of care?*

Children are, of course, not in nappies for ever. Over time 'toddlers' begin to understand about their bodies and begin to associate certain feelings with different causes and outcomes. One of the biggest physical changes is when children begin to be ready to control their own bodily functions. This is generally known as 'toileting'.

There is often great pressure on children – and their parents – to toilet train children as soon as possible, but trying to get a child to use the toilet too early can lead to many problems. Sometimes there almost seems to be a 'race' between parents to see whose child is 'dry' earliest! Early years settings too can often inadvertently put pressure on parents by admission policies, which only allow children over 3 who are toilet trained to come to the setting. The information set out below will help you support children during this phase.

How to help children with their toilet training

The golden rule about toilet training is that it should only be started when the child is ready. It is the child who should lead the way – not the adult. Many children develop the physical and cognitive skills needed sometime between 18 months and 2 years. However, there are always children who may be ready a little earlier and children who may not be quite ready until around 3 years. Some children may even be slightly older than this. Toilet training also takes time. It can take three months for the child to get the idea, and then this may only be daytime success! The other thing to remember is that girls appear to be easier to toilet train than boys, but no one really knows why.

The following checklist shows the ways in which a child will 'tell' the parent or carer that they are ready.

- The child begins to have bowel movements more regularly and often at predictable times, for example in the morning after breakfast, or will 'pee' about an hour after a big drink.
- The child is physically able to pull pants up and down or at least makes some effort to do so.
- The child is beginning to show interest in what happens in the bathroom and may also show an interest in wearing pants rather than nappies.
- The child shows signs of active awareness that a bowel movement is happening such as grunting, squatting, telling you, etc. Compare this to how a baby seems unaware of bowel movements and this development shows you that bodily sensations are changing.
- The child has words for stool and urine such as 'poo' and 'wee' or 'wee wee,' etc. (It is helpful to find out what words the family uses for these functions so that a child with minimal language can be understood.)
- The toddler must be able to follow simple instructions such as 'go get your shoes', otherwise he or she is simply not going to understand anything you are trying to do!
- Toddlers begin to show that they understand the feelings they have in their bodies which mean they need to 'go'. Over time they will be able to signal or tell you that they need the potty or the toilet. In the early stages, signals such as the child holding himself or herself in the groin area, wriggling, looking uncomfortable or pulling at clothing may all be letting you know that the child is aware of different sensations.
- The child may dislike the feeling of being in a dirty nappy.
- Just as bowel actions are becoming more regular and predictable, another sign is that the child can be 'dry' for three of even four hours at a time. This shows that the bladder muscles are now developed enough to hold and store the urine. What is also noticeable is that the child will release more urine at one go rather than smaller amounts more often.

Another useful milestone showing readiness for toilet training is that the child is positive about it. The child has now understood that many things have a 'place' and that it is important to put things where they belong – and this includes bodily waste! It is important that the child is also beginning to want to be independent and do things for himself or herself. Being able to manage bodily functions is a huge step towards becoming independent.

The child must also be able to physically walk and sit down safely and comfortably. This may seem obvious but these are all skills that have to be learned.

Finally, children need to be motivated to be toilet trained. The child's desire to please parents and other key adults is what helps here. It is important that parents or key workers show pleasure when the child uses the potty or toilet and do not show anger or disgust when the child has 'accidents'.

Some do's and don'ts to help a child

- Do make sure you have found out what the parents' wishes are and how they are managing this important stage. There must be consistency between home and setting. If the parents appear to be over anxious, senior colleagues should be able to help and support the parents in good practice. Health visitors are often a very good source of additional information and advice for both parents and staff in settings.
- Do take things slowly. Some children become dry during the day very quickly and others take much longer – so be patient.
- Do praise the child when successful but don't make such a fuss that the child begins to become anxious and fretful.
- Do be 'low key' if a child has an 'accident'. Toilet training like any other skill needs lots of practice so 'accidents' are bound to happen. Never make a child feel stupid or 'bad' if they wet or mess their pants.
- Don't put pressure on the child – slow and steady is the rule, and be guided by the child's pace. If the child starts to appear anxious or worried, don't persist. Gentle encouragement, stories, songs and fun potties or using the toilet with specially adapted seats and steps are all good ideas, so long as the child does not see going to the toilet as a 'performance' which must be achieved at all costs!

When *not* to start or be persistent in toilet training

Toddlers are often creatures of habit and routine. Any changes in routine may mean their behaviour 'regresses'. This means that a child may begin to behave in a way more appropriate for a younger child. Toilet training should be 'on hold' if the family are involved in a house move, a new baby, change in parental relationships, illness, etc. Toilet training requires a lot of learning and effort on the part of the child, so not asking them to cope with too many new things at once is helpful.

Evidence collector
This evidence collector supports elements CCLD 203.1,203.2,203.3

Key Skills

1 Find two children in your workplace of different ages in the birth to 3 age range. For each one note down their different routines. How do the different routines meet their different needs?

2 Suggest one play activity for each child and write down how the activity would benefit the child.

3 Using a computer put your notes into a short presentation to give your assessor or your colleagues. Make sure you note down the times and dates that you observed the routines.

End-of-unit knowledge check

1 Give three reasons why it is important to observe babies and children.

2 Suggest at least two games you could play with babies aged:
- under 3 months
- 6–9 months
- 3–6 months
- 9–12 months.

3 State which senses or areas of development they encourage.

4 Identify at least five safety considerations when selecting toys and play materials for a baby who is crawling.

5 Identify at least two reasons why it is important to talk to babies when carrying out care routines

6 List five ways of making changing fun for babies.

7 Name at least three conditions you might observe when changing a baby and state what you would do about them.

8 How frequently should you change a baby's nappy?

9 Name two types of nappy that may be used and state how they should be disposed of when soiled.

10 What safety issues should be considered when changing babies or helping a child use the toilet?

Support a child with disabilities or special educational needs

Over the past few years, the rights and needs of children have been taken more seriously. People in society are becoming more aware that children who have physical disabilities or learning difficulties have the same right to learn and be cared for as other children. This means that settings are welcoming children who previously would not have been offered a place. Working with these children and families is hugely rewarding, but also requires high levels of skill and flexibility.

What you must know and understand:

- Why it is important to understand the requirements of legislation and codes of practice (K2P142)
- What local and national support and information is available (K2M143)
- How to work in partnership with parents (K2D144)
- How to work with children and avoid labelling (K2P145–146)
- How to plan for children's individual requirements (K2D149)
- How to remove barriers that prevent children's participation (K2D150)
- Ways of working with children who have particular needs (K2D147–148)
- How to ensure that what you do is suitable for all the children you work with (K2D151)
- How to use aids and equipment safely to support children (K2D152)
- The impact of having a child with additional needs within a family (K2D153)

Key principles

It is essential that you understand certain key principles and issues if you wish to work effectively in early years settings. These principles apply to all settings and practitioners in the UK. They form the basis for current thinking and also underpin much of the recent legislation. You therefore need to be familiar with these terms and to be able to use them properly and sensitively.

Inclusion

A good starting point is to understand the term **inclusion**. This means looking for ways of helping children to join in who would traditionally have been excluded from settings or activities. This way of thinking has enormous impact on the way you work with children. In some ways it turns things around. Instead of expecting children to fit in with what you are doing, it means looking at what you are doing and checking that it meets with children's needs. You have to be ready to adapt activities, change routines and sometimes even alter the layout of the setting so that children can join in.

Inclusion is important because it is fair. It means:

- that all children have the same chances to play and learn
- that children do not have to be segregated from others just because they are not 'the same'
- that groups of children learn that all people are different, all are special and yet all have some similar needs.

This unit looks at disabled children and children with special educational needs. However, inclusion is also about checking that children whose language, culture, home background or religion is different to others can join in and fulfil their potential.

Special educational needs

The term **special educational needs** (SEN) is used to describe children who need more help in order to learn or to access the curriculum. The term is not perfect as it could be argued that all children are special and so they all have needs! Some parents also dislike their children being labelled or categorised. They feel that this will disadvantage them as others may treat their children less favourably. This is one reason why Scotland is likely to adopt the term 'Additional Support for Learning'.

Key terms

Inclusion: a process of identifying, understanding and breaking down barriers to participation and belonging.

Key terms

Special educational needs: children who may need extra or different support from other children of the same age.

Key terms

Impairment: the loss or abnormality of development of growth. For example, hearing impairment means that a person has a loss of hearing.

Restrictions caused by a child's impairment: a physical or mental impairment that has a significant and long-term effect on a child's ability to carry out normal activities.

Disabled

The term 'disabled' is used when a person with impairment faces restrictions as a result of their impairment. It is also a tricky term as again it can lead to labelling. A child with a hearing loss is not disabled when doing a jigsaw puzzle, but might be disabled if he or she cannot lip-read the person reading a story. The danger with any term is that people tend to jump to conclusions about what a person can and cannot do.

● *Inclusion means that all children have the same chances to play and learn.*

Using language

Some language that you might hear people using to describe certain groups of children and adults is old-fashioned. It often reflects attitudes that date back to when disabilities were not fully understood. It is therefore important to be aware of language that is now considered to be offensive. As language can change, it is also important for you to keep up to date. Remember that it might not be the word itself that is offensive but the way it is used. For example, 'handicap' refers to the disadvantage that the person has compared to other people but the term 'handicapped' was frequently used in the past to describe the person. This is no longer acceptable. Some people regard the term 'disabled' in the same way.

Did you know?

The terms 'imbecile' and 'idiot' were used to describe children with learning difficulties in the Mental Deficiency Act 1913. Under this Act, children could be permanently removed from their families. This is why these terms are considered to be offensive.

Terms to avoid	Terms that are preferred
Handicapped person	Disabled person
Invalid	Disabled person
Wheelchair bound	Wheelchair user
Sufferer, victim of, crippled by, afflicted	Person who has…
Spastic	Person with cerebral palsy
Mongoloid, mongol	Person with Down's syndrome
Mental handicap	Learning difficulty
Congenital	Genetically impaired
Disabled toilet	Accessible toilet

Terms to use when talking about children with disabilities

emphasises their rights to make choices and be independent. It also challenges society to become more inclusive so that disabled people are not seen as being 'problems that need sorting out' or 'victims that need pity'.

Why it is important to understand the requirements of legislation and codes of practice

Laws and policies reflect society's views and attitudes. As a result of campaigning by organisations, the rights of children who have disabilities or special educational needs have been strengthened. This section outlines some of the key legislation that will affect your work with children.

It is essential to keep up to date, especially if you work in Northern Ireland or Scotland as some of the legislation at the time of writing is still in draft form. Look out for the Additional Support for Learning Bill if you live in Scotland and the Special Educational Needs and Disability Bill if you live in Northern Ireland.

Common principles across the four countries within the UK

Many common approaches across the countries in the UK are seen in legislation and regulations. These all reflect the need to include children with additional needs rather than to separate them from other children. In England and Wales these common principles can be seen in the SEN (Special Educational Needs) Code of Practice 2001 (see page 000). In Northern Ireland and Scotland legislation is still being written, but draft versions reflect these principles.

The right to mainstream education

The right to **mainstream education** is about children being able to attend the school of their choice. Mainstream schools may have to make physical adaptations to their buildings such as putting in ramps, widening doors, etc. They will also have to look at their teaching methods to ensure that children can learn. For children with complex needs, specialist provision is likely to continue although specialist units will probably be placed within schools.

Support for children in the early years

All the countries in the UK recognise the need for early identification and support for children with additional needs in the early years. This is important, as there are many benefits to the child when help and support are given early on. In some cases, such as difficulties with speech, hearing and vision, early identification can prevent the child from having problems in other areas such as behaviour and concentration.

Did you know?

The policy of inclusion is a controversial one for some parents. In some areas, parents have opposed the closure of special schools. They are not sure that providing mainstream education will best suit the needs of their children. On the other hand, other parents have fought hard to get their children into mainstream education.

Key terms

Mainstream education: schools and colleges that all children can attend regardless of their race, culture or ability.

Support and rights for parents

Current legislation and proposals in each of the four countries strengthen parents' rights. They have to be kept informed of what is happening and their views and ideas must be taken seriously. To help parents gain information and also to act as mediators, parent partnership services are being set up in England and Wales (see page 00). At the time of writing, these services have not been set up in Scotland and Northern Ireland so if you live there, you will need to find out what the latest plans are.

● *Working with parents to identify a child's needs*

Empowerment of children

Listening to children's views is also of major importance. Adults have to listen to children's thoughts about their education. In England and Wales, under the SEN Code of Practice 2001, adults are expected to take into account children's interests and views when drawing up plans for them. This approach will also be echoed by Scotland and Northern Ireland in their proposed legislation.

Individual plans for children

All countries are keen to provide individual support and programmes for children. In Scotland, these are likely to be called Individual Education Programmes, while in England and Wales they are known as Individual Education Plans. The idea behind this approach is to ensure that adults working with children think about their needs and provide focused strategies and teaching to help children fulfil their potential. Individual

Early years services

Advice and support can also be gained from early years services; the way in which these services are organised depends on the area and the country in which you live. In many areas, early years teams are connected to the education department of the borough council. Early years teams usually have experienced practitioners who in many cases will visit and advise your setting.

Local support groups

Local support groups are often organised by parents who find it helpful to meet with others and share experiences, information and advice. You will probably be able to find out about what is available in your local area from the library, education department or more easily from parents.

Check it out

Find out what facilities are available in your local area for children who have special educational needs.

National support organisations

National organisations, such as Epilepsy Action, provide a range of services. They not only provide support for children and their families, but also produce information for the general public. Some organisations provide helplines and leaflets, and also run training courses for professionals. Many organisations aim to raise public awareness and may campaign for better services and rights for children. National organisations will often have a website where you can access information.

Health professionals and social services

Health professionals may support some of the children with whom you work. They may be able to give you additional information, strategies or advice to help you work more effectively. In some cases, they may need you to assist them by working in particular ways with children. Health professionals are bound by a strict code of confidentiality. This means that you need to ask parents' permission before approaching them. The table below outlines the roles of some of the principal services that are usually available.

Service	Role
Speech and language team	Speech and language teams include speech therapists. They assess, diagnose and work out a programme of exercises to help children's communication and speech.
Sensory impairment team	Many education services have a team dedicated to helping children with a visual or hearing impairment. They may visit homes and settings to advise on how best to help the child and how to use equipment effectively.

continued on next page

Service	Role
Health visiting service	Health visitors are trained to promote health across all age ranges in the local community. Health visitors can provide advice for parents about care and development.
Occupational therapy service	Occupational therapists work to maximise physical movements and development. In many areas there are specialised occupational therapists who work with children. They usually work closely with families but may also advise how best to make a setting accessible.
Physiotherapists	Physiotherapists are usually provided by the health service. They work directly with children and their parents to provide exercises and movements that will help the child to strengthen an area of the body or reduce the impact of a medical condition.
Social services	Social services support children and their families by providing funding and support to meet children's needs. Children who are defined as 'in need' because their needs are complex and severe are likely to have a social worker assigned to them. Respite care, a service which allows parents some time off, is usually organised by social services.

● *The role of health professionals and social services*

Educational psychologists

Educational psychologists are professionals who have been trained to assess children's development and learning. They are able to identify children's needs and help parents and professionals meet them. Parents with concerns about children's learning or behaviour can refer children to educational psychologists, as can professionals with parents' consent. Educational psychologists often watch a child in the setting in order to build a picture of how the child is coping, as well as seeing the child separately. They are then able to give advice and suggest a programme to assist the child.

Internet

The Internet can be a good source of information. A search on the Internet can help you find out what support organisations are available and also give you more information about the child's needs. It is important though to realise that some information on the web may not be accurate.

Toy libraries

Toy libraries lend large and small toys and equipment to families and also to organisations. If you have a toy library in your area, it is worth visiting as libraries usually stock equipment that meets the needs of children with sensory impairments.

Check it out

Think of a child in your setting who has additional needs. Make a list of possible sources of support and information about the child's particular needs.

● *Parents know how best to help and support their child*

How to work in partnership with parents

Working in partnership with parents is probably one of the best ways of finding out information about children. Parents know their children well. They will be aware of their child's interests, strengths and needs. Parents have usually learned how best to help their child and will have developed strategies that support the child. Many parents will also have researched extensively in order to work out how to help their child, especially where the child has a medical or physical disability. They may have contacted support organisations, seen other professionals and met other families with similar circumstances.

The SEN Code of Practice 2001

The SEN (Special Educational Needs) Code of Practice 2001, which is used in England, outlines seven key principles when working with children. These principles are based on good practice and are worth reading even if you do not work in England. The box opposite shows these principles.

Providing support for parents and families

Everyone needs support from time to time. Parents of children are no different. You can support them effectively by making time for them and communicating well. You may at times be able to support them by putting them in contact with professionals, organisations or other parents.

1   **Acknowledge and draw on parental knowledge and expertise in relation to their child.**
    This principle recognises that parents will usually be able to share some valuable advice, thoughts and strategies with practitioners.

2   **Focus on the children's strengths as well as areas of additional need.**
    This principle is about remembering that children are 'whole people' and are not problems that need curing or sorting out. Think about the language you are using and also about how it might sound if it was said to you.

3   **Recognise the personal and emotional investment of parents and be aware of their feelings.**
    Parents love their children unconditionally and see them as valuable. If you focus only on the child's areas of needs, parents will feel that you do not really know their child.

4   **Ensure that parents understand procedures, are aware of how to access support in preparing their contribution and are given documents to be discussed well before the meeting.**
    Meeting with parents and working through individual learning plans is an essential part of supporting children. This principle is about making parents feel at ease and ensuring that they can properly contribute to a meeting.

5   **Respect the validity of differing perspectives and seek constructive ways of reconciling different viewpoints.**
    This principle is about understanding that parents are entitled to their own opinions about what is best for their child.

6   **Respect the differing needs that parents themselves may have, such as a disability or communication and linguistic barriers.**
    Some parents may have particular needs that may prevent them from contributing. Inclusion means thinking about parents' needs and looking for ways of meeting them. This might mean translating documents, encouraging parents to bring along a friend or putting up a travel cot so that a baby can be brought along to a meeting.

7   **Recognise the need for flexibility in the timing and structure of meetings.**
    This principle reminds you that parents may have jobs, difficulty with transport or other commitments. Partnership with parents means looking for times that everyone finds convenient, not just you!

● *Seven principles of working with parents*

It is usual for individual learning plans to be drawn up in consultation with parents. In many cases, it is the person who works closely with the child who puts the plan together, although in some settings this can be done by the person who co-ordinates special educational needs.

The plan usually consists of three or four targets for the child's development and contains activities and strategies to be used. The plan is then reviewed using information gained from observations and parents.

Using individual plans/programmes

If you know a child has an individual plan, it is important to read through it and use it to adapt or plan activities. Some settings show how the main curriculum plan is to be adapted to meet the needs of individual children. Others record the adaptations onto their activity plans. You will need to find out what the arrangement is in your setting. You may also need to seek advice as to how best to adapt an activity to suit the needs of the child. This will ensure it is not a wasted opportunity to help a child make progress and will avoid a child becoming frustrated because he or she cannot manage an activity.

Name: Daniel   **Early Years Action**

Area/s of concern: Fine motor skills/concentration

Review date: 14th March 2003

Early years practitioner: Miss Fletcher   Start date: Jan 2003

DOB: 4-12-99   IEP No.1

Proposed support:

Support began: Jan 2003

Targets to be achieved	Achievement Criteria	Possible resources/techniques	Possible class strategies	Ideas for support/assistant	Outcome
1. To grasp a small object between finger(s) and thumb	**1.** Pick up 5 beads and transfer to a pot in under 3 minutes.	**1.** Sorting activities e.g. beads, using spoons in sand tray Play-doh	**1.** Provide a variety of small objects within Daniel's reach. Encourage him to pick them up with fingers.	**1.** Demonstrate how to pick up objects with a pincer grip. Praise success.	
2. To maintain attention in a small group activity and participate appropriately	**2.** To participate fully in a sensory activity for 10 minutes.	**2.** Building sand castles. Sorting objects that float and sink	**2.** Provide opportunity for Daniel to participate and take turns at an appropriate level with 1:1 support.	**2.** Encourage Daniel to participate and take turns. Praise him.	

Parents/practitioner contribution Work with Daniel on related activities at home. Practise taking turns at home. Playing games.

Parent's signature _____

Practitioner's signature _____

● *An individual learning plan*

Keys to good practice: How to meet children's individual needs

✓ Find out from colleagues and parents about a child's individual needs.

✓ Use observations to help you work out how best to help a child.

✓ Make sure that your work supports a child's individual plan.

✓ Adapt activities in order to meet children's individual needs.

Case study 2: The importance of reading children's individual plans

Liam is 4 years old. His individual education plan for this term focuses on building his hand–eye co-ordination. Maria is an early years worker who is new to the setting. A small group of children are playing in the sand tray. She notices that Liam is spilling quite a lot of the sand. She tells him that he must stop playing if he carries on making such a mess.

1 *Why is it important for adults to find out about children's individual needs?*
2 *How might Maria have worked differently with Liam if she had read his IEP?*
3 *Explain why Maria's response to Liam was an example of exclusion.*

Valuing and empowering children

All children need to gain confidence and to feel valued. Your work with children with additional needs must allow this to happen. However, many children learn that they are not the same as other children and so think they are in some way inferior. This is sometimes because adults around them forget to focus on the whole child's needs and think about the child only in terms of what they cannot do or need help with. This can mean that children are not given the same opportunities as others.

Check it out

What term does your setting use for an individual plan that is provided for a child?

Choices and control

Children gain in confidence and improve their skills when they are able to do things by and for themselves. When you work with children, you should avoid doing things that they can do for themselves. A child might not be able to feed himself or herself but might still want to hold a spoon. And a child who finds it hard to do puzzles might still enjoy choosing one and tidying it away.

You should look for ways of helping children feel responsible and independent. Even if this is only in tiny ways, it is still important as choice and control over their actions is the basis for children's individuality.

Children's behaviour can also be affected by lack of choice. Sometimes unwanted behaviour, such as tantrums or throwing objects, is a sign that the child is not getting enough freedom.

Test yourself

Think of a child with whom you work. Explain how you help this child to make choices and develop self-help skills.

Case Study 3: Empowering children

Kieran has a limited amount of control over his hand movements. This means that he needs support to do some everyday tasks such as feeding and dressing. Kieran enjoys being with other children and has definite preferences when it comes to choosing who and what to play with. Kieran becomes frustrated when he cannot make his hands do what he wants them to. He has tried to move a piece of railway track, but in doing so has knocked over the tunnel that he has spent time assembling. His key worker asks Kieran if he would like him to reassemble the tunnel. Kieran nods and carries on assembling the track.

1   *Why might Kieran's behaviour be linked to his physical impairment?*
2   *Explain why Kieran's key worker asks Kieran first before putting the tunnel back together.*
3   *Why is it important to look for ways of giving children as much control and choice as possible?*

Being sensitive to children

Adults working with children must try hard to be sensitive. Many children simply want to play and enjoy being with other children. They do not want adults reminding them about their additional needs or talking about them in a loud voice. Some children's physical needs might be quite intimate and these children will need privacy and for adults to be discreet.

Supporting children with medical conditions

Some of the children that you work with might have a medical condition. The medical condition itself will rarely affect children's potential to learn, so some children will not be seen as having special educational needs. On the other hand, frequent absences because of illness, hospital visits and treatment may affect children's learning. This is because they may miss out on activities. It can also affect young children's friendships as children often form close friendships with those who they see frequently.

Gaining information

Parents are likely to be able to give you most of the information you need about the medical condition. This includes what to look out for and when you should seek emergency help or contact the parents. It can also be helpful to gain more information from the relevant support organisation.

Helping children

Children may need plenty of acknowledgement, praise and opportunities to be independent. Some older children may also at times become frustrated and depressed by the condition and it is important to act as a good listener. Where children have been absent, you will need to help them get back into the routine of the setting gently. Young children may need more adult attention, while older children may need adults to organise activities that will allow them to ease themselves back into their group of friends. If children have missed out on some learning during their absence, adults may need to spend a little more time with them.

How to remove barriers that prevent children's participation

Inclusion means making sure that all children can have access to the same opportunities. This sounds easy, but in practice it means identifying possible hurdles or barriers that children face.

Attitudes of adults

Possibly the biggest barrier to participation is adults! This is rarely deliberate, but is still a problem. Adults may not realise that a child can manage an activity and so it may not be offered to the child. At other times, adults may not think hard enough about how to change the activity in order that the child can still have a go. Some adults still take the attitude that it is up to children to 'fit in' rather than for activities to be changed so that children can join in. Hopefully, this will become rarer in the future.

Communication

Some children need support in order to communicate. This means that they might not be able to tell you what they want to do or what they need. A variety of strategies can be used to help overcome this barrier.

Physical barriers

Sometimes barriers are physical. For example, doors may not be wide enough to accommodate children using mobility aids, toys may not be large enough or tables may not be at the right height. Physical access will

Key terms

Barriers to communication: anything that prevents a child communicating with others or forming relationships with them. This might be hearing, speech or visual loss, learning disabilities, mental health issues or a lack of support services.

gradually become less of an issue in the future, as all new buildings have to be accessible to wheelchair users, but older buildings still need to be adapted to improve accessibility wherever possible.

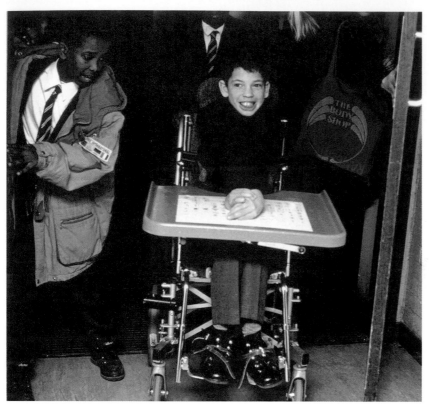

● New buildings have to be accessible to wheelchair users, but older buildings still need to be adapted.

Ways of working with children who have particular needs

Supporting children's communication and interaction

Some children may have difficulties with communication and interaction. Their difficulties in communicating their needs, or in not being able to understand what is happening, may make them feel frustrated and isolated.

Being a language partner

Some children need additional time with an adult in order to boost and develop their language and communication skills. If you are working with children in this way, think of yourself as a language partner. Children learn best when they are enjoying themselves and have a warm relationship with the adult. You may work with one child at a time or have a small group with whom you play games. It is essential that this type of work is fun for the child.

● *Parents can be language partners*

 Keys to good practice: How to be a language partner

✓ Avoid taking the child away from what he or she is doing – consider whether you can be a language partner and play alongside the child.

✓ Choose times when the child is relaxed and not overtired.

✓ Make eye contact with the child.

✓ Plan activities that are enjoyable and are play based.

✓ Use puppets and props to help the child communicate.

✓ Acknowledge the child's communication positively.

✓ Do not correct the child's speech.

✓ Speak clearly and adjust your language to suit the child.

✓ Be ready to stop before the child's concentration slips.

Helping children who cannot hear fully

Many young children have temporary hearing loss, especially in the winter months. Long bouts of hearing loss may affect some children's speech. Other children will have been identified with a hearing loss early on in their lives and may be using hearing aids. For children using hearing aids, it is important to find out from the parents about how best to help the child and to learn a little about how their hearing device works.

 Did you know?

In the winter months, as many as one in four children will have a temporary hearing loss. This is often caused by colds.

Keys to good practice: How to support a child who cannot hear fully

✓ Check that you have the child's attention before speaking.

✓ Maintain eye contact with the child.

✓ Speak normally, but speak clearly.

✓ Do not speak extra loudly.

✓ Do not put your hand over your face.

✓ Be expressive with your speech and body language.

✓ Make sure that you face into the light so that a child who is lip-reading can clearly see your face.

✓ Identify the topic of conversation early on, for example point at what you are talking about.

✓ Use props, pictures and visual aids to support your speech.

✓ If a hearing device is used, make sure that you know how to check if it is working and, if necessary, change the battery.

Stammering (dysfluency)

Stammering affects the fluency in children's speech and so is also known as dysfluency. While many children between the ages of 2 and 3 years will stammer, this is usually temporary. It is often a result of the child knowing what to say and finding it hard to get the words out quickly enough. For some children, however, stammering becomes more permanent, and this can affect their confidence.

The best way to help children is to reduce the amount of tension and pressure on the child. Relaxing the child can help them to speak more fluently. Situations that cause the child to feel nervous, excited or tense are likely to cause stammering.

Early speech therapy can be effective for children. If adults notice that stammering in a young child is becoming more frequent, they should follow their setting's procedures in sharing this information with parents.

 Keys to good practice: How to support a child who stammers

✓ Avoid situations when all the focus is on the child, for example circle times.

✓ Make sure that the child feels that you have plenty of time for them. Sit down and make eye contact.

✓ Reduce the speed at which you talk. This can help the child to relax and speak more slowly.

✓ Avoid asking direct questions as they can put the child under pressure.

✓ Do not finish off the child's sentence to 'help' or let other children interrupt.

Alternative and augmentative communication

Alternative and augmentative communication methods can help children to communicate and interact with others.

The decision to use alternative and augmentative methods of communication is often taken by speech therapists and specialists alongside parents. Over the past few years, the range of methods has increased and technology is being used more and more. For example, voice simulation allows children to press a picture or type a word to generate a voice. In the same way, children who find it hard to write can use voice recognition to put their thoughts into writing.

Visual systems

Some children will need visual cues in order to make sense of language. If the child you are working with uses a system of visual communication like those below, you will need to spend time learning how to use it quickly and fluently.

Picture representations

Some children benefit from using pictures to supplement communication. For example, you may show a child a picture of an apron and at the same time say the word so that the child knows that he or she needs to get an apron.

Picture-exchange system

This system is based on pictures. This not only helps children to understand the meaning of words, but also helps them to think about the way in which communication is a shared and two way process. The child takes and also receives pictures and so learns about interaction. A picture-exchange system is an augmentative method as speech is still used. For example, a child who wants to paint may go to their carer with a picture of the painting area. The carer would take the card and say 'so you would like to paint?' The carer might give the child a picture of an apron and tell the child to get an apron first.

Sign representations

Some children's cognitive development is the reason why they find it hard to talk and communicate. Babies first learn about language by seeing the object being talked about at the same time as hearing the word. You may point to a cat and say 'cat'. The child then remembers the word and so eventually does not need to see the cat to know what the word means. But for some children, sounds alone are not enough and they need to have their language supported by signs.

A common sign system is Makaton, which helps children link the word to an action or object. This makes it easier for them to understand the word.

Makaton should not be confused with British Sign Language. Makaton is not a language in itself, but a tool to help language. For example, a child who wants a drink cups the hands as if holding a beaker. The teacher acknowledges the child by saying 'Did you want a drink?'

British Sign Language

British Sign Language is an alternative form of communication. It is a complete language and is used instead of speech. Most users have significant hearing loss and so need a different way of communicating, but they do not have learning difficulties.

Check it out

It is useful to learn a few of the common Makaton symbols. Find out where you can take a basic Makaton course in your area.

Supporting children's cognition and learning

How and why some children learn more easily than others is still not fully understood. The way in which the brain takes in and handles information is quite complex. Children may be good at some types of learning and thinking and have weaknesses in others. Some children's difficulty in learning is also linked to their language development. This is because language and thought are closely connected (see Unit 203).

Concentration

Some children have difficulties in concentrating and you will have to adapt the way in which you work to meet their needs.

Keys to good practice: How to support a child who has difficulties in concentrating

✓ Base learning on activities that already appeal to the child.

✓ Be ready to change activities before the child's attention wanes.

✓ Look for activities that keep the child active.

✓ Avoid activities where the child is expected to wait or sit for periods of time.

✓ Give simple clear instructions – one at a time.

✓ Observe the child and notice what holds his or her attention.

✓ Use props and visual aids.

Using a multi-sensory approach

The brain takes in information through the five senses. Many children who have difficulties in learning will therefore be helped if early years workers present information in a more sensory way. The following are examples of activities that involve the child in doing, touching and seeing while also learning:

- counting sand castles and knocking them down at the same time
- drawing letter shapes in shaving foam.

Consolidation

Children may need to repeat an activity several times before they are completely confident. They may also benefit from the same idea being presented in a variety of ways. This is called consolidation. You could, for example, play the same game several times, but change one feature each time.

Timing

Some children are able to respond better at certain times of the day or in the week. This information can be gained by talking to parents or by observing the child. You should keep an eye on the length of activities and notice whether or not the child's concentration is waning.

Success

Enjoyment is key to learning. Children who have done well and enjoyed an activity are more likely to want to return to the activity another day. It is important to make sure that children feel some success or satisfaction.

Careful observation and realistic expectations of the child are the keys to ensuring success. You might, for example, make sure that a child, who normally gives up quickly when doing a jigsaw, tries one that is within his or her capabilities. By being successful, the child is more likely to have a go at another jigsaw in the future.

Memorable

To learn something effectively means having a good memory of it. One way in which you can help children to learn is to look for ways of making an activity memorable. It might mean looking for activities that are new or surprising, or using a puppet. The puppet might be holding an object of interest or just be making an activity feel more fun. It can also help children if they see a photograph of themselves doing the activity later on.

Supporting children's sensory development

Some children may have sensory impairments that may mean they have difficulty with hearing, touching or seeing. As children need their senses to help them find out about the world, this can have an impact on other areas of their development such as concentration, cognition and language. On page 00, you looked at ways of helping children with hearing impairment. This section looks at ways of helping children with visual impairment and touch.

Helping children with visual impairment

The best advice for working with children who do not see fully will probably come from parents and/or other professionals. Some adaptations to help children can be quite simple, such as rubber mats on tables to avoid

Children use play to make sense of their lives.

Play is now actively encouraged where children are in unfamiliar settings, for example hospitals and social services units, and increasingly in doctors' and dentists' surgeries. Quality play can help a child to express fears about procedures in hospital, or can be used to explain what is going to happen.

How play can help development

The aspects of development that can be helped through play can be remembered by the acronym **SPICE**, as shown in the diagram below.

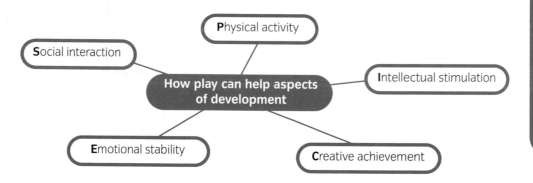

So, how can play help all these aspects of development? Over the page are some possibilities.

Social interaction involves any kind of interaction, for example when the child or young person:

- takes turns
- shares
- relates to relatives and friends
- leads or works as part of a team
- co-operates with others
- relates to other adults or children.

Physical activity includes developing fine and gross motor skills, for example when the child or young person:

- uses hand–eye co-ordination
- uses balancing skills
- practises or learns new skills
- uses whole body co-ordination
- uses fine finger control
- uses and controls muscles.

Intellectual stimulation is gaining or improving knowledge, for example when the child or young person:

- experiments
- is creative
- uses imagination
- uses memory
- thinks carefully
- experiences concepts
- solves problems
- uses and learns terminology.

Creative achievement involves anything that a child or young person creates using his or her imagination, for example when the child or young person:

- uses practical/theoretical skills
- produces something
- creates an object or image
- uses imagination or initiative.

Emotional stability involves personal feelings, for example when the child or young person is:

- confident
- relaxed
- amused
- loving
- resentful
- cross
- thrilled
- confused
- proud
- distressed
- angry
- sad
- happy
- pleased
- wary.

Developmental areas of play are sometimes described differently or include more categories such as:

- **social and moral** – including acceptable behaviour within society, consideration for others, behaving responsibly
- **aesthetic and spiritual** – including appreciating and creating beauty, inspiring creativity, life and cultural experiences, acceptance and belonging
- **sensory** – relating to the five senses

Check it out

Look at the diagram opposite about how play can help aspects of development. Think about any game you might have played as a child. How was each aspect of development helped by hat game?

Key terms

Physical play: play that is physically active, for example football, rounders or tag.

- **linguistic** – development of vocabulary and understanding of terminology.

One play activity can meet many developmental categories, for example the developmental value of outdoor **physical play** is shown in the diagram below.

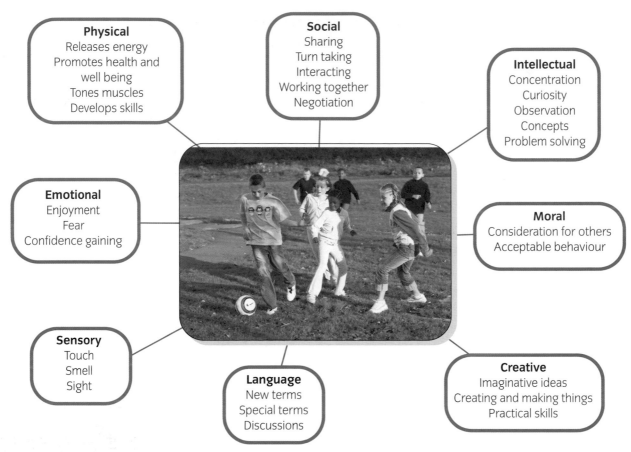

Physical
Releases energy
Promotes health and well being
Tones muscles
Develops skills

Social
Sharing
Turn taking
Interacting
Working together
Negotiation

Intellectual
Concentration
Curiosity
Observation
Concepts
Problem solving

Emotional
Enjoyment
Fear
Confidence gaining

Moral
Consideration for others
Acceptable behaviour

Sensory
Touch
Smell
Sight

Language
New terms
Special terms
Discussions

Creative
Imaginative ideas
Creating and making things
Practical skills

- *One physical play activity, such as football, can meet many developmental categories*

Why it is important that children and young people's play should be self-directed and focus on their needs (K3/4)

The children should always be at the centre of any play activity; this means that the play opportunities should focus on the children, on what they want and need. Playworkers need to provide sufficient opportunities, **resources** and activities to encourage children to use their senses to gain experiences and knowledge they can use in later life.

While children and young people are playing, they may from time to time make mistakes. This is not a failure but part of a learning curve. By making mistakes, a child or young person will learn from them and be able to redirect their aim.

Key terms

Resources: Equipment and materials that will stimulate play.

Case study 1

How a child or young person plays can be classified as follows:

- observation – copying an action demonstrated to them, for example hitting a ball with a racquet
- exploration – trying a new activity, for example go-karting or tag games, where they will be acquiring new skills and socialising
- experimentation – having time and space to try out an activity in a relaxed environment
- repetitiveness – repeating a particular activity or skill to gain more of an understanding of it.

Another way children and young people gather information is by using their five senses: sight, smell, taste, touch and hearing. For example, if the children ask for an activity about food and you provide a food tasting opportunity, it would involve using the senses as shown in the table below.

Sense	Example of information
Sight	Comparing fruit from different countries, and of different colours, shapes, sizes.
Hearing	Learning about the produce, where it comes from and how it grows.
Taste	Tasting the produce (bitter, sweet, sour).
Touch	Feeling the texture (hard, soft, prickly).
Smell	Deciding whether the scent of the produce is pleasant or unpleasant.

- *Senses used during food tasting activity*

There are many different types of play. Below are examples which playworkers need to provide for.

- **Environmental play** takes place in the environment in cities as well as rural areas. It can be indoors or outdoors. It raises awareness to or involves natural elements and can lead on to craftwork, artwork or drama.
- **Creative play** is when children and young people use their imagination to create, invent or produce things. Creative play is an important way to encourage children to experiment and explore the world around them. They discover things by using their senses.

Key terms

Environmental play: play that involves and/or raises awareness of natural elements and/or wildlife and their survival.

Key terms

Creative play: play that is inventive and/or productive, for example writing, construction, artwork, music.

- **Cultural play** values, celebrates and raises awareness of different cultures. Play can enhance learning, understanding and acceptance.
- **Imaginative play** is where children and young people use their imagination, 'pretend' or act out situations of fantasy. It is sometimes called role play. It allows children and young people to explore a variety of different situations. Sometimes the roles are portrayed through other objects, for example puppets.
- **Physical play** involves physical activity. It can include play that exercises muscles, develops eye–hand co-ordination, develops fine and gross motor skills, etc.

A playworker should understand and be aware that children and young people can and will want to play without adult involvement. Providing a safe physical environment will ensure that children play more creatively and develop through play.

Supervision levels and ratios within the setting should meet the inspection requirements. This will help to ensure the safety and security of the children and young people in your care. Playworkers should understand the different levels of supervision and use their own initiative and intuition to judge if their involvement in play will enhance or inhibit. This approach will help the play to be self-directed.

Play should be self-directed for the following reasons:

- to encourage independence
- to help children learn through play
- to give freedom of choice to encourage decision making
- to help children excel in their own achievements
- to boost self-esteem
- to help all-round development
- to help build confidence
- to encourage discovery and exploration
- to help children interpret meaning
- to help children learn about the consequences of their decisions.

Key terms

Cultural play: play that celebrates and/or raises awareness of different cultures and their values and practices.

Key terms

Imaginative play: play that involves 'pretend' roles or acting out fantasy situations.

● *Self-directed physical play in the environment*

Whatever play opportunities are available, they should focus on the children and young people's interests and needs. Play opportunities should be developmentally appropriate, stimulating and appealing. All children are different. Their needs can be very simple or very complex and will constantly be changing and developing.

The play opportunities you offer should be geared towards meeting these needs, especially any particular or additional needs a child may have. To identify these needs, you should have knowledge of the individual children or young people in your setting, plus a good knowledge of child development. If the setting does not meet the needs of the children and young people attending, then the children will become bored and it is highly likely that attendances will fall.

Case study 2: Supporting children in physical play

A group of children aged 8 to 13 are playing bulldog. It is largely going well but the older children tend to target the younger ones to catch and the younger ones are getting upset.

1   *What kind of play is this game supporting?*
2   *What might be the benefits of the different age groups playing together?*
3   *What might be the disadvantages?*
4   *What could happen if the game continues unsupervised?*
5   *How might the playworker encourage the children to continue to play safely and happily without taking over?*

How to identify children and young people's play needs and involve them in decisions about their play (K5/6)

Children and young people will have different interests and needs. It is important that the play setting reflects this by providing a variety of environments that will enhance development. A setting should provide a range of opportunities that cover all the different types of play and meet the development needs of the different children and young people who attend. The term used for this is 'child centred'.

When creating a play environment, it is advisable to ask the children or young people in your setting what they would like. If you do not ask those in your care and set out activities you think that they would like, you will be disappointed at the lack of interest a child or young person may show. Also, if certain aspects of your setting do not appear stimulating or challenging to a child or young person, the child will be reluctant to attend.

These aspects could be in relation to the physical environment, from the decoration and the layout to the equipment and materials that you provide. The setting therefore needs to be child centred. Asking the children and young people what they want will help them to feel that the environment is their own.

There are many benefits to the children and young people, the staff and the parents of a child-centred setting. Some examples of why the setting should be child centred are shown in the diagram below.

Playworkers can contribute to a child-centred setting by helping to make the environment friendly, attractive, stimulating and challenging. Think about these ideas:

Friendly

- Look and be enthusiastic.
- Show an interest in the children.
- Use a range of techniques to welcome children and young people and create a welcoming atmosphere.
- Invite children to do things and ask for things.

Attractive

- Use screens to display pictures or interesting posters that will encourage creativity.
- Involve the children in decorating the setting
- Use materials and displays that reflect a range of interests and ages.

Stimulating and challenging

- Have activities where children can succeed but that include a challenge.
- Recognise effort and achievement.
- Use praise and encouragement.
- Review and develop decor and layout.
- Change things around frequently.

How to identify children's play needs

The play needs of the children and young people in your setting can be identified:

- through the use of trained staff who have sound knowledge of the children's needs
- by giving children choices
- by using effective listening and communication skills
- by asking the children for input, and valuing and implementing their ideas.

Group: [   ]   Age range: [   ]   Date: [   ]

Activity: [   ]

Number of children/young people in the group: [   ]

Length of activity (minutes/hours): [   ]

Changes suggested by children/young people in the group:

[   ]

Level of enjoyment of children/young people in the group:

[   ]

Any other comments:

[   ]

● *Monitoring form*

Check it out

1 Think of a time when you asked for feedback in your setting.
   a Which method was used?
   b What was the response of the children?
   c How was the feedback used?

Design a questionnaire to give out at your setting about what play the children and young people would like.

To ensure that the environment is meeting the needs of the children and young people that attend, feedback from them will enable you to assess and improve the service you provide. To monitor children or young people's involvement in a setting you can use the following techniques.

- Observation – do the children or young people look bored or only half interested in the activity?
- Questionnaires – some settings distribute questionnaires to find out which activities the children enjoyed.
- Monitoring forms – these are similar to questionnaires; staff complete them with the children each evening to monitor the success of the **play opportunity**.
- Suggestion box – this is emptied weekly, and is another way children and young people can contribute to the weekly planning of activities.
- Children forums – where staff and children can discuss future events, needs and equipment, etc.
- Chats – every day you will talk to the children; you can encourage them to provide you with feedback by asking them, 'Did you enjoy that activity? Would you do it again?'

Key terms

Play opportunity: any type of resource or activity that provides the children or young people with opportunities to play.

Case study 3: Involving children in decisions

A group of children aged 9–11 in your club are having a snack, and they begin to discuss their plans for the summer holidays.

1 *How would you use this opportunity to improve and plan for the club's summer activities?*
2 *What would you suggest happens next?*
3 *Who else would need to be involved?*

How to help to provide the type of play environment that stimulates children and young people's play (K7)

Examples of the types of environments within a play setting that can stimulate children and young people's play are given in the table at the top of the next page.

Playworkers should help by providing resources, materials and equipment. However, the more involvement the children and young people have, the more child centred the setting becomes.

To ensure the play environment is stimulating, you need to be aware of the following as a playworker.

Environment	Materials and equipment
Craft area	Paint, malleable materials, crayons, boxes
Role play area	Dressing up clothes, cooking utensils, pretend food
Quiet area	Books, tapes, soft cushions, bean bags
Soft play area	Large, soft shapes, balls
Computer corner	Computer/video games, play station
Construction area	Lego, small- and large-scale construction toys
Music area	Musical instruments, radios, tapes, TV, video, karaoke machine, dance mats
Physical area (indoors/outdoors)	Bats, balls, bicycles, skipping ropes, pool table, football table
Games	Board games, fantasy games, quiz games
Food area	Cooking equipment, utensils, chairs, tables, snacks and drinks

● *Environments, materials and equipment that can stimulate play*

- Age range – in a play setting the age range can be vast; through experience you will learn to adapt activities to meet the different ages and developmental levels.
- Abilities – if the equipment and materials promote activities that are too easy, the children will become bored; if they are too difficult, they may become frustrated or lose interest in the activity. Find the level that is appropriate.
- Interests – by knowing the children you will have a better understanding of the type of opportunities and activities they like to participate in, and you can then make these available.
- Staff supervision – different activities require various levels of supervision. This may mean that you need to have a rota or a programme to include everyone's requests.
- Resources – make sure you have sufficient equipment for all to participate and that equipment is in good working order.
- Play space – check that your floor space can house activities safely. Again, you may need a floor rota to create opportunities for all.
- Number of participants – too many children and insufficient resources increase the risk of danger. Children and young people can take turns as long as they are informed beforehand.
- Sufficient time – there is no point starting a long activity 15 minutes before the end of a session. Participants will feel frustrated that they cannot complete the task.

If all of the above are taken into consideration then a play opportunity should be fun and run smoothly, and children or young people will feel they have both enjoyed it and gained something from it.

Check it out

Plan an activity or discussion about what the children and young people in your setting would do if you won the lottery and had unlimited funds to spend on the setting. You could provide catalogues and magazines to help them decide, and encourage the children and young people to think of ways to present their ideas.

Case study 4: Finding suitable play opportunities

Tom is 12 years old and enjoys environmental play outside; he particularly enjoys building. However, today it has rained constantly. Finally, he comes over to you and says, 'I'm bored!'

1   *What would be your reply?*
2   *How could you use this situation to help Tom find play opportunities of interest?*

How to balance the need for risk and challenge in play against the requirements of health and safety (K8)

When providing play opportunities an acceptable level of challenge and risk should be incorporated. Playworkers need to understand the difference between a **risk** and a **hazard**.

- A **risk** is a potential danger. A climbing frame is a potential danger if it is not in a fit state for use and there is nothing to protect a child who might fall. Ensuring it meets safety standards and that it is only used under supervision makes it an acceptable risk rather than a hazard.
- A **hazard** is something in a play setting that has the potential to cause someone harm, for example not cleaning up spillage of a liquid, or leaving equipment out where someone could trip over it.

Children need to be encouraged to experiment and take risks to help them learn techniques and strategies to deal with risks. However, it is the playworker's responsibility to ensure the safety of children and young people in their care. Supervision and, if necessary, intervention can effectively allow for children to take up challenges and risks.

It is safe to say that most children will not undertake something that they are not comfortable with. The danger lies in less confident children being encouraged by a bolder one to do something they are not comfortable with. They then realise they are outside their own boundaries of safety.

- *An acceptable level of suggestion allows children to take up challenges and risks*

Case study 5: Dealing with risk

Joe is extremely agile and can climb trees and climbing frames with no problems. His friend Jem, however, has never climbed a tree before, but doesn't want to seem 'soft' and so, encouraged by Joe, follows him. Part way up, Jem looks down and realises he is very scared and cannot get down.

1   *What would happen next?*
2   *If you had seen this happen, how would you have dealt with it at the time?*
3   *What, if anything, would you do afterwards?*

Case study 6: Ensuring safety during imaginative play

Jill and Aysah are in the outside area and have built a den by stacking boxes. They have decided to secure the 'roof' by balancing on the top of the boxes.

1   *How would you highlight health and safety rules without stifling play?*
2   *How could you encourage the imaginative play to continue?*

Why children and young people need variety and choice in the play setting and how to involve them in creating their own play environments (K9/11)

Always remember that children and young people are all individuals. One child may like a particular type of food and another may not – the same principle can be applied to play. Throughout a play session or day children need variety in the activities on offer to them.

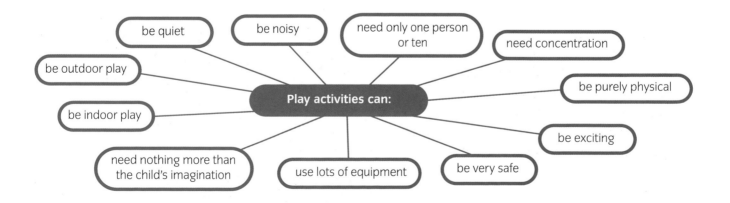

The list of variations in play is endless – can you think of other descriptors of types of play?

It is important to think about the different needs of the children you are working with as well as the time of day when you are planning activities. Even the most active child or young person will need some 'time out' to recover from activities. It may be that an activity that kept a child engrossed on one day simply does not appeal to them on another, so alternatives are needed.

The second value of play talks about choice within the setting (see page 22). Think about this quote from a child about choice of play.

I hate it when I'm not allowed to play like I want to. You know, when they all tell you to be quiet, or come in the middle of something you are doing and want to know why you are doing it.

Ashok, 10 (Berkshire)

Check it out

How does your setting involve children and young people in the planning and creation of their own play environment?

The best way of making sure that the opportunities on offer to the children and young people provide the variety and choice they want is to involve them in the planning. You have already thought about how to find out their views (see page 11).

Why it is important to plan play opportunities that are easily adapted by children and young people to their own needs (K10)

Your responsibility as a playworker is to facilitate play. Some play settings have a programme of activities and this can be a useful tool for creating opportunities for children to develop and adapt their play. Providing a programme enables settings to plan in advance. The programme can also be made available to children and their parents or carers so they know what is happening.

Despite this, some of the most effective play settings operate without a programme – a lot will depend upon the type of setting in which you work, the age of the children and young people that attend your setting, the expectations of the parents and carers (especially if they pay for the care that you provide) and the setting's management ethos.

Programmes can have the following benefits for staff and children.

- They help staff to work together and know what is required.
- They help ensure that equipment and materials are available.
- They help with planning any visits or celebrations for special occasions.
- They ensure staffing levels meet requirements.
- They help children and young people feel more secure.

- They help ensure children and young people attend in appropriate dress and footwear.
- They help to motivate children and young people.
- Children and young people can see when their ideas are put on the programme.

Programmes also help to meet parental expectations; parents often have more confidence in the play setting if the setting seems well organised. However, if a programme is strict and rigid this will hinder play; children do not need to spend too much time on structured activities, which they do all day at school. Flexibility within the play programme is therefore vital.

If you are to offer a play opportunity or an activity, it is useful to plan so that you are prepared and the equipment and materials are ready for the session. Before the activity, discuss your ideas with your supervisor to ensure that it is a suitable activity for the children and young people in your setting. You can follow set activity plans or use a less formal model. Whatever method you choose, make sure that you cover all the possible eventualities and planning guidelines. Some tips and hints are set out below to help you.

- Beforehand – ask the children and young people to think of some ideas and then complete the activity plan.
- The activity – write what you are going to do. Remember, an activity can be any interaction between you and one or more children, or between children. It does not have to have an end product.
- Aim – state what you and the children or young people hope to achieve from the activity and why you have decided to do it.
- Playworker input – highlight any specific role you will have, either practically or to promote development, for example new vocabulary to be introduced.
- Health and safety – highlight any aspects you and the children need to consider with regard to both resources and the environment, including a list of who you should notify.
- Development value – write what skills and knowledge the children will learn, linking them to SPICE (see page 7). Your supervisor may have some helpful suggestions.
- Resources – state clearly all the resources you will need and use this as a checklist when you set up the activity.
- Plan of activity – make notes on your activity. These can include diagrams if applicable and instruction points.
- Implementing the activity – remember, it is your activity; get involved without stifling the play. Interact and supervise the children as appropriate. Think about the presentation when setting up the activity; if it looks appealing the children are more likely to take part. Make it enjoyable for both the children and yourself. Remember to encourage

them to adapt and change things.

- Evaluation – write up how it went. Be honest; say if it was a huge success or a terrible disaster. Describe how the children reacted. What surprised you? Did the children gain what you thought they would (look back at your aim and development value) or did the activity promote areas you had not considered? Would you do anything different next time? Did the children deviate from your plan?

At first, planning and doing the activities may not be easy, and recording may be a chore. It will get easier and quicker as you develop, enabling you to link theory to practice and to add value to the input you give to the children or young people. Your setting may have its own guidelines for planning activities, or you could use a similar format to the one in the play activity plan below.

PLAY ACTIVITY PLAN

Activity title: Bubble making

Play opportunity: Environmental/physical/outdoor play

Aim: To provide a variety of resources that can be used to make bubbles; to encourage the young people to use and develop these different bubbles

Location: Outside play area

Number of children/young people: 1–20

Age range: 5–15 years

Number of staff: 1–2 depending on number of participating children

Playworker input: To provide bubble liquid and resources, to encourage imagination and adaptation, to introduce scientific and special vocabulary, to aid participation and give encouragement

Health and safety: Large open space: ensure it is rubbish free, check materials for sharp edges, etc. Highlight the dangers to children/young people regarding:

- bubble liquid in eyes
- slipping on spilt liquid
- bubble liquid in mouth.

Development value:

Social – sharing, taking turns, discussing, helping each other, working together

Physical – dexterity, fine and gross motor skills, exercising lungs, blowing

Intellectual – problem solving, how to get bigger bubbles, using terminology relating to scientific concepts

Creative – making shapes to dip in liquid, finding other materials to use

Emotional – experiences, success and failure, dealing with emotions

Resources: Bubble liquid in large bowls, bubble pipes, rings, wire, small hoops, curtain wire, plastic six pack holders, coat hangers, pliers, water aprons for younger children

Plan: Try it out prior to the activity, get equipment out and readily available, enlist the help of the children to make/decant the liquid into the bowls, explain the health and safety issues, encourage children/young people to take part and experiment, top up materials, help as required, collect more resources if requested

After the activity, it will help if you evaluate. This will enable you to highlight positive and negative aspects and improve the activity if it is repeated. It may also be useful to discuss the activity with the children and your colleagues and ask them for feedback. Most play settings have a file of activity plans as a central resource, so if the activity is repeated by another playworker he or she will be aware of any aspects to repeat or exclude.

Even though you have planned an activity, the children or young people may adapt the resources and completely change it from your plan. This is fine; your role is to provide resources and opportunities which children and young people are free to choose (or not) and adapt as they wish.

Check it out

Plan, implement (carry out) and review an activity that you are going to provide for the children and young people in your setting.

Case study 7: Helping children to take their ideas forward

A group of children ask if they could do some 'cutting out' and whether you have any catalogues they could use. You only have old catalogues from buying equipment. When you get these out the children become engrossed in the range of outdoor equipment.

1 *What should you do now?*
2 *How could you help the children to take their ideas forward?*
3 *What value will the children be gaining from this activity?*
4 *What could you do to help with new ideas for play opportunities?*

How to make sure play environments meet both legal requirements and the needs of your organisation (K12/13)

Guidelines are set out to help playworkers focus on the play opportunities that they should provide and to ensure that the setting is safe, hygienic and secure. You will find guidelines in your setting about the **requirements of your organisation**. These will include the organisation's policies and procedures that will relate to the Standards for children as laid down by Ofsted in England, National Care Standards and HMIE (Scottish) in Scotland and Estyn in Wales.

A job description for a playworker will usually involve points that focus on the working environment, for example: Help provide a safe and welcoming child-centred environment which meets the needs of all the children attending.

A job description sets out the basis for your expected performance and duties. Once you sign your contract it will be a legal document.

Key terms

Requirements of your organisation: the procedures and policies of your play setting as they apply to children and young people's rights, health and safety.

The values of play also include sections about the environment, for example the fourth value of play states:

Every child has a right to a play environment which stimulates and provides opportunities for risks and challenges and the growth of confidence and self-esteem.

These guidelines help playworkers to determine the type of environment that is needed. Each setting will have its own aims and objectives that will include aspects relating to the environment. You may find that your setting's aims are similar to the ones below.

The overall aims of the Louistown out-of-school club are to:
- recruit and monitor high quality staff who meet the needs of all children
- encourage progress by providing a safe, nurturing and stimulating environment
- generate a happy environment with warm and caring staff.

Your setting's policies and procedures should meet the National Standards for your region. Standard 4 'Safe settings' of the English Standard states:

The premises should be safe, secure and suitable for their purpose. They provide adequate space in an appropriate location, are welcoming to children and offer access to the necessary facilities for a range of activities which promote their development. The space standards provide minimum space requirements for the whole provision. The registered person shows how this space will be divided up and used to provide activities for children and how staff will be deployed within it.

Provision is made (space or partitioned area) for children who wish to relax or play quietly, equipped with appropriate furniture. This area may be converted from normal play space, provided children can rest safely without disturbance.

Play areas are large enough to give scope for free movement and well spread out activities. There are separate areas for different activities.

The implementation of these guidelines will be checked by Ofsted, HMIE (Scottish) or Estyn at inspection and any that are not adhered to will form part of the setting's action plan.

You may find that your playwork team has set practices that it follows with regard to the environment. These may not be legal obligations, or even set in the guidelines, but may well be instances of good playwork practice, for example reviewing and updating the environment on a regular basis. This is important in order to ensure that the environment meets the children's changing needs. It also helps with:

- keeping the environment challenging, stimulating and interesting
- meeting the developmental changes of the children
- keeping the environment welcoming in appearance, safe and hygienic
- relieving boredom and lack of interest
- updating the environment to meet current interests and developments.

When reviewing the environment, it is good practice to involve a variety of people, such as those shown in the table below.

People involved	Why
Children	It is their facility; they should feel it is a child-centred environment
Staff	To gain ideas, to enlist help, to enhance team work
Parents/family	To gain ideas and opinions, to enlist help, to enhance participation
Other facility users	To ensure the facility is still appropriate to their needs

 Involving people in reviewing the environment

Keys to good practice: Creating a range of play environments

When you are planning play activities always make sure they meet the needs of the children and young people.

✓ Ask them what they want.

✓ Use feedback from them.

✓ Where possible involve them in creating the play environment.

✓ Make sure there is variety and flexibility in the planning.

✓ Make sure there are enough resources for all.

✓ Make sure that you are meeting the requirements of your setting and relevant laws (see page 27 in Unit 202).

Check it out

At a staff meeting you are asked to prepare a cultural play environment. You are allocated a display board and a corner of the setting.

Discuss the following:
- what you would do
- the resources you would need
- why you would do it
- how you would organise it.

Check it out

Recall a time when you created a themed play area within your setting as a result of suggestions and ideas from the children or young people.

If you have not experienced this, try to encourage the children or young people to think of an idea (or theme) that you can help them implement.

Key terms

Relevant laws: laws that are relevant to a play setting such as the Health and Safety at Work Act, Control of Substances Hazardous to Health regulations, the Children Act.

How to offer play opportunities that respect children or young people's right to adapt the opportunities to their own needs (K14)

An organised play setting should help children and young people feel secure. To meet inspection requirements and parental expectations, a programme of opportunities and activities is usually available. However, when planning opportunities within this programme playworkers need to ensure that they are flexible and easily adapted by the children and young people.

For example a playworker may provide craft equipment for kite making. The children may decide to develop and adapt the activity to create other things that are seen in the sky, for example hot air balloons and aeroplanes, or they may change it into a Chinese theme and make a dragon.

Free and spontaneous play is important and should be in every session. Some people think that structure and play do not go together. However, by giving children and young people opportunities to choose and adapt activities within a flexible programme, play can be enhanced and children can be motivated to create stimulating opportunities.

Some sessions on the programme may be left blank to indicate total free play. Spontaneous play can motivate children to create stimulating opportunities

The example of the kite making activity could progress throughout the afternoon and be further developed by the children and young people. Once an idea is suggested, you as the playworker can build on this and explore different options and opportunities relating to the idea. You should discuss your ideas (taken from the children and young people's suggestions) with colleagues and parents or carers. They can contribute in several ways and this will help:

- to ensure co-operation from everyone involved
- to respond to all needs
- to show respect for the opinions and views of others involved
- to make all feel they are actively involve
- to provide resources.

The activities you select should be safe and stimulating for the children and young people. You may have to consider the following to ensure this:

- whether the setting can afford any resources needed
- whether the children are being challenged to an acceptable level by the activity
- whether enough staff are available
- whether all resources and equipment are safe before use
- the age and stage of development of the children likely to be taking part
- what the children like to do

Check it out

1 If you have a programme of opportunities and activities at your setting, look at this week's programme. Identify the opportunities for free play and play that can be adapted by the children and young people.
2 Try and introduce more opportunities for free play.

- any special needs
- any relevant medical details.

It is also important to provide a variety of opportunities that offer choice. There are several reasons for this:
- to ensure that each member of the group feels important and valued
- to ensure your play setting is offering quality care that responds appropriately to the needs of the children
- to create a truly child-centred play environment that the children want to attend
- to avoid boredom which, in turn, avoids unwanted behaviour.

Plans need to be flexible and to give children the opportunity to create and control play themselves. This is to ensure that:
- play opportunities are child centred
- children feel 'ownership' of the play setting
- children are empowered
- children feel more confident and their self-esteem is enhanced
- decision making and independence are encouraged.

Playworkers can play a vital role in instigating and providing for play. They can provide a range of resources, as shown in the table below.

Resources	Example
Natural materials	Sand, water, clay, puddles, wood, sawdust
Construction materials	Lego, building bricks, stickle bricks, Meccano
IT materials and electrical equipment	Computers and games, activity disks, TV, video
Tools	Hammer, screwdriver, saw, craft knife, spade
Outdoor play equipment	Bikes, trolley, swings, climbing frame, seesaw
Craft materials	Collage, boxes, paint, glue, scissors, brushes
Imaginative play materials	Dressing up clothes, jewellery, drapes, tents
Research material	Books, disks, magazines, journals, catalogues
Games and equipment	Board games, footballs, bats and balls
Scrap materials	Empty boxes, tubes, cloth, off cuts of wood, packaging

● Resources that can be provided for play

Why it is important to involve children and young people in discussing and agreeing ground rules (K15)

Each setting will have set **ground rules** for behaviour. These may be included in the setting's behaviour policy and be of a general nature, focusing on the type of behaviour expected within the setting. Additional ground rules may be set out at the start of an activity to focus specifically on the type of activity the children and young people will be engaged in.

Ground rules should include boundaries and constraints as well as directives for appropriate behaviour. A playworker should focus on positive re-enforcement of these rules. It is good practice to involve the children and young people in setting the ground rules so they will:

- understand the reasoning behind the rules and be more likely to keep to them
- understand the rules and hopefully think they are fair
- understand why the rules are necessary
- learn what rules are for.

You can talk to the children and explain why the ground rules are necessary. Ask them if there are any issues they would like to include, and create a list, ensuring that the reason for the rule is properly discussed and explained. Regularly review and update the list in conjunction with the children. If you are re-negotiating ground rules with the children and young people you must ensure that any changes or adaptations are in line with your organisation's policies and procedures. It may help to check the ground rules out with your colleagues or senior playworker.

Key terms

Ground rules: agreed rules for a play opportunity; this will usually cover issues such as behaviour, health and safety, co-operation, respect or other issues requested by the children and young people.

Test yourself

1 You are asked to provide an environmental play opportunity outdoors for a summer play scheme for 15 children.
2 You are asked to become involved in a creative play planning session for children with a range of disabilities.

For each case identify:
- what you would do
- how you would organise the session
- why you would do it
- how you would set the ground rules
- what resources you would need
- what opportunities you would make available for free play.

How to balance the rights of a child or young person to play in a self-directed way against the rights of others (K17)

The main focus of the Children Act, which became law in 1989, was to protect children and ensure their rights were upheld. Before the Children Act came into force, the United Nations Convention on the Rights of the Child (1959) gave directives with regard to children's rights, which influenced how children were treated. The wording of the convention is now out of date but the message remains valid: children have rights and they should be empowered to exert these rights.

The values of play (see page 4) also relate closely to the rights of children and young people. As a playworker your role is to incorporate these values into your work practice and help empower children to exert these rights.

Check it out

1 Research into the United Nations Convention on the Rights of the Child and compare it to your own thoughts on children's rights.
2 Look at the values of play (on page 4) and see which ones relate to children's rights.

Balancing children and young people's needs and rights

In empowering children and young people, a playworker needs to be aware of the need to balance the rights of all the children and young people in the setting. This can involve a range of techniques and strategies including:
- good listening and communication skills
- awareness and understanding of equality of opportunity
- sensitivity to the young people in your care and to their individual needs.

The members of the playwork team can work together to ensure a consistent approach is adopted while still treating children according to their individual needs. If the balance between the individual rights of a child or young person and the rights of others is not addressed, the possible effects could be that the whole group of children suffer as well as individuals for the following reasons:
- children will not feel valued as individuals
- resentment and jealousy may occur
- health, security and safety directives may be breached
- children may feel neglected
- children may no longer reach their full potential in play, as they feel that the playworkers have favourites or have taken sides.

Check it out

Think of an instance when you have used discussion and negotiation to help with ensuring all children's rights are met.

How to encourage children and young people to extend themselves through play and adapt play opportunities (K16/18/19)

At times children and young people will need support in their play, but any support given by the playworker should focus on encouraging independence and getting them to practise skills for themselves. In providing stimulating, interesting and challenging play opportunities that are developmentally appropriate, a playworker is providing the potential for children and young people to extend themselves, as shown in the diagram below.

I want to be able to do stuff I like, because I want to. My Mum and Dad are always on at me about everything, it's like they don't think I can do stuff. At the adventure playground I like it because they are really cool and they stay out of your face when you want them to.

Toby, 9 (Berkshire)

You, as the playworker, must ensure that the opportunities provided are stimulating and appropriate for the age and stage of development of each child. You should give children and young people choices and involve them in decision making. Being appropriately involved in play will often extend the activity and gently lead children towards new goals and ideas. Make sure you give support when needed in a sensitive manner.

Support should be provided without the playworker taking control or undermining the child or young person. Support can include:

- encouragement and praise
- re-stocking or providing materials and equipment
- physical help with moving, opening or manoeuvring things
- providing information to help with decision making
- pointing out the options available to enable the child to make choices
- negotiating or reiterating ground rules
- highlighting and discussing health, hygiene and safety issues
- acting as mediator in conflict situations
- assessing risks.

Support should be offered but not forced on the children and young people (except in hazardous situations). The playworker needs to be aware of when to withdraw and become unobtrusive in play.

While providing stimulating and challenging environments that offer play opportunities and activities in which children and young people want to participate, you should be sensitive to individual needs by acknowledging that all children are different and have differing needs. By building an

● *Playworkers should support children without taking control*

Check it out

Think of an instance when you have provided support by helping children to do any of the suggestions above.

appropriate and caring relationship with the children or young people, you will gain their respect and trust. To maintain the relationship you should ensure that you do not undermine their confidence and self-esteem by 'pushing' children and young people too far.

It is important for children to explore play opportunities for themselves as it encourages independence, freedom of choice and decision making. It also enables them to excel in their own achievements, which will boost their confidence and increase their self-esteem.

Some children and young people are outgoing and need little support or encouragement to take part in play. Others may stand on the sideline, looking as though they want to join in, but lacking the confidence to do so. It is your duty as a playworker to help these children gain confidence. This can be achieved in a number of ways:

● by playing alongside them, giving moral support
● by giving them assistance, for example when walking along a balancing beam you may hold both hands, then hold one until the child or young person has the confidence to do it without help
● by giving them time and space to try (and to practise) an activity, for example skipping
● by providing praise to increase their self-esteem and confidence
● by finding out what they would like to do and, if possible, offering the play opportunity.

● *Playing alongside a young person can give confidence and moral support*

Test yourself

Complete the chart below by indicating the appropriate level of support.

Age	Activity	No support	Little support	Lots of support
5–6 years	Cooking activity			
11–16 years	Game of basketball			
7–8 years	Sewing activity			
11–15 years	Playing computer games			
4–5 years	On a swing			
9–12 years	Making jewellery			
8–10 years	Playing a board game			
15 years	Watching a video			
5–8 years	Playing in then paddling pool			

Discuss your answers with a colleague as you will need to focus on the setting in which you work.

Children and young people require different types of support and encouragement, as shown in the table below.

Age	Support needed
5–7	Children may need a great deal of additional support with basic skills to help them achieve the desired result
	Lots of praise and encouragement is needed to acknowledge effort rather than the end product
8–12	Children may need occasional support but usually only when it is asked for They can be fiercely independent, but usually respond well to praise and encouragement
13+	Young people are usually very capable and are unlikely to need direct support Some discrete assistance may be required from time to time
	The may appear disdainful of praise, as they fear ridicule from their peers if they respond positively to praise

● *The support and encouragement children need*

Although the previous table is directed towards the different age ranges, it is important to balance these with the child or young person's developmental level. The age ranges are only an approximate guide.

Playworkers can improve their practice by becoming reflective practitioners. They can think back and assess their practice to identify things that could or should be changed, or can ask colleagues to reflect on their practice.

How to identify when a child or young person may have been pushed too far and how to avoid undermining their self-esteem (K20)

Adults involved in working with children and young people sometimes forget that children need to make mistakes in their drive for independence. All children are working towards the ultimate goal of full independence in all areas of life and of having a clear view of the answer to 'who am I?' As playworkers your role is to support them in reaching this to a level appropriate to their age and stage of development.

Self-esteem is when a child or adult feels good about themselves. Children or adults who feel it is not worth other people taking time with them have low self-esteem. Of course the opposite is high self-esteem when children or adults feel it is worth other people taking time with them and taking notice of them. Self-esteem is important for children in middle childhood – from about the age 7 or 8. Their concept of self-esteem is developed from the reactions of other people to them.

How do you think constantly being told you are useless will affect a child's self-esteem? Or always being ignored in favour of an older brother or sister?

Self-confidence is linked to self-esteem. How can children be confident about themselves and happy to engage with others, if they have low self-esteem? It is easier for a child with high self-esteem to try out new things, make friends and find out about the world.

Promoting self-confidence is part of your role as a playworker with children and young people. How can you create opportunities for a child to feel good?

Although it is important to support and help children who may have poor self-esteem and are not self-confident, making them join in or pushing them to the front can be very damaging for them. It can take a considerable amount of time to gain confidence. Remember that the current situation has taken all the child's life to develop – you will not change the child overnight.

Check it out

Think about games you plan for children.

1 Do you make it possible for everyone to win sometimes?
2 How does a child react if they don't win?
3 How can you make sure everyone has a turn?
4 How can you give a shy child a gentle helping hand to go first for once?
5 How to you stop more assertive children overwhelming others?

Case study 8: Supporting children who lack self-confidence

You have organised a morning of team games for the children in a holiday club. Two of the more outgoing children have taken over as team leaders and chosen 'their teams'. During the choosing three children were not picked and you had to put them into the teams, although they said they didn't want to take part. You notice that the team leaders and some of the other children are making unpleasant remarks about them.

1 *What has gone wrong?*
2 *How should the team session have been arranged?*
3 *How could you support the three children involved?*

How to offer appropriate support to children and young people during a play opportunity (K21/22/23)

Play is all about children enjoying themselves and developing their skills. Play can at times be challenging to children; at other times they may be reluctant to extend themselves to develop skills. As a playworker you need to be able to:

- identify when children need support and when they don't
- know what type of support is needed and when to offer it
- know how to offer support without taking over.

Activities should always be planned to meet the needs of individual children. Sometimes one child may need a particular focus. For example, a child may already be identified as having specific needs due to delayed development or behaviour issues. Some children may have programmes designed by other professionals, such as physiotherapists, or by their parents. It may be necessary to extend an activity for a child who is particularly advanced in an area of development to make sure that he or she is being challenged enough.

If you are involved in planning and offering support to a child during a play activity make sure that you have:

- identified the child's needs
- set clear aims for the support
- produced a plan for the support
- integrated the support with the overall plan
- reviewed the support after the event.

Support may be of any type depending on the play activity involved.

Case study 9: Supporting a child with specific needs

Kane has some problems with his mobility – he cannot walk very well. You notice him watching the other children on the outdoor equipment, but not attempting to join in.

1   *How could you help him to use the equipment?*
2   *How would you involve the other children?*
3   *What would you need to consider to make sure Kane safely enjoys his play?*

Case study 10: Planning for a child who finishes activities quickly

Jade always finishes activities in the creative area long before the other children. When she has finished she tends to start to interfere with other children's work and this often leads to them getting upset.

1   *Why might this be happening?*
2   *What could you do to prevent the situation?*
3   *What impact might this have on your future planning?*

There is danger in always making special arrangements for a child or young person as this may well set them apart from their friends. Ideally you should be planning activities that allow all children to be equally involved according to their skills and abilities.

Sometimes all the support that is needed is a steadying hand from an adult or gentle encouragement to be involved. The skill is in recognising when and how to offer this without singling a child or young person out.

Why it is important to recognise children and young people's play cues (K24)

To empower children is to encourage and support them, and the role that you as the playworker should adopt should be sensitive. You need to be aware of the **play cues** (the verbal language, body language or facial expressions) that children show, which may indicate that they are not happy with a situation.

For example, a child has been struggling to tie his shoelaces in response to a request to do so before he can go outside to play. His cues will show that he is not happy, is frustrated and is becoming distressed. The playworker should be aware of these cues and assist the child in a way that does not undermine his confidence.

The same kind of thing may happen during play and the playworker should be able to pick up cues and act accordingly. The more time that a playworker spends working with children and young people, the more accustomed he or she will become to recognising and acting upon children's play cues.

Play cues can be varied or similar. Set responses are recognised especially from children and young people who are:
- related
- spend a lot of time together
- attend the same school
- are in the same class
- live in the same area
- watch the same TV programmes.

Key terms

Play cues: facial expressions, language or body language that communicate the child's or young person's wish to play or invite others to play.

Check it out

Observe a specific child at your setting with whom you have built up a good relationship. Look out for and assess his or her cues.

● *Examples of play cues – how would you respond to these?*

Even if the play cues are similar, a playworker should respond to the children according to their individual needs.

Case study 11: Responding to a child's play cues

You have a creative table where some of the older children are making masks. You notice that Sam, an 8 year old, is standing watching. He picks up some card and glances round the room, and then he catches your eye and quickly puts the card down.

1 *How could you respond to this cue?*
2 *How could you help him join in?*
3 *How could you support him without undermining his control and involvement?*

How to recognise when your involvement in children and young people's play could increase their involvement (K25)

It's great. Nobody on your back about homework, or doing everything in a certain way because that's how they say you should. They are like friends, the Playworkers, except they are adults.

Hannah, 12 (Nottingham)

There are times when a playworker is required or invited to participate in play opportunities. This may be to join in or to support the children and young people. A playworker should only become involved in play in the following circumstances:

- If invited to by the children and young people – it feels good to be invited to do something and it is a compliment to you if children invite you to play. However, it is important not to take over or stifle their play.

- If the children need help to achieve their aims – this may be physical help, to move or provide something or to collect materials and equipment, or it may be to support children with individual needs to enable them to participate fully.

- To reduce potential hazards and to assess risks – if there is a risk to health, safety or security, your presence may be required. To assess and deal with the issue you should encourage the children to try to identify and deal with it rather than taking over yourself.

- If a conflict situation arises that the children seem unable to resolve – to encourage the children and young people to resolve the conflict themselves is the best course of action. This can often be achieved by negotiation and compromise (you assist as a facilitator if necessary).

- If the children are looking bored and uninterested – your presence may enthuse and motivate the children and young people, or you could give them an idea to extend or redirect the opportunity.

- During a team game when a team member has to leave – it is important that you do not always win, but are seen to take an active part.

There are times when children and young people would love you to join in, but also times when your presence will inhibit their play. As a playworker you should be aware of these different requirements. You should only participate in play activities if invited to do so.

There are times when a playworker should not join in children's play for a number of reasons, some of which are shown in the following diagram.

Check it out

Think of the last time you joined in play. Were you invited? Did you meet the guidelines above?

Keys to good practice: How to join in play

✓ Do not use equipment that is not suitable or designed for adults.

✓ Try not to take over the game or activity.

✓ Wait to be invited to join in.

✓ Be aware of health and safety issues.

✓ Do not become too competitive.

✓ Try to empower the children to take control.

✓ Assess whether your involvement is stifling or inhibiting play.

✓ Encourage, praise and enthuse the children.

✓ Be a good role model.

Check it out

1 A new playworker has become involved in a team game and has become very competitive; the opposing team ask you to join their side. State what you would do and why.

2 Recall an instance when you have responded to a child or young person's play cue and either joined in or not taken part in play.

How to bring a play session to an end so that it respects the participants' needs and meets your setting's requirements (K26)

Play opportunities sometimes come to a natural end and this is the best option for the children and young people. Children should be encouraged and allowed to complete their play wherever possible. However, there are often times when, and reasons why, play opportunities need to be brought to an end. It is the playworker's role to facilitate this in a sensitive and appropriate manner so that the children do not feel disappointed.

There are a variety of reasons why play opportunities need to be brought to an end, for example for snack time, to clear away messy creative play, because a parent or carer has arrived for a particular child, or because it is the end of the session.

Play opportunities need to be ended at an appropriate pace for the children participating in them in order to:

- avoid frustration – children will easily become frustrated if their play is terminated while they are busy
- allow children time to complete their tasks and games
- demonstrate that you care about the children and value their play
- encourage them to continue or play again – if children do not complete their play they may refuse to play in the future.

In any of the above situations, it is important to provide the group with a timescale and explanation of how long they have left to complete the activity, why they need to stop what they are doing and, if applicable, when they can pick it up again. If you are able to give a timescale and aim for the activity, the children or young people can adapt their play to accommodate this. Free play opportunities can often be terminated more easily. If a time restraint occurs, the children can change and adapt the activity to meet these deadlines. They can also take a break for lunch or a snack and return to the activity, often without too much disturbance.

Situations sometimes arise that mean you have to break or end the play suddenly. You will need to make contingency plans for these occasions. For example, if the activity is outside and the weather changes, space can often be made available indoors unless the activity requires specific equipment and/or a larger space. For emergency evacuation, fire drills and health and safety issues, it is often possible to take a break and then return to resume play after the all clear has been given.

The arrival of parents or carers may cause disruption to play, so it is important when planning play activities that this is considered. When children start an activity it should be explained that the arrival of parents is at a set time, so they are aware and can plan for this.

Check it out

List the most usual reasons for ending play sessions at your setting.

Case study 12: Ending an activity appropriately

As it has been raining all afternoon, you arrange for the children to watch a video. The children decide to turn the video watching into a 'cinema experience' by putting the chairs in lines and selling pretend tickets and refreshments. By 4pm the video has not finished but several parents and carers have arrived to collect their children.

1   *What would you do?*
2   *How could you have avoided this?*

Case study 13: Avoiding disruption to play

It is a lovely summer day and the children are outside making a den in the corner of the outdoor space. They start this in the morning and it extends to become a 'camp site'. It is now dinner time, play is still in full swing and the children need to eat their packed lunches The children are clearly reluctant to break off from their play. The afternoon session starts at 1pm and this involves some of the children going on an outing with another member of the team.

1   *What do you do now?*
2   *How could you have prevented the situation developing?*
3   *How could this be used for future activities?*

Keys to good practice: How to end play activities

✓ Try to pre-warn children of end times.

✓ Negotiate and discuss end times.

✓ Always give explanations for immediate ends.

✓ Try 'take a break' tactics.

✓ Try and plan for disruptions by having other options available.

Your organisation's procedures for tidying up the play setting (K27)

Each setting should have a set policy that involves a tidying up routine and sometimes a rota that staff and children follow for packing away activities. Tidying away will take place as an ongoing process:

- when children and young people move to another activity
- when the area is required for another activity, for example snack time
- at the end of an activity
- at the end of the session
- for health and safety reasons, for example sweeping up spilt sand.

Most tidying up tasks are appropriate for children or young people to take part in. However, there may be times when the playworker will need to be present usually for health and safety reasons, for example when washing sharp knives. Tidying up is an important part of development for children and young people so that they understand the importance of leaving the areas clean and tidy and ready for the next person to use.

Tidying up develops social skills such as:

- working together to achieve the task
- co-operating with others
- improving self-help skills and independence
- sharing ideas with others as to how to do it as quickly as possible
- acting in a socially acceptable manner.

It also develops physical skills such as:

- hand–eye co-ordination
- fine and gross motor skills.

Children and young people should be involved in tidying up for the reasons given in the diagram below.

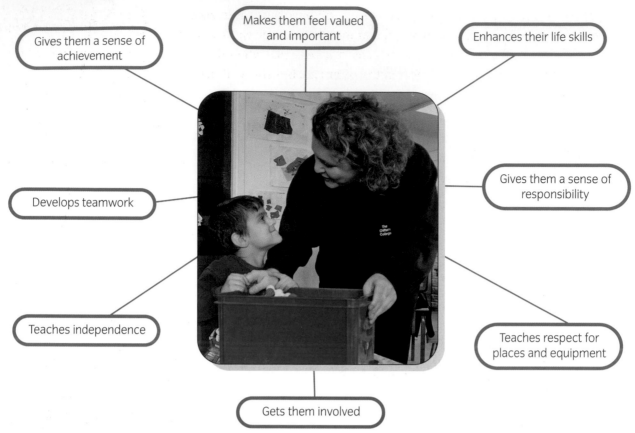

Gives them a sense of achievement

Makes them feel valued and important

Enhances their life skills

Develops teamwork

Gives them a sense of responsibility

Teaches independence

Teaches respect for places and equipment

Gets them involved

● *Why involve children and young people in tidying up?*

While it is appropriate for children and young people to tidy up after themselves, this will be dependent on:

- the age, size and development of the children or young people
- the type of materials and equipment and where they are stored
- the risks involved, for example the safety of using high shelves would need to be assessed before enlisting the help of children and young people.

Case study 14: Ensuring an activity is tidied away

After an afternoon visit to the local farm, you return to the play setting with an hour left before parents and carers are due to arrive to collect their children. The children start drawing and making animals on the creative table.

1 *How could you bring the session to an end?*
2 *How could you get feedback on the activity?*
3 *How would you ensure the activity is tidied away?*

The procedures that you follow in your setting will have taken into account the type of setting in which you work, the amount of storage space and the number of staff available. Clearing away usually takes place when the children and young people have vacated the premises, but this will depend upon the hours the staff are expected to work.

 Keys to good practice: How to tidy up

✓ Encourage children to help with tidying up.

✓ Move only small equipment until children have gone.

✓ Ensure you have enough staff.

✓ Move children to another area.

Your organisation's procedures for the children and young people's departure (K28)

It is very important that, as a playworker, you are aware of children leaving the site, whether the setting operates an open or closed access. Generally, in open access settings, the children or young people are encouraged to sign in and out, for health and safety and legal reasons. In closed access settings, children are not allowed to leave the building without a designated parent or carer, who should be listed on their registration form. The parent or carer would normally sign their child out of a setting.

Government guidelines state that arrangements should be made with parents about the arrival and departure of their children to and from the provision, and staff should make sure that they are collected by the correct person. The guidelines also state that children should be released from the provision to individuals named by the parent only.

 **Check it out**

Think about the equipment you have at your setting that the children and young people can tidy away themselves. Is it always the same children or young people who do it?

● *Giving rewards boosts a child's sense of achievement*

 Case study 15: Making sure a child is collected by the correct person

One day a woman appears at your setting and says that she has come to collect Pamjit. She tells you that she is Pamjit's aunty and that Pamjit's mum has sent her.

1 *What would you do?*
2 *Would you let Pamjit go with the woman? Justify your answer.*

Your organisation's record keeping procedures (K29)

The Childcare Act (2006) in England and Wales and the National Care Standards in Scotland set out requirements regarding the records that settings are required to keep, which include the following:

- a daily attendance register to indicate clearly the children present at any given time
- current information on all children, to be reviewed regularly and including details of medical and dietary requirements plus emergency contact details
- accident and incident books
- staff and volunteer records.

Most settings adhere to this and often keep other records that will be of benefit to the children and young people and to the setting. Throughout a session a number of records may be made. The following are some examples.

- The register will be completed on arrival and again on departure. This is a very important document and must be kept up to date for legal as well as health and safety reasons.
- Any accidents or illnesses that occur and any medication administered during the session need to be written up in the accident book, and the parents or carers informed.
- Any incidents should be noted. The setting usually has one book for positive or negative behaviour, and one for health and safety monitoring (for example faulty equipment, appliances that need checking, etc.).
- Items bought with petty cash or grants need to be recorded, as well as payments from parents or carers for the service of the setting.
- Fire drills need to be recorded. This will be done on a legal document that includes details of when the fire fighting equipment was checked.

When children and young people join a setting, personal records are set up that provide the staff with the necessary information should an emergency arise. These records also inform the staff of any medical conditions or allergies that the children may have. Once all records are complete, they must be locked away and stored in a secure cabinet. Access to children's files is limited. All records that are kept should be accurate and legible so that, if and when they are required, they can be easily read and understood.

Check it out

Find out from your placement the regulations that apply in your area.

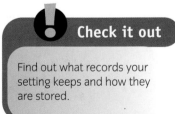

Check it out

Find out what records your setting keeps and how they are stored.

Your role as a playworker is very important.

Design a booklet that shows the children and young people at your setting what you can do to support them. This should be done on a computer.

Include:
- rules and guidelines
- possible activities
- how the children and young people are involved in deciding on activities
- the roles and responsibilities of children, young people and workers in preparing, planning and ending activities.

End-of-unit knowledge check

1 List two ways you can obtain feedback from children and young people on what they want in the play environment.

2 Give four examples of equipment suitable for young people aged 12–16 years.

3 Suggest some materials that you would make available to encourage free play outside.

4 Explain why children and young people should be involved in creating play environments and how you would go about involving them.

5 Describe the types of support that children and young people might need to adapt to a play opportunity and how you might provide this support without taking control.

6 How would you identify if and when children and young people need support during a play opportunity?

7 Give three reasons why it is important to involve children in tidying up.

8 Explain how to bring a play session to an end in a way that respects the children and young people's needs and involvement, but meets the requirements of your play setting.

9 Describe your organisation's procedures for children and young people's departure.

10 What are the records that the Childcare Act 2006 requires a playsetting to keep?

Useful addresses

Every effort has been made to ensure that all details were up to date at the time of publication.

Many of the details below are for each organisation's head office, which should be able to provide local contact numbers.

ADD/ADHD Family Support Group
1a The High Street
Dilton Marsh
Nr Westbury
Wilts BA13 4DL

Association for Spina Bifida and Hydrocephalus (ASBAH)
42 Park Road
Peterborough PE1 2UQ
Tel.: 01733 555988
Web: www.asbah.org

Awdurdod Cymysterau Cwricwlwm ac Asesu Cymru (ACCAC)
Castle Buildings
Womanby Street
Cardiff CF10 1SX
Tel.: 029 2037 5400
Web: www.ccw.org.uk

Barnardo's
Tanners Lane
Barkingside
Ilford
Essex
IG6 1QG
Tel.: 020 8550 8822
Web: www.barnardos.org.uk

British Allergy Foundation
Deepdene House
30 Bellgrove Road
Welling
Kent DA16 3PY
Tel.: 020 8303 8525
Web: www.allergyfoundation.com

British Deaf Association
1–3 Worship Street
London EC2A 2AB
Text phone: 020 7588 3529
Video phone 020 7496 9539
Voice phone 020 7588 3520
Web: www.bda.org.uk

British Dyslexia Association
98 London Road
Reading
RG1 5AU
Helpline: 0118 966 8271
Web: www.bda-dyslexia.org.uk

British Dyspraxia Foundation
8 West Alley
Hitchin
Herts
SG5 1EG
Helpline: 01462 454986
Web: www.dyspraxiafoundation.org.uk

British Nutrition Foundation (BNF)
High Holborn House
52–54 High Holborn
London WC1V 6RQ
Tel.: 020 7404 6504
Fax 020 7404 6747
Email: postbox@nutrition.org.uk
Web: www.nutrition.org.uk

British Red Cross Society (BRCS)
10th Floor Westminster Tower
3 Albert Embankment
London SE1 7SX
Training tel.: 020 7388 8777
Web: www.redcross.org.uk

Child Accident Prevention Trust (CAPT)
18–20 Farringdon Lane
London EC1R 3AU
Tel.: 020 7608 3828
Web: www.capt.org.uk

ChildLine
Studd Street
London N1 0QW
Helpline: 0800 1111
Web: www.childline.org.uk

Children's Society
Edward Rudolf House
Margery Street
London
WC1X 0JL
Tel.: 020 7841 4436
Web: www.the-childrens-society.org.uk

Coeliac UK
PO Box 220
High Wycombe
Bucks HP11 2HY
Tel: 01494 437 278
Web: www.coeliac.co.uk

Commission for Racial Equality
Elliot House
10–12 Allington Street
London SW1E 5EH
Tel.: 0207 828 7022
Fax: 0207 630 7605
Email: info@cre.gov.uk
Web: www.cre.gov.uk

National Drugs Helpline
Helpline: 0800 77 66 00
Email: helpline@ndh.org.uk
Web: www.ndh.org.uk

National Eczema Society (NES)
Hill House
Highgate Hill
London N19 5NA
Tel.: 020 7281 3553
Fax: 020 7281 6395
Helpline: 0870 241 3604
Web: www.eczema.org/

National Federation of Families with Visually Impaired Children
c/o Queen Alexandra College
49 Court Oak Road
Birmingham
B17 9TG

NSPCC
42 Curtain Road
London EC2A 3NH
Tel.: 020 7825 2500
Fax: 020 7825 2525
Helpline: 0808 800 5000
Textphone: 0800 056 0566
Web: www.nspcc.org.uk

National Toy and Leisure Libraries
68 Churchway
London
NW1 1LT
Tel: 020 7387 9592
Fax: 020 7383 2714
Email: admin@natll.ukf.net
Web: www.natll.org.uk

Nursery World
Admiral House
66 – 68 East Smithfield
London
E1W 1BX
Tel: 020 7782 3000
Web: www.nursery-world.com

Ofsted
Alexandra House
33 Kingsway
London
WC2B 6SE
Tel.: 020 7421 6744
Web: www.ofsted.gov.uk

Parentline Plus
520 Highgate Studios
53–79 Highgate Road
Kentish Town
London NW5 1TL
Tel.: 020 7284 5500
Web: www.parentlineplus.org.uk

Parents Advice Centre
Franklin House
12 Brunswick Street
Belfast BT2 7GE
Tel.: 028 9031 0891
Helpline: 028 9023 8800
Email: Belfast@pachelp.org
Web: parentsadvicecentre.org/

Qualifications and Curriculum Authority (QCA)
83 Piccadilly
London W1J 8QA
Tel.: 020 7509 5555
Fax: 020 7509 6666
Minicom: 020 7509 6546
Web: www.qca.org.uk

Royal National Institute for the Blind (RNIB)
Customer Services
PO Box 173
Peterborough PE2 6WS
Tel.: 0845 702 3153
Minicom: 0856 58 56 91
Helpline: 0845 766 9999
Fax: 020 7388 2034
Textphone: 0800 51 51 52
Email: helpline@rnib.org.uk
Web: www.rnib.org.uk

Royal Society for the Prevention of Accidents (RoSPA)
Edgbaston Park
353 Bristol Road
Edgbaston
Birmingham B5 7ST
Tel.: 0121 248 2000
Email: help@rospa.co.uk
Web: www.rospa.co.uk

Samaritans
The Samaritans
The Upper Mill
Kingston Road
Ewell
Surrey KT17 2AF
Tel.: 020 8394 8300
Helpline: 08457 909090
Fax: 020 8394 8301
Email: admin@samaritans.org
Web: www.samaritans.co.uk

SCOPE
6 Market Road
London N7 9PW
Helpline: 0800 800 333
Email: cphelpline@scope.org.uk
Web: www.scope.org.uk

SENSE
11–13 Clifton Terrace
Finsbury Park
London N4 3SR
Tel.: 020 7272 7774
Minicom: 020 7272 9648
Fax: 020 7272 6012
Email: enquiries@sense.org.uk
Web: www.sense.org.uk

Sickle Cell Society
54 Station Road
Harlesden
London NW10 4UA
Tel.: 020 8961 7795
Email:
sickleinfo.line@btinternet.com
Web: www.sicklecellsociety.org/

St. John Ambulance
27 St John's Lane
London EC1M 4BU
Tel.: 08700 10 49 50
Email: info@sja.org.uk
Web: www.sja.org.uk

Stillbirth and Neonatal Death Society (SANDS)
28 Portland Place
London W1B 1LY
Tel.: 020 7436 7940
Helpline: 020 7436 5881
Email: support@uk-sands.org
Web: uk-sands.org/

Sure Start
Sure Start Unit
Department for Education and
Skills and Department for Work
and Pensions
Level 2
Caxton House
Tothill Street
London
SW1H 9NA

Tel: 0870 0002288
Email:
info.surestart@dfes.gsi.gov.uk
Web:
www.surestart.gov.uk/contacts/

Terrence Higgins Trust (THT)
52–54 Gray's Inn Road
London
WC1X 8JU
Tel.: 020 7831 0330
Fax: 020 7242 0121
Email: info@tht.org.uk
Web: www.tht.org.uk

Twins and Multiple Births Association (TAMBA)
2 The Willows
Gardner Road
Guildford
Surrey
GU1 4PG
Tel.: 0870 770 3305
Email: enquiries@tamba.org.uk
Web: www.tamba.org.uk

Vegetarian Society of the United Kingdom
Parkdale
Dunham Road
Altrincham
Cheshire WA14 4QG
Tel.: 0161 925 2000
Email: info@vegsoc.org
Web: www.vegsoc.org.uk

World Health Organisation (WHO)
Avenue Appia 20
1211 Geneva 27
Switzerland
Tel.: (+00 41 22) 791 21 11
Web: www.who/int/en/

Glossary

Abusive behaviour	– behaviour which hurts feelings or insults another child or causes physical harm
Adolescence	– a period in which children are developing into adulthood
Appraisal	– formal feedback about your job
Assessing	– interpreting what you have seen
Attachment	– relationship with primary carer
Birth to Three Matters	– a curriculum for children under 3
Carer	– the individual looking after a child at any point
Child centred	– when the curriculum and other activities consider the needs of the child first and foremost
Cognitive development	– a child's process of thinking, organising information and learning abstract concepts
Cold cooking	– could include making sandwiches, milk shakes, instant whip, marzipan sweets, decorated biscuits
Confidentiality regulations	– the rules on which the setting has decided to control the spread of information which it is inappropriate to disseminate or share
Constructive feedback	– honest opinions designed to help the recipient
Creative play	– children create and explore through play
Creativity	– bringing into existence something original
Curriculum	– all the activities and experiences which enable children to learn, both those planned with specific learning aims and unexpected events which are turned into opportunities for learning
Curriculum plans	– what is to be done in the long-, medium- and short-term so that children will achieve the learning outcomes set (usually written down)
Data Protection Act	– a Government act which states what documentation should be made available and who has access to it
DfES	– Department for Education and Skills
Disability	– a physical or mental impairment that has a significant long-term effect on a person's ability to carry out normal activities
Disabled	– a person with impairment who faces restrictions because of this

Discrimination	– the practice of treating one person or group of people less fairly than other people or groups
Diversity	– accepting and celebrating people's differences
Emotional development	– a child's development which enables him/her to understand and cope with emotions and feelings, and to develop a sense of security and a positive self-image
Environment	– the place, setting or service where you work with children
Equality of opportunity	– all people have access to the same opportunities
Families	– parents, carers and extended family who contribute to the welfare of the child
Fine manipulative skills	– small and often intricate operations made primarily with the hands (fine motor skills)
Formula milk	– made for babies as near to breast milk as possible
Formal support systems	– support from manager, supervisor, etc.
Foundation Stage	– curriculum for 3–5-year-olds
Gross motor skills	– could include throwing, catching, striking, kicking, bouncing, whirling, spinning, walking, jumping (large motor skills)
Imaginative play	– children's pretend play in groups or alone
Inclusion	– a process of identifying, understanding and breaking down barriers to enable participation and belonging
Informal support systems	– support from team colleagues, other colleagues, etc.
Integration	– inclusion of children with special needs
Key stage	– a stage of the National Curriculum (there are 3 stages)
Learning outcomes	– what children learn as a result of their activity/experience
Musical activities	– songs, rhymes, tapping out rhythms, humming, moving to music, dancing, playing instruments, listening to tapes, clapping, responding to songs and rhymes with actions
National Curriculum	– a school curriculum for children aged 6(?) to 16 years
Negative behaviour	– when a child behaves in an unacceptable way that is detrimental to themselves or others

Non-verbal communication	–	communicating through gestures and body language
Observing	–	watching children, noting, thinking
OFSTED	–	Office for Standards in Education
Open-ended questions	–	questions that necessitate other than yes/no response, e.g. What do you think? Why did that happen? How did you manage that?
Palmer grasp	–	when a child holds objects in the palm of his/her hand
Physical play	–	children using their fine and gross motor skills in play
Pincer grip	–	when a child holds items between his/her thumb and forefinger
Policies	–	written documents of protocols, procedures and requirements that state how a setting should be run
Positive behaviour	–	when a child acts in an acceptable way
Positive images	–	those which counter common negative stereotypes, e.g. girls in active and leadership roles; boys in caring roles; black people in positions of authority and responsibility; people with disabilities taking part in active pursuits
Positive reinforcement	–	praise and other confirmatory actions endorsing an achievement with the objective of making the achievement a part of regular activity
Primary carer	–	the main person caring for a child
Procedures	–	ways of implementing policies
Professional development	–	progressing in a chosen career
QCA	–	Qualifications and Curriculum Authority
Recall memory	–	description or demonstration of events, actions and emotions previously observed or experienced, with or without assistance
Recognition memory	–	ability to recognise from visual (such as photographs or drawings), aural, smell, taste, written or tactile cues, things that have been experienced or observed in the past
Respect	–	showing interest in and consideration for the opinions/wishes/judgements of others even though they may differ from your own and you may not agree with them

Role play	–	children exploring their world through play
SATs	–	key assessment tasks of the National Curriculum
Self-esteem	–	feeling that one is a person of worth, valued by others
Self-image	–	the picture one has of oneself
Sensory	–	associated with hearing, sight, feeling, taste and smell
Significant person	–	the person who has prime responsibility for observation of, records of and planning for an individual child and liaising with her/his parents. This person may also have primary care of the child for most of her/his time spent in the setting, especially for babies and toddlers
Social development	–	how a child learns to live and operate with others
Solitary play	–	a child playing alone
Special educational needs	–	children who may need help to learn or access the curriculum
Stepping stones	–	stages in which children meet the early learning goals of the Foundation Stage
Stereotype	–	over-simplified generalisation about a particular group which usually carries derogatory implications; taking a particular assumed characteristic of one person (which may or not be correct) and applying it to all members of that group
Summative assessment	–	summarising findings
Sure Start	–	a government initiative designed to improve the well-being of young children and their families
Unwanted behaviour	–	behaviour that is not accepted by the policy of the setting
Verbal communication	–	communicating through language
Weaning	–	the process of taking a baby from milk feeds to solid food

A

abuse

avoiding 59–61

bullying 57

children's awareness of 58–61

emotional 55–6

harassment 57

importance of recognising 52–8

Keepsafe Code 60

Laming Report 53

neglect 56

physical 54–5

position of injuries on body 54

protecting children 59–61

response to disclosure 61

sexual 56–7

signs and indicators 52–8

accidents 36–46

deaths 26

hazardous substances 32–3

minimising 32

'accommodation' 112

achievement recognition 164–5

active involvement 162–3

activities

encouraging babies 273

setting up 239–40

addresses 346–50, 389–93

allergies 188, 287, 295

ambulances 48

American Sign Language 278

animals 29, 30–31

anxiety 173

attachment theory 169

attachments 121–2

B

Bandura, Albert 114–15

behaviour

boundaries 62, 66, 225–6

consistency 61–3

expectations 225–6

factors affecting 128–9

negative 63, 66–7

policies and procedures 66

positive 62, 64–7

relative 65

rewards 67

rules 61–3, 66

unwanted 63, 66–7

best friends 127–8

Birth to Three Matters framework 194–5, 261–3

bleeding 48

body language 9–10

body shape changes 102

bottle feeding

common problems 285–7

equipment washing 282

formula, preparing 279

giving 284–5

making up 280–1

preparation 284

safety 283–4

settling baby after feed 285

storage 282–3

warming and temperature 281–2

boundaries 225–6

boundaries for behaviour 62, 66

Bowlby, John 121–2, 169

British Sign Language 121, 278, 334

Bruner, Jerome 113

buildings 33

bullying 57

C

case studies

accident prevention 37

activities adaptation to meet all needs 377

anxious behaviour 174

assessing ability to write name 73

behaviour, negative 63

body language 9

bruising suspicion 55

bullying 58

collection procedure 254, 385

communication encouragement 195

confidential information 21

confidentiality, maintaining 74

construction activity 217

cooking activity 238

decisions, involving children in 358

display effectively 230

distressed baby 264

dress code policy 247

emotional need to be independent 161

empowering children 328

encouraging with praise 165

ending activities appropriately 382

feeding babies 280

grouping 231

hats in role play 211

head lice 190

health and safety improvements 253

health and safety outside 34, 361

individual plans, importance of 327

injured child 50

job description 251

jumping to conclusions 55

knowledge gaps 150

labelling children 314

learning from reaction of adults 125

learning from watching others 115

learning when activities enjoyable 114

mathematics through play 209

mature trainee 145

music and movement 204

nappy changing 307

neglect possibility 56

outdoor activities, risk assessment 44, 361

outing to the park 69

E